Learning HTML5 Game Programming

Addison-Wesley Learning Series

✦ Addison-Wesley

Visit **informit.com/learningseries** for a complete list of available publications.

The **Addison-Wesley Learning Series** is a collection of hands-on programming guides that help you quickly learn a new technology or language so you can apply what you've learned right away.

Each title comes with sample code for the application or applications built in the text. This code is fully annotated and can be reused in your own projects with no strings attached. Many chapters end with a series of exercises to encourage you to reexamine what you have just learned, and to tweak or adjust the code as a way of learning.

Titles in this series take a simple approach: they get you going right away and leave you with the ability to walk off and build your own application and apply the language or technology to whatever you are working on.

✦ Addison-Wesley   **informIT.com** | **Safari** Books Online

Learning HTML5 Game Programming

A Hands-on Guide to Building Online Games Using Canvas, SVG, and WebGL

James L. Williams

✦Addison-Wesley

Upper Saddle River, NJ · Boston · Indianapolis · San Francisco
New York · Toronto · Montreal · London · Munich · Paris · Madrid
Cape Town · Sydney · Tokyo · Singapore · Mexico City

The publisher offers excellent discounts on this book when ordered in quantity for bulk purchases or special sales, which may include electronic versions and/or custom covers and content particular to your business, training goals, marketing focus, and branding interests. For more information, please contact:

U.S. Corporate and Government Sales
(800) 382-3419
corpsales@pearsontechgroup.com

For sales outside the United States, please contact:

International Sales
international@pearson.com

Visit us on the Web: informit.com/aw

Library of Congress Cataloging-in-Publication Data:

Williams, James L. (James Lamar), 1981-
  Learning HTML5 game programming : a hands-on guide to building online games using Canvas, SVG, and WebGL / James L. Williams.
     p. cm.
  ISBN 978-0-321-76736-3 (pbk. : alk. paper) 1. Computer games—Programming. 2. HTML (Document markup language) I. Title.
  QA76.76.C672W546 2011
  794.8'1526—dc23

                              2011027527

ISBN-13: 978-0-321-76736-3
ISBN-10: 0-321-76736-5

Text printed in the United States on recycled paper at RR Donnelly in Crawfordsville, Indiana.

First printing September 2011

Associate Publisher
Mark Taub

Senior Acquisitions Editor
Trina MacDonald

Development Editor
Songlin Qiu

Managing Editor
Kristy Hart

Project Editor
Anne Goebel

Copy Editor
Bart Reed

Indexer
Tim Wright

Proofreader
Sheri Cain

Technical Reviewers
Romin Irani
Pascal Rettig
Robert Schwentker

Publishing Coordinator
Olivia Basegio

Cover Designer
Chuti Prasertsith

Senior Compositor
Gloria Schurick

To Inspiration

Came over for a midnight rendezvous

And is gone by morning as if by cue

—Author

❖

Table of Contents

Preface

I wrote this book to scratch an itch, but also because I could see the potential in the (at the time) nascent HTML5 gaming community. I wanted to help developers navigate the wilderness of HTML5 and learn about Canvas, WebGL, and SVG, along with best practices for each.

It sometimes took a bit of discussion to convince developers that HTML5 wasn't just a plaything. They were surprised to learn they could have rich content with all the niceties of a desktop application—such as double buffering, hardware acceleration, and caching inside the confines of the browser without a plugin. Many of them considered Flash as the sole option. It was interesting to watch the tides turn from "Flash for everything" to "Use Flash only where there are HTML5 gaps."

During my writing of this book, the ecosystem around HTML5 game programming has rapidly evolved and matured. I am sure the technologies will continue to evolve, and I look forward to the advances the next year brings.

Key Features of This Book

This book covers areas contained in the "loose" definition of HTML5, meaning the HTML5 specification, WebGL, SVG, and JavaScript as they pertain to game programming. It includes sections on the math behind popular game effects, teaching you the hard way before providing the one to two lines of code solution. For those who are still getting accustomed to JavaScript, there is a chapter on alternative languages that can be used to produce games. These include languages that run directly in the JavaScript engine, those that compile to JavaScript, or those that are a combination of the two. Server-side JavaScript has taken the programming world by storm in recent months. For games, it presents an extra level of flexibility to structure games. Logic can start in a self-contained client instance and then progress to a scalable server instance with few changes in code. The book closes with a discussion of how and where you might publish your games. You have a multitude of choices for game engines and libraries. All the libraries used in this book are unobtrusive in their handling of data, and you could easily take the lessons learned and apply them to other libraries. This book does not discuss the low-level details of WebGL, instead opting for the use of a high-level library that permits low-level API access when needed. The goal of this book is to get you quickly up and running, not to teach you all there is to know about WebGL, which could be a book all by itself.

Target Audience for This Book

This book is intended for application developers who use or would like to learn how to use HTML5 and associated web technologies to create interactive games. It assumes knowledge of some programming languages and some basic math skills.

Code Examples and Exercises for This Book

The code listings as well as the answers for the exercises included in this book are available on the book's website. You can download chapter code and answers to the chapter exercises (if they are included in the chapter) at http://www.informit.com/title/9780321767363. The code listings are also available on Github at https://github.com/jwill/html5-game-book.

Acknowledgments

I have several people to thank for this book. The Pearson team (including Trina MacDonald, Songlin Qiu, and Olivia Basegio) has been invaluable during the project. Their goal is to make one's work that much more awesome, and I think they succeeded. Writing a book on a topic that's evolving rapidly involves a certain measure of guessing where the market will go. I'm glad to have had technical reviewers (Romin Irani, Pascal Rettig, and Robert Schwentker) who shared my passion for the subject matter, gave me speedy and precise feedback, and validated my predictions when I was right, yet got me back on track when I veered slightly off course. And lastly, to my family and friends who listened patiently without judgment, let me off easy when I flaked, and other times forced me to take a break; thanks, I needed that.

About the Author

James L. Williams is a developer based in Silicon Valley and frequent conference speaker, domestically and internationally. He was a successful participant in the 2007 Google Summer of Code, working to bring easy access to SwingLabs UI components to Groovy. He is a co-creator of the Griffon project, a rich desktop framework for Java applications. He and his team, WalkIN, created a product on a coach bus while riding to SXSW and were crowned winners of StartupBus 2011. His first video game was *Buck Rogers: Planet of Zoom* on the Coleco Adam, a beast of a machine with a blistering 3.58MHz CPU, a high-speed tape drive, and a propensity to erase floppy disks at bootup. He blogs at http://jameswilliams.be/blog and tweets as @ecspike.

1

Introducing HTML5

HTML5 is a draft specification for the next major iteration of HTML. It represents a break from its predecessors, HTML4 and XHTML. Some elements have been removed and it is no longer based on SGML, an older standard for document markup. HTML5 also has more allowances for incorrect syntax than were present in HTML4. It has rules for parsing to allow different browsers to display the same incorrectly formatted document in the same fashion. There are many notable additions to HTML, such as native drawing support and audiovisual elements. In this chapter, we discuss the features added by HTML5 and the associated JavaScript APIs.

Beyond Basic HTML

HTML (Hypertext Markup Language), invented by Tim Berners-Lee, has come a long way since its inception in 1990. Figure 1-1 shows an abbreviated timeline of HTML from the HTML5Rocks slides (http://slides.html5rocks.com/#slide3).

Although all the advancements were critical in pushing standards forward, of particular interest to our pursuits is the introduction of JavaScript in 1996 and AJAX in 2005. Those additions transformed the Web from a medium that presented static unidirectional data, like a newspaper or book, to a bidirectional medium allowing communication in both directions.

JavaScript

JavaScript (née LiveScript and formally known as ECMAScript) started as a scripting language for the browser from Netscape Communications. It is a loosely typed scripting language that is prototype-based and can be object-oriented or functional. Despite the name, JavaScript is most similar to the C programming language, although it does inherit some aspects from Java.

The language was renamed JavaScript as part of a marketing agreement between Sun Microsystems (now Oracle Corporation) and Netscape to promote the scripting language alongside Sun's Java applet technology. It become widely used for scripting client-side

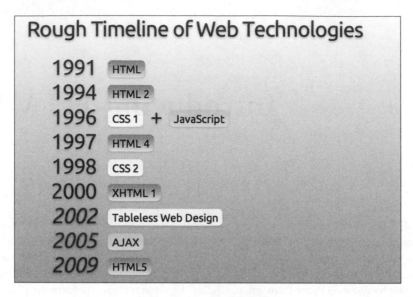

Figure 1-1   HTML timeline

web pages, and Microsoft released a compatible version named JScript, with some additions and changes, because Sun held the trademark on the name "JavaScript."

AJAX

AJAX (Asynchronous JavaScript and XML) started a new wave of interest in JavaScript programming. Once regarded as a toy for amateurs and script kiddies, AJAX helped developers solve more complex problems.

At the epicenter of AJAX is the `XMLHttpRequest` object invented by Microsoft in the late 1990s. `XMLHttpRequest` allows a website to connect to a remote server and receive structured data. As opposed to creating a set of static pages, a developer was empowered to create highly dynamic applications. Gmail, Twitter, and Facebook are examples of these types of applications.

We are currently in the midst of another JavaScript renaissance, as the major browser makers have been using the speed of their JavaScript engines as a benchmark for comparison. JavaScript as a primary programming language has found its way into server-side web components, such as Node.js, and mobile application frameworks, such as WebOS and PhoneGap.

Bridging the Divide

Even the best of standards takes a while to gain uptake. As a means to not let the lack of features limit innovation, Google created Chrome Frame and Google Gears (later, simply Gears) to bring advanced features to older browsers.

Google Gears

Google Gears, which was initially released in May 2007, has come to define some of the advanced features of the HTML5 draft specification. Before the advent of HTML5, many applications used Gears in some way, including Google properties (Gmail, YouTube, Doc, Reader, and so on), MySpace, Remember the Milk, and WordPress, among others. Gears is composed of several modules that add functionality more typical of desktop applications to the browser. Let's take a moment and talk about some of its features.

In its first release, Gears introduced the Database, LocalServer, and WorkerPool modules. Gears' Database API uses an SQLite-like syntax to create relational data storage for web applications. The data is localized to the specific application and complies with generalized cross-site scripting rules in that an application cannot access data outside its domain. The LocalServer module enables web applications to save and retrieve assets to a local cache even if an Internet connection is not present. The assets to serve from local cache are specified in a site manifest file. When an asset matching a URL in the manifest file is requested, the LocalServer module intercepts the request and serves it from the local store.

The WorkerPool module helps address one of the prevalent problems with JavaScript-intensive websites: long-running scripts that block website interaction. A website by default has a single thread to do its work. This is generally not a problem for very short, bursty actions (such as simple DOM manipulation) that return quickly. Any long-running task, such as file input/output or trying to retrieve assets from a slow server, can block interaction and convince the browser that the script is unresponsive and should be forcefully ended. The WorkerPool module brought the concept of multithreading computing to the browser by letting your WorkerPool create "workers" that can execute arbitrary JavaScript. Workers can send and receive messages to and from each other, provided they are in the same WorkerPool, so they can cooperate on tasks. Workers can work cross-origin but inherit the policy from where they are retrieved. To account for the fact that several properties such as `Timer` and `HttpRequest` are exposed by the `window` object, which is not accessible to workers, Gears provides its own implementations.

Another API of interest is the Geolocation API. The Geolocation API attempts to get a fix on a visitor by using available data such as the IP address, available Wi-Fi routers with a known location, cell towers, and other associated data.

Google ceased principal development of Gears in November 2009 and has since shifted focus to getting the features into HTML5. Thankfully, all these features we've discussed found their way into HTML5 in some shape or form.

Chrome Frame

Chrome Frame is a project that embeds Google Chrome as a plugin for Internet Explorer 6 and higher versions, which have weak HTML5 support. Chrome Frame is activated upon recognition of a meta tag. Chrome Frame currently does not require admin rights to be installed, thus opening opportunities on systems that are otherwise locked down.

You can find more information about Chrome Frame at http://code.google.com/chrome/chromeframe/.

Getting Things Done with WebSockets and Web Workers

One of the additions to HTML5 is APIs that help the web application communicate and do work. WebSockets allow web applications to open a channel to interact with web services. Web Workers permit them to run nontrivial tasks without locking the browser.

WebSockets

WebSockets allow applications to have a bidirectional channel to a URI endpoint. Sockets can send and receive messages and respond to opening or closing a WebSocket. Although not part of the specification, two-way communication can be achieved in several other ways, including Comet (AJAX with long polling), Bayeux, and BOSH.

Listing 1-1 shows the code to create a WebSocket that talks to the echo server endpoint. After creating the socket, we set up the functions to be executed when the socket is opened, closed, receives a message, or throws an error. Next, a "Hello World!" message is sent, and the browser displays "Hello World!" upon receipt of the return message.

Listing 1-1   **WebSocket Code for Echoing a Message**

```
var socket = new WebSocket(ws://websockets.org:8787/echo);
socket.onopen = function(evt) { console.log("Socket opened");};
socket.onclose = function(evt) {console.log("Socket closed");};
socket.onmessage = function(evt){console.log(evt.data);};
socket.onerror = function(evt) {console.log("Error: "+evt.data);};

socket.send("Hello World!");
```

Web Workers

Web Workers are the HTML5 incarnation of WorkerPools in Google Gears. Unlike WorkerPools, we don't have to create a pool to house our Web Workers. Listing 1-2 shows the code to create a simple worker and set a function for it to execute upon receipt of a message. Listings 1-2 and 1-3 show the HTML code for creating a web page with a Web Worker that displays the current date and time on two-second intervals.

Listing 1-2   **Web Page for Requesting the Time**

```
<!DOCTYPE HTML>
<html>
 <head>
  <title>Web Worker example</title>
```

```
 </head>
 <body>
  <p>The time is now: <span id="result" /></p>
  <script>
   var worker = new Worker('worker.js');
   worker.onmessage = function (event) {
     document.getElementById('result').innerText = event.data;
   };
  </script>
 </body>
</html>
```

The associated JavaScript worker.js file is shown in Listing 1-3.

Listing 1-3   **Worker.js File for Getting a Date and Time**

```
setInterval(function() {w
    postMessage(new Date());
}, 2000);
```

In the two listings, we see that workers can send messages using `postMessage()` and can listen for messages on the closure `onmessage`. We can also respond to errors and terminate workers by passing a function to `onerror` and executing `terminate()`, respectively.

Workers can be shared and send messages on MessagePorts. As with other aspects of the Web Worker spec, this portion is in a state of flux and somewhat outside the needs of the examples in this book. Therefore, using SharedWorkers is left as an exercise for the reader to investigate.

Application Cache

Application Cache provides a method of running applications while offline, much like the LocalServer feature in Gears. A point of distinction between the two features is that Application Cache doesn't use a JSON file, using a flat file instead to specify which files to cache. A simple manifest file to cache assets is shown in Listing 1-4.

Listing 1-4   **Sample Application Manifest**

```
CACHE MANIFEST
# above line is required, this line is a comment
mygame/game.html
mygame/images/image1.png
mygame/assets/sound2.ogg
```

The Application Cache has several events it can respond to: `onchecking`, `error`, `cached`, `noupdate`, `progress`, `updateready`, and `obsolete`. You can use these events to keep your users informed about the application's status. Using the Application Cache can make your game more tolerant to connectivity outages, and it can make your users happy by letting them start game play quicker (after the assets are cached). Also, if you choose, Application Cache can be used to allow users to play your game offline. Don't worry too much about it right now. In Chapter 11, "Publishing Your Games," we discuss using the Application Cache in more detail.

Database API

At present, there are multiple ways to store structured data using HTML5, including the WebSQL API implemented by Webkit browsers and the competing IndexedDB API spearheaded by Firefox.

WebSQL API

WebSQL provides structured data storage by implementing an SQL-like syntax. Currently, implementations have centralized around SQLite, but that isn't a specific requirement.

There isn't a "createDatabase" function in WebSQL. The function `openDatabase` optimistically creates a database with the given parameters if one doesn't already exist. To create a database name `myDB`, we would need to make a call in the form

```
var db = openDatabase("myDB", "1.0", "myDB Database", 100000);
```

where we pass `"myDB"` as the name, assign the version `"1.0"`, specify a display name of `"myDB Database"`, and give it an estimated size of 100KB. We could have optionally specified a callback to be executed upon creation. Figure 1-2 shows the content of the Chrome Developer Tools Storage tab, which we will cover in more detail in Chapter 2, "Setting Up Your Development Environment," after executing the preceding line of code.

Figure 1-2   Storage tab showing a created database

In the window to the right, we can run arbitrary SQL code, as shown in Figure 1-3, where we created a table, inserted some information, and ran a query.

Figure 1-3   Storage tab showing SQL statements

Although not universally supported, the specification does call out the existence of both asynchronous and synchronous database connections and transactions. Our current example creates an asynchronous connection; to create a synchronous one, we would call `openDatabaseSync` with the same parameters. After the initial connection, there is no distinction when it comes to database transactions besides calling `transaction(...)` for read/write transactions and `readTransaction` for read-only transactions.

A word of caution: Synchronous connections are not well supported and, in general, you should structure your code to run asynchronously.

IndexedDB API

IndexedDB stores objects directly in object stores. This makes it easier to implement JavaScript versions of NoSQL databases, like those of the object databases MongoDB, CouchDB, and SimpleDB. At the time of this writing, the implementations of the APIs weren't synchronized and used different naming schemes and strictness to the specification. The Internet Explorer implementation requires an ActiveX plugin. I encourage you to check out http://nparashuram.com/trialtool/index.html#example=/ttd/IndexedDB/all.html to see some examples in action on Firefox, Chrome, and Internet Explorer. The Chrome code in most cases will work seamlessly on Safari.

Web Storage

Web Storage provides several APIs for saving data on the client in a fashion similar to browser cookies. There is a Storage object for data that needs to persist between restarts named `localStorage` and one for data that will be purged once the session ends named `sessionStorage`. The data is stored as key/value pairs. These two objects implement the functions listed in Table 1-1.

Table 1-1   **Web Storage Functions**

Function Name	Description
`setItem(key:String, value)`	Creates a key/value pair given the specified values. Some implementations require the value to be a string.
`getItem(key:String)`	Returns the item specified by the given key.
`removeItem(key:String)`	Removes the item identified by the given key.
`clear()`	Clears all key/value pairs from the Storage object.
`key(index:long)`	Returns the key for the specific index.

Each Storage object also has a `length` property indicating the number of present key/value pairs.

Web Storage offers a more fluent API we can use in lieu of the `getItem` and `setItem` functions listed in Table 1-1. The alternate API uses an array-like means of referencing a key. To set a `localStorage` key/value pair with the values of a hometown newspaper, we could use the following, for example:

```
localStorage['newspaper'] = 'The Baltimore Sun';
```

Likewise, we could retrieve that value with just the left half of the preceding expression:

```
localStorage['newspaper'];
```

In the context of game programming, we could use Web Storage to store user high scores as well as data for saved games.

Geolocation

The Geolocation API doesn't have an explicit function to ask for the user's permission to track his or her position. Instead, the browser handles this transparently for us. When the Geolocation API first requests position information from a website for which it doesn't have permission, a contextual pop-up appears to request permission from the user.

We can check to see if the browser supports the Geolocation API by checking for the following object:

```
navigator.geolocation
```

If it resolves to a non-null value, we have the ability to geolocate.

The calculated position of a user is defined by the Position object, which contains a Coordinates object named `coords` and a timestamp indicating when the fix was retrieved. Table 1-2 shows the properties of the `coords` object.

Table 1-2   **Coordinates Object Properties**

Property Name	Return Value	Description
latitude	double	The latitude of the position fix.
longitude	double	The longitude of the position fix.
altitude	double	The altitude of the position fix in meters. If this is unavailable, the value will be null.
accuracy	double	The margin of error of the lat-long fix in meters. If this is unavailable, the value will be null.
altitudeAccuracy	double	The margin of error of the altitude value. If this is unavailable, the value will be null.
heading	double	The direction in which the device is traveling in degrees (0° to 360°, inclusive). If this is unavailable, the value will be NaN.
speed	double	The speed in meters that the device is traveling. If this is unavailable, the value will be null.

After we have verified that geolocation is available, obtaining a position fix on a device is simple. We just call `getCurrentPosition` with either one, two, or three parameters, corresponding to the functions to run if getting a fix is successful, if it fails, and the options on the request, respectively.

Listing 1-5 shows the code needed to retrieve a location, draw it on a map with a marker, and draw a proximity circle around the marker.

Listing 1-5   Drawing a Map with Geolocation

```
if(navigator.geolocation) {
    navigator.geolocation.getCurrentPosition(function(pos) {
        var latitude = pos.coords.latitude;
        var longitude = pos.coords.longitude;

        var options = {
            position:new google.maps.LatLng(latitude, longitude)
            ,title:"Your location"};

        var marker = new google.maps.Marker(options);

        var circle = new google.maps.Circle({
            map:map, radius:pos.coords.accuracy
        });
        circle.bindTo('center', marker, 'position');

        marker.setMap(map);

        map.setCenter( new google.maps.LatLng(latitude, longitude));
    },
    function(error) {
        console.log(error.message);
    });
}
```

After verifying that geolocation is available, we first attempt to retrieve a fix on the position of the device. In this example, we are passing in the two parameter functions of `getCurrentPosition` to execute if successful, an error occurs, or if the user declines geolocation. After getting the latitude and longitude portions, we create a marker centered at that position with the title "Your location." To the marker, we attach a circle whose radius is equivalent to the accuracy of the position fix. Lastly, if there is an error, our error-handling function prints out the error message to the console. Figure 1-4 shows a sample position fix using the OpenStreetMap tile set.

Although we did not use it, we could have also specified an options object that indicates several preferences on the retrieved data. We could also set up a listener to execute every time there is a position change returned from the `watchPosition` function. Geolocation is an expensive API. Use it judiciously and don't be afraid to cache the location.

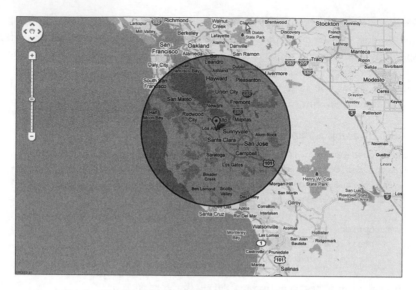

Figure 1-4   Geolocation from the browser

We could use geolocation to create localized leader boards, or on a multiplayer server to match players who are physically close to one another.

Getting Users' Attention with Notifications

In HTML4, the options to communicate messages to the user were limited. You could show the user an alert window or show a message in a `div` element. Showing an alert window is well supported on all browsers, but it is highly disruptive. It is something that requires immediate attention and doesn't let you move on until you have handled it. One sure way to annoy a user is by making him lose a life because some message obscured his view. Showing a message in a `div` element fares slightly better, but there isn't a standard way to add them. These types of messages can be easily ignored. On one side we have notifications that crave attention, and on the other we have notifications that can be easily ignored. There has to be a middle ground. Enter web notifications.

On the Mac OS X and Ubuntu platforms natively, and with a plugin on Windows, an application can send configurable messages to users and notify them of events or changes it deems important. An example of such a notification is shown in Figure 1-5.

Figure 1-5   Desktop notification message

Like their desktop counterparts, web notifications can contain an image along with a contextual message.

Requesting Permission to Display Notifications

Before we can display notifications to users, we first have to get their permission. Explicit permission protects the users from being bombarded with unwanted notifications. We can request permission to display notifications by executing the following:

```
window.webkitNotifications.requestPermission();
```

This will show a contextual message in the browser to allow the user to approve or deny access, as shown in Figure 1-6. Instead of a no-argument function call, we can also pass a function to execute when the user responds to the prompt.

Figure 1-6   Web notification permissions message

We can likewise verify permission by running the following command:

```
window.webkitNotifications.checkPermission();
```

In this case, checkPermission() returns an integer that indicates the permission level, as shown in Table 1-3.

Table 1-3   **Notification Permission Level**

Constant Name	Value
PERMISSION_ALLOWED	0
PERMISSION_UNKNOWN	1
PERMISSION_DENIED	2

Looking at the name, you would expect notifications to work in at least the major Webkit browsers, namely Chrome and Apple Safari. Although Safari uses Webkit, it doesn't implement the Notification API. If the spec is implemented globally, the namespace could presumably change from webkitNotifications to simply notifications.

Creating Notifications

You can create two types of notifications: simple and HTML. Simple notifications display a simple message with an optional title and icon image, whereas HTML notifications display an arbitrary URL. For example, we can create a simple notification by executing the following:

```
var msg = window.webkitNotifications.createNotification(
     '', 'Test Notification', 'Hello World'
);
```

Our notification will have the title "Test Notification" with the message "Hello World." Because we passed an empty string for the icon image, the API omits it. We can do this for any other parameter. Do this to hide parameters you don't want displayed. Passing no value to the function will cause a text message of "undefined" or a broken image link. Figure 1-7 shows our notification running in the browser. As you can see, it is pretty Spartan, and we have no control over the design besides the parameters we passed it.

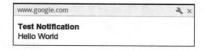

Figure 1-7   Simple web notification

As mentioned before, HTML notifications can get their content from an arbitrary URL such as a website or an image. The function just takes the desired URL to display in the form:

```
var msg =window.webkitNotifications.createHTMLNotification(
     'http://example.com'
);
```

HTML notifications give you no means to resize them, and unless the URL has code to optimize the notification for small screens, scroll bars will probably be included. On a 1680×1050 screen, the default size seems to be approximately 300 pixels wide by 50 pixels high, but because the notifications API is still a draft at the time of this writing, that is certainly subject to change. Until fine-grained height and width attributes are added, stick with simple notifications.

Interacting with Notifications

The resulting notification has two basic functions for controlling it: `show()`, which surfaces the notification to the user, and `cancel()`, which hides the notification if it's currently visible or prevents it from being displayed if it is not visible. Web notifications can also execute functions in response to notification events. Table 1-4 shows a list of the applicable functions you can specify to respond to events.

Table 1-4   **Web Notification Functions**

Function Name	Description
onclick	This function will execute if the notification is clicked *and* the underlying platform supports it. Avoid this event if at all possible.
onclose	This function will execute after the `close` event is fired. This could be when the user closes the notification or if it is closed programmatically.

Table 1-4   **Web Notification Functions**

Function Name	Description
ondisplay	This function will execute after the show() function is called and the notification is visible to the user.
onerror	This function executes after show() is called in the event of an error.

You can check the current status of the draft specification at http://dev.chromium.org/developers/design-documents/desktop-notifications/api-specification.

Media Elements

When HTML was originally designed, it was concerned with mostly textual links. Native display of images would come much later. It is not hard to understand why you would need a plugin or browser extension to play audio or video. In most cases, this meant Flash. HTML5 has tried to address that issue with the inclusion of the audio and video tags.

The audio and video tags allow us to play media in the browser natively. Also, a group of properties can be set to control playback. Here is the most basic HTML form for embedded media (in this case, an audio file):

```
<audio src="song.mp3" autoplay />
```

This creates an audio HTML element, assigns the source to song.mp3, and instructs the page to "autoplay" the content. It is equivalent to the following JavaScript code:

```
var song = new Audio();
song.src = "song.mp3";
song.autoplay = true;
song.load();
```

Controlling Media

In addition to the autoplay attribute listed in the previous example, several other attributes can be used to control our media. For example,

```
<video src="vid.avi" controls />
```

or

```
var vid = new Video();
vid.src = "vid.avi";
vid.controls = true;
```

tells the browser to provide a default set of controls for starting and pausing playback, setting the volume level, and seeking in the stream. In the absence of such a property, the

developer can provide a custom set of controls using the JavaScript functions and properties listed in Tables 1-5 and 1-6.

Table 1-5   **Media Tag Functions**

Function Name	Description
play()	Starts playing the media from the current position and sets the paused property to false
pause()	Halts playing the media and sets the paused property to true
load()	Resets the element and applies any settings, such as pre-fetching

Table 1-6   **Media Element Properties**

Property Name	Accepted Values	Description
currentTime	integer	Sets the position in the media stream for playback
duration	N/A (read-only)	Indicates the length of the source media in seconds
loop	true or false	Specifies whether or not to play the media from the beginning when the end of the stream is reached
autoplay	true or false	Specifies whether or not to play the media as soon as possible
muted	true or false	Specifies whether or not to set the volume at 0.0

The list of properties has been truncated for brevity and usefulness. To see a full list of
available properties, check out the HTML5 draft spec at http://dev.w3.org/html5/spec.

Handling Unsupported Formats

At the time of this writing, the audio and video elements in different browsers don't nec-
essarily all support the same types of audio and video. The reason a particular browser
doesn't support a particular format might be due to the age of the format, competition
with an endorsed format, or patent restrictions that the browser's parent company doesn't
want to deal with. Media tags have several methods to deal with this.

Listing Multiple Sources

Instead of specifying a single source, the developer can choose to list multiple sources to
let the browser choose the appropriate one to use. The following snippet lists two sources

for a video tag and the fallback message if neither format is supported or the browser doesn't support the video tag.

```
<video>
    <source src="video.ogv" />
    <source src="video.avi" />
    <!- Neither is supported, can show message or fallback to Flash ->
    <div><span>Use a modern browser</span></div>
</video>
```

Although listing multiple sources is an option for a static page, it's not great for applications with dynamic content. For those instances, using the tool Modernizr is recommended. We'll discuss Modernizr in more detail in Chapter 2, but consider this a primer.

Using Modernizr

Modernizr (www.modernizr.com) inspects browser capabilities at runtime and injects the properties into a JavaScript object. To see whether the browser can play audio or video, we would check the value of `Modernizr.audio` or `Modernizr.video` to see if it evaluates to true.

Checking support for a particular format is slightly different. Verifying support for MP3 files is done by checking the value of `Modernizr.audio.mp3`, but the value returned isn't true or false. The HTML5 spec states that the browser should return its confidence level that it can play the format. The return value will be "probably," "maybe," or an empty string. When we use `Modernizr.audio.mp3` in a conditional clause, any non-empty value is treated as true and the empty string is treated as false.

> ### CSS3
>
> CSS3 doesn't fit the scope of this book, and readers are encouraged to explore the specification if they are interested in it. Like HTML5, CSS3 extends its predecessor (CSS2) by adding new features and codifying previous proposals, such as web fonts and speech, which were introduced in previous versions but not widely supported. A useful website for further information is http://www.css3.info.

HTML5 Drawing APIs

An interesting area of the HTML5 spec is the new drawing APIs. Canvas, SVG, and WebGL provide bitmapped, vector, and three-dimensional drawing capabilities, respectively.

Canvas

The canvas element started its life as an Apple extension to Webkit, the layout engine powering Safari and Chrome, to display Dashboard gadgets and additions to the Safari browser. It was later adopted by Opera, Firefox, and related browsers, eventually becoming a component of the HTML5 specification. The beta release of Internet Explorer 9 (IE9) has brought native support to all major browsers, although support in IE9 is not as complete as the aforementioned browsers.

The canvas element can be most simply described as a drawable region with height and width attributes using JavaScript as the medium to draw and animate complex graphics such as graphs and images. A full set of 2D drawing functions is exposed by the JavaScript language. Given the close relationship between JavaScript and ActionScript, a Flash drawing or animation using ActionScript can be easily ported to JavaScript with only moderate effort. Canvas will be covered in more detail in Chapter 5, "Creating Games with the Canvas Tag."

SVG

SVG (Scalable Vector Graphics) is a mature W3C specification for drawing static or animated graphics. The ability to inline SVG without the use of an object or embed tag was added in HTML5. Vector graphics use groupings of mathematics formulas to draw primitives such as arcs, lines, paths, and rectangles to create graphics that contain the same quality when rendered at any scale. This is a marked benefit over images whose discernible quality degrades when they are displayed at a scale larger than that for which they were designed.

SVG takes a markedly different approach from the canvas element in that it represents drawings in XML files instead of purely in code. XML is not the more concise representation of data, so a file may contain many repeated sections. This can be addressed by compressing the file, which can greatly reduce its size. As with the canvas element, interaction can be scripted using JavaScript. Prior to IE9, IE supported an incompatible vector format called VML. As of IE9, all major desktop browsers support a fairly common feature set of SVG 1.1. Chapter 6, "Creating Games with SVG and RaphaëlJS," puts SVG front and center.

WebGL

WebGL is a JavaScript API for 3D drawing that enables the developer to assess graphics hardware and control minute details of the rendering pipeline. It is managed by the Khronos group and shares much of its syntax with OpenGL 2.0 ES. At the time of this writing, WebGL is not supported in Internet Explorer 6+ or the stable branches of Opera and Safari. It is available in the stable builds of Firefox and Chrome/Chromium and in development builds of Opera and Safari. Chapter 7, "Creating Games with WebGL and Three.js," dives into WebGL.

Conveying Information with Microdata

A web application or API parsing a page can interpret HTML marked up with microdata and respond to it. For instance, a search engine that returns results marked up with microdata could be parsed by a browser extension or script to better present the data to a visually impaired or colorblind user. Microformats are a preceding concept that serves the same goal. One key difference between microformats and HTML5 microdata is the way that the data is denoted. As shown in Listing 1-6, microformats use the `class` property of an object to indicate the fields on an object.

Listing 1-6   **hCard Microformat Example**

```
<div class="vcard">
    <div class="fn">James Williams</div>
    <div class="org">Some Company</div>
    <div class="tel">650-555-3055</div>
    <a class="url" href="http://example.com/">http://example.com/</a>
</div>
```

Microdata uses the same concept with slightly different notation. Instead of marking properties using classes, the `itemprop` keyword is used. The keyword `itemscope` marks an individual unit. At its core, microdata is a set of name/value pairs composed into items. Listing 1-7 shows a microdata example. The `itemtype` property indicates a definition of the object and specifies valid properties. You could use microdata to encode the names and scores on a leader board page or instructions and screenshots from a game.

Listing 1-7   **Microdata Example**

```
<p itemprop="address" itemscope
     itemtype="http://data-vocabulary.org/Address">

<span itemprop="street-address">1600 Amphitheatre Parkway</span><br>

<span itemprop="locality">Mountain View</span>,
     <span itemprop="region">CA</span>

<span itemprop="postal-code">94043</span><br>

<span itemprop="country-name">USA</span>

</p>
```

Summary

HTML5 marks a groundbreaking change in how we interact with the browser. This chapter highlighted the major additions that apply to our needs. You learned how Google Chrome Frame brings HTML5 features to IE browsers as well as the multiple ways to draw assets.

In exploring HTML5, in addition to its drawing APIs, you learned about features that allow you to run computationally heavy tasks without blocking the browser, setting up bidirectional communications channels between applications, and enabling offline execution of applications.

You can download chapter code at www.informit.com/title/9780321767363.

2

Setting Up Your Development Environment

One of the great things about HTML5 is that having a computer with a reliable Internet connection is the main barrier to starting development. All the other tools you will need can be obtained freely on the Internet. Some specialized applications require a license, but we will focus on their free counterparts.

In this chapter, you will install the tools needed to make applications for HTML5 games. We will also examine some of these tools in detail.

Development Tools

Some developers swear by a bare-bones command-line editor, such as emacs, vim, and (one of my personal favorites) Redcar. However, for medium to large projects, as the number of files increases, using an Integrated Development Environment (IDE) brings numerous advantages, including easier file management and renaming, code-hinting and syntax checking, and automated builds. Because of its great extensibility and because we will be using it for our Java-specific examples, we will be installing the Eclipse IDE and the Java platform upon which it runs. Although installing Java and Eclipse is optional for the basic examples, our examples involving the Google Web Toolkit (GWT) will require Java to be installed. Feel free to substitute your own preferred tool chain.

Installing Java

As mentioned before, Eclipse and GWT run on Java. They require Java 5 SDK or higher. Generally, most people will have a fairly recent version of Java on their machines. You can find out if you have the proper Java SDK installed by running the following at a command prompt:

```
$ javac -version
```

If that command fails, you don't have the Java SDK installed. However, if you get a response similar to the following snippet, with a number of 1.5 or higher, you are good to go:

```
javac 1.6.0_17
```

For the Mac platform, the Java SDK comes preinstalled on versions prior to OS X 10.7 (codenamed Lion). Computers using OS X version 10.5 (codenamed Leopard) already have Java 1.5, and those with version 10.6 (codenamed Snow Leopard) have Java 1.6.

Windows users can download an executable of the Java SDK from http://java.sun.com/javase/downloads/index.jsp, making sure to select a download that includes the "JDK." Once the file is downloaded, executing it will install Java.

Java installation on Linux is a bit trickier. Although installation differs slightly from distribution to distribution, Java 6–compatible binaries are available in the package managers of all major distributions. Failing that, you can install Java using the downloads on Sun/Oracle's website.

Installing the Eclipse IDE and Google Plugin

Eclipse is a multipurpose IDE primarily used by Java developers. Eclipse is modular in design and has a plugin architecture that exposes new features to the IDE. Due to this plugin architecture, there is support for other programming languages, including C++, Python, Ruby, and PHP. It also forms the basis for many specialized IDEs, some of which we will explore later in this chapter.

The installation of the Eclipse IDE is rather straightforward on all platforms. Figure 2-1 shows the Eclipse loading screen. Instead of an installer application, the Eclipse foundation (the makers of Eclipse) ships a self-contained archive file. You download the archive and extract it somewhere on your machine, and you are ready to go. You can download the latest version of Eclipse at http://www.eclipse.org/downloads/. Make sure you grab the package "Eclipse IDE for Java Developers."

Figure 2-1   Eclipse loading screen

After you have Eclipse installed, double-click the executable file (possibly eclipse.exe or simply eclipse) to open it. If you have come back to this section from one of the later chapters dealing with the App Engine, you might want to change the perspective to the Java Perspective by selecting Window | Open Perspective | Java. To get App Engine integration in Eclipse, you have to install several packages. Here are the steps to follow:

1. Select Help | Install New Software. There might be an option titled "Software Updates" instead.

2. Click the Add button to add a new software site. You can alternatively install the package from your hard drive, but adding a site allows Eclipse to routinely check for software updates.

3. You can name the site anything you want because it is just an identifier for housekeeping purposes. I titled it "Google App Engine Plugin" in Figure 2-2. Add one of the following URLs to the Location text box and click OK (check code.google.com for versions higher than 3.5):

   - For Eclipse 3.5 (Galileo): http://dl.google.com/eclipse/plugin/3.5

   - For Eclipse 3.4 (Ganymede): http://dl.google.com/eclipse/plugin/3.4

   - For Eclipse 3.3 (Europa): http://dl.google.com/eclipse/plugin/3.3

4. Check the boxes next to "Google Plugin for Eclipse" and "Google Web Toolkit," as shown in Figure 2-3, and then click Next. You can install support for Google Web Toolkit at this time as well. Your versions might be higher.

5. Confirm that the two plugins appear in the list under Install Details and then click Next.

6. Review the licenses and indicate that you agree to the terms by clicking the appropriate radio button. The Google Plugin has several Eclipse dependencies, so don't be alarmed if you see several other plugins listed. After you have downloaded the required packages, Eclipse will prompt you to restart it. When it returns, you'll be all set.

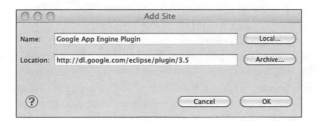

Figure 2-2   Eclipse Add Site dialog panel

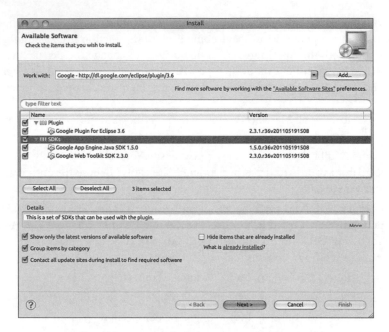

Figure 2-3   Eclipse Available Software dialog panel

Google Web Toolkit

The Google Web Toolkit (GWT) is a set of libraries that allows developers to write rich Internet applications in the Java programming language and have them converted into cross-platform Asynchronous JavaScript and XML (AJAX) applications without worrying about the individual quirks or incompatibilities of the target browsers. This allows developers to write an application from front to back in the same language.

If Java isn't your cup of tea, open-source ports of GWT are available for Python and Ruby called Pyjamas and RubyJS, respectively. The ports tend to lag quite a bit behind the most recent version of GWT, so we won't be using them directly in any examples. However, much of the core GWT code will have similar Pyjamas code. You can find more information about Pyjamas and RubyJS at http://code.google.com/p/pyjamas and http://rubyforge.org/projects/rubyjs/, respectively.

GWT requires at least Java 1.5 to be installed on the target machine. You can install GWT by downloading it from http://code.google.com/webtoolkit/download.html and extracting it somewhere on your machine. The Google Plugin for Eclipse supports GWT, so revisit the previous section to see the instructions for installing the plugin.

Chapter 8, "Creating Games Without JavaScript," will cover using GWT with Canvas, WebGL, and SVG in more detail.

Web Server Tools and Options

Unless you plan to keep your game all to yourself or to package it as a mobile application, chances are that you will need a web server of some shape or form. In this section, we will discuss some of the options for deploying your game.

Google App Engine

Google App Engine is a hosting environment for Java and Python that permits you to host your application on Google's infrastructure. In theory, your application can scale almost infinitely. To operate in this way, there are some trade-offs, such as the use of an untraditional data store, limited access to the file system, and special APIs for authentication, mail, and fetching. One of the other benefits of the App Engine is that you can write applications using Rhino, the Java platform implementation of JavaScript, so that you can run JavaScript from back to front. Using App Engine also gives you a little extra value from installing Eclipse. The Google plugin lets you deploy to App Engine with just a couple button clicks.

You can install Google App Engine or read about the plugin for Eclipse at http://code.google.com/appengine/.

Opera Unite

The Opera browser, since version 10.0, has packaged an embedded web service called Opera Unite. Unite has built-in applications for streaming files and sharing photos, chatting, and hosting a site. To host a website, you would normally have to register a domain, find a web host, and upload your files. Unite lets you do this all with the click of a button. When you start the Unite service, it registers your computer with a proxy server run by Opera. Thus, visitors to

http://*your_device.your_username.operaunite.com/*
(where *your_device* is the name of your computer)
get routed correctly. The proxy server allows you to set up a service without having to punch a hole through your router. Unite's web server runs using server-side JavaScript and allows file system access. You can even package and publish your game so that others can install it without needing to connect to your Unite instance.

Unite is great for putting something out there to share with friends or testers, but it requires the browser to be running, so it isn't a great option for anything that needs 24/7 uptime. We will discuss packaging applications for distribution in Chapter 11, "Publishing Your Games."

Node.js and RingoJS

RingoJS is a web framework that runs on Rhino and implements specifications and proposals from the CommonJS API. Given that JavaScript evolved into being without a discrete spec, CommonJS seeks to set standards for things that may have been originally outside the scope of a JavaScript application—such as access to the local file system.

Node.js and RingoJS both implement parts of CommonJS, with RingoJS being a bit more API-compliant. One major point of divergence is that Node.js runs on Google's V8-engine, which powers JavaScript support in Google Chrome and is implemented in C++.

We will discuss server-side JavaScript, specifically Node.js, in more detail in Chapter 9, "Building a Multiplayer Game Server."

Browser Tools

An important piece in developing HTML5 applications is a browser that implements most of the spec and has decent debugging tools. Google Chrome, Mozilla Firefox (and its derivatives), Apple Safari, and Opera have outstanding HTML5 compliance and debugging tools. Internet Explorer 9, which was released in March 2011, is much more HTML5 standards-compliant than its predecessor, but it lags in terms of support compared to the aforementioned browsers.

Inside the Chrome Developer Tools

Using Chrome's debugger tools, we can dynamically inspect the page's DOM, view resource loading times, and run arbitrary JavaScript. We can view the Developer Tools console for any page by selecting View | Developer | Developer Tools. Figure 2-4 shows the console window for Google.com. With the Elements tab selected, we have a nested view of the DOM with associated styles for the document elements. Hovering over an element tag will highlight it in the browser window. This is really useful when trying to figure out which element is the one that is off by several pixels.

Figure 2-4   Chrome Developer Tools Elements tab

The other two tabs in the Developer Tools console that are incredibly useful to game developers are the Resources and JavaScript Console tabs. The Resources tab, shown in Figure 2-5, allows you to track on an asset-by-asset basis what exactly is slowing your gadget from showing in Waves quickly. The first time you run it on a new site, you can decide to activate it just for this session or forever. Resource tracking does a bit of overhead to page loading times, so it is best to use it sparingly.

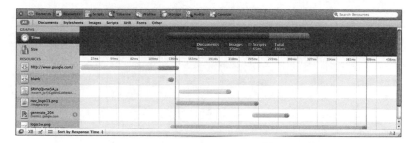

Figure 2-5   Chrome Developer Tools Resources tab

The last tab I'll highlight in this section is the JavaScript Console tab, as shown in Figure 2-6. For those of us who aren't exactly JavaScript gurus, it's a godsend because it, along with the `console.log()` command, frees us from the most dreaded acts in programming: `println` (or in this case, `alert`) debugging. You can also use it to inspect the DOM programmatically or run arbitrary JavaScript.

Figure 2-6   Chrome Developer Tools Console tab

Chrome Extensions

Similar to the Eclipse IDE, the functionality of Google Chrome can be enhanced and extended with extensions. Extensions range in purpose from RSS readers and site-specific enhancements or notifiers to games. A full list can be found at https://chrome.google.com/extensions. Let's take a moment to call out a couple that will make our lives a little bit easier in creating gadgets.

We can install these extensions in Chrome by clicking the Install button from the Chrome Extensions page, as shown in Figure 2-7, and following the prompts. Two useful plugins for developers are JSONView and YSlow. JSONView allows you to view JSON data formatted to increase readability. YSlow analyzes web pages and gives tips on how to improve performance.

Figure 2-7   Installing a Chrome extension

Safari Developer Tools

The Developer tools in Apple's Safari are quite similar to their counterparts in Google Chrome. By default, they are hidden to the end user.

To enable them, select Preferences in your title or icon bar and navigate to the Advanced tab. As shown in Figure 2-8, make sure that "Show Develop menu in menu bar" is checked. Visit the previous section on the Chrome Developer tools for an overview of what is present.

Figure 2-8   Enabling the Developer menu

Firebug

Firebug is an extension for Mozilla Firefox that allows developers to debug a website's HTML, CSS, and JavaScript. Although originally designed for Firefox, Firebug also has a "Lite" version that will run in Google Chrome and complements the tools already present in that browser.

You might have noticed that the core components and tabs of Firebug look very similar to those of Chrome and Safari. As in Chrome, there are add-ons for Firefox and Firebug to expose more developer capabilities (such as DOM manipulation and introspection) for several programming languages (such as PHP and Python). You can find instructions on installing Firebug or Firebug Lite by visiting http://getfirebug.com.

HTML5 Tools

In this section, we will discuss some tools that allow us to easily create assets for our games. In the case of Raphaël and ProcessingJS, these are lightweight graphics libraries.

ProcessingJS

ProcessingJS is a JavaScript library that can act as an abstraction layer over the canvas tag to draw primitives, respond to user interaction, and draw and manipulate images. ProcessingJS was created in the summer of 2008 by John Resig, the creator of the popular JavaScript library jQuery, who ported it from of the similarly named Processing Java Library. As a result, the functions and API calls are syntactically identical to the Java version. Likewise, many of the Java samples can be ported with no code changes. It must, however, be noted that ProcessingJS doesn't implement the full Java API. This doesn't matter that much for our purposes because most of those features would be things we would rather do with WebGL.

You can view some examples and the API reference at http://processingjs.org.

Inkscape

Inkscape is a mature cross-platform vector graphics editor using SVG. It is comparable to the commercial applications Adobe Illustrator and CorelDRAW. Although the most recent release is only 0.48, there has been a vibrant community dating back to its inception in 2003. The version number is more of an indication of how much of the SVG 1.1 spec the application implements. Although it doesn't support the complete SVG spec, and some might argue that no application does, the Inkscape community has made up for this with plugins that enhance the platform.

You can download the application at http://inkscape.org.

SVG-edit

SVG-edit is a web-based, JavaScript-powered, SVG creation tool. SVG-edit is great for simplified drawings that will have a limited amount of effects applied to them. The interface, as shown in Figure 2-9, has controls for creating text and simple primitives as well as embedding images.

If you have to create, say, a checkerboard in a pinch, SVG-edit would be great for that. It doesn't include file management and is only able to display the raw SVG code for you to copy and paste into a text editor, as shown in Figure 2-10.

You can download the source or try it online at http://code.google.com/p/svg-edit/.

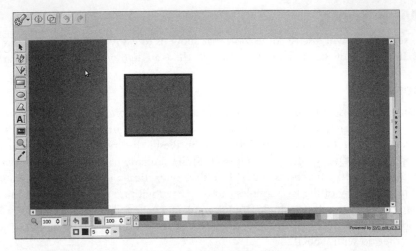

Figure 2-9   SVG-edit interface

Figure 2-10   SVG-edit code view

Raphaël

In the two previous sections, we discussed lightweight and advanced tools for creating SVG files using a user interface. Those are appropriate for games where all the assets are pre-fabricated—for a chess game, for example. For SVG games where assets would need to be created dynamically or for those developers who prefer to use code to create SVG graphics, there is Raphaël. Raphaël is a JavaScript library that provides primitive shape, font, and animation support and is evaluated to embedded SVG at runtime. There is also a compatibility layer that renders using Vector Markup Language (VML) if the browser implements VML in lieu of SVG (namely, IE browsers prior to IE9). Raphaël can be downloaded at http://raphaeljs.com/.

We will take advantage of these tools in Chapter 6, "Creating Games with SVG and RaphaëlJS."

3D Modeling Tools

In Chapter 7, "Creating Games with WebGL and Three.js," we will discuss creating games using WebGL. We need tools to create assets for those games. In the games industry, that usually means applications such as 3D Studio Max and Maya. With prices ranging from just south of a thousand dollars to more than several thousand dollars, these applications can be cost prohibitive for the hobbyist game programmer. As is the case with commercial vector graphics applications, very capable open-source applications are available to fill this need for the hobbyist or professional.

Blender

Blender, shown in Figure 2-11, is a cross-platform open-source 3D modeling, rendering, and animation application. Among its features are cloth, skeletal, and rigid body simulation, texturing, particle dynamics, and compositing. Blender can import and export to many different graphics file formats. It also has a Python API that can be used to extend the application. Blender has been used in pre- and post-production on several television commercials, television shows, and feature films.

You can find out more information about Blender and download it at http://blender.org.

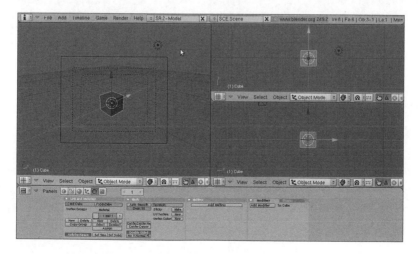

Figure 2-11   Blender interface

Summary

In this chapter, we identified some of the tool and frameworks that will best serve our needs in creating HTML5 games. We installed the Java SDK and the Eclipse IDE and also discussed the SVG and 3D modeling tools and libraries we will use throughout the book to create assets for our games.

You can download chapter code at www.informit.com/title/9780321767363.

3

Learning JavaScript

Although the title of the book explicitly calls out SVG, HTML5 Canvas, and WebGL, they wouldn't be able to do much without the help of JavaScript. SVG, Canvas, and WebGL need JavaScript to drive the interactions between the user and the game. JavaScript also provides the basis for libraries and languages such as GWT and Coffee-Script, which are referenced later in the book. Node.js, also covered later in the book, uses JavaScript to run server-side code. In this chapter, we will cover the basics of JavaScript, along with some useful utilities and libraries that will aid in creating games, and use a JavaScript library to create your first game.

What Is JavaScript?

JavaScript is a loosely typed dynamic language that began its life as a Netscape Communications project named LiveScript. It was renamed to JavaScript roughly around the time plugin support for the Java programming language was added to Netscape, much to the chagrin of developers everywhere. Despite the name, JavaScript and Java are only loosely related in that both of them are influenced by C and share some of the same keywords and structures.

JavaScript's Basic Types

Certain types of objects are guaranteed to exist in every JavaScript implementation. They can also be thought of as the building blocks to create other types of objects. The JavaScript basic types are as follows:

- **Array**—A collection of things.
- **Boolean**—A value of true or false.
- **Function**—A piece of code that does some work.
- **Number**—Examples include 42, 3.54e-3, and 3.14159.
- **String**—A collection of characters in single or double quotes, such as "Hello".
- **Object**—The base type from which all other types descend.

- **undefined**—The referenced object doesn't exist.
- **null**—The object exists with no value, but JavaScript makes a specific distinction as to if the object exists and has no value or if it doesn't know about the object. If you execute the code

```
var x = null;
```

you are telling JavaScript that you are defining an object that doesn't have a value at this time but might be used in the future. On the other hand, if you just execute

```
var x;
```

the value of x, in this case, would be undefined.

Understanding Arithmetic Operators

We learned in the first grade that the basic arithmetic operators are +, −, /, ★, and = for adding, subtracting, dividing, multiplying, and assigning values. Although the first four are generally used for numeric values, some programming languages allow you to redefine how they interact with user-defined objects. JavaScript isn't one of those languages. You should stay away from using the operators on your objects unless they are Numbers; this way, you'll avoid unexpected results. For example, given that adding two Strings together concatenates them, you might expect that subtracting them will remove an instance of the second String from the first. That's how it works in some other languages, but not in JavaScript. JavaScript throws Exceptions after trying to evaluate them as Numbers.

Understanding JavaScript Functions

Let's begin by looking at the simple JavaScript function shown in Listing 3-1. In the code, we first declare a function named HelloWorld (which prints "Hello, World!" to the console) and then we execute it.

Listing 3-1   Hello World JavaScript

```
function HelloWorld() {
    console.log("Hello, World!");
}
HelloWorld();
```

The function keyword tells the application running the code that the enclosed code will do some task. In this case, our function doesn't take in any parameters to manipulate or use to do its work or return anything. Some other programming languages require specifying a return type for the object the function will return. In JavaScript, however, regardless of whether the function returns anything, we always start its declaration with the function keyword. Listing 3-2 shows a function that takes two values and adds them together.

Listing 3-2   Adding Two Objects

```
function add(one, two) {
    return one + two;
}
```

This listing introduces two new concepts: function parameters and the `return` keyword. Function parameters give us a way to provide data that the function needs to do its work, and the `return` keyword sends us an object after the work is completed. If we call the function

```
add(23, 43);
```

it returns 66. We can also call it with any other object, such as a String, and it concatenates the String values that describe those objects.

Functions as First-class Objects

Functions in JavaScript not only can be executed, they can also be constructed and modified at runtime, assigned to variables, and returned by other functions. Objects with the latter capabilities (everything but the ability to be executed) are known as **first-class objects**. These capabilities give us a structure that roughly approximates the `class` keyword from other programming languages such as Java and C#. In those languages, classes define a prototype for the variables and functions that objects of those classes will contain. Also, functions, even if they have some first-class citizen properties, are not allowed to be nested in one another. In this capacity, JavaScript straddles the line between classes and functions, so some refer to a function that returns the same type as itself as a class. Listing 3-3 shows a `Car` "class" that contains functions to start, accelerate, and apply the brakes.

Listing 3-3   JavaScript `Car` "Class"

```
function Car() {
    var self = this;
    self.speed = 0;
    self.start = function() {
        console.log("Car started.");
    }
    self.accelerate = function() {
        self.speed = self.speed + 10;
        console.log("Speed is now:"+self.speed+ " mph");
    }
    self.applyBrakes = function() {
        self.speed = 0;
        console.log("Brakes applied.");
    }
}
```

One thing to note from this listing is that we are using an alternate form to declare our function by defining variables that will hold the functions and then assigning anonymous functions to them. We can create a instance of `Car` and start it by executing the following:

```
myCar = new Car();
myCar.start();
```

The key difference from before is that instead of executing the function directly, we are requesting to have an instance, or copy, of it stored into the global variable `myCar`. This allows us to call member functions on the object. Another new concept is assigning variables using the `var` keyword. Using `var` is generally optional, but it does affect variable scope. A variable's scope determines the visibility, and as a result, the value held in it. Let's say that outside of the `Car` function we had a variable named `self` declared using the following code:

```
self = "me"
```

The `self` variable with the value `"me"` is declared with a global scope and is viewable anywhere; however, the `self` that `Car` uses is only visible to functions inside `Car`. The object that the `this` keyword points to can change based on where it is called from. Using a local `self` variable gives us assurance that the calls within the object will function properly.

Comparison Operators

Comparison operators test whether two objects are equal or their relative value. For example, we could use the operators shown in Table 3-1 to test whether the String `"abc"` is equal to `"def"` by executing

```
"abc" == "def"
```

The result would be false.

Table 3-1   **Comparison Operators**

Operator	Description
!	Reverses the result of a logic operator, making a true value false and vice versa.
&&	Both sides of the expression must resolve to true in order for true to be returned.
||	If either side of the expression resolves to true, then true will be returned.
==, ===	Returns true if the two objects are equal. == attempts to forcefully convert both objects into the same type and then compares them. === requires that the objects be the same type.

Table 3-1   **Comparison Operators**

Operator	Description
!=, !==	Returns true if the two objects are not equal. != attempts to forcefully convert both objects into the same type and then compares them. !== requires that the objects be the same type.
<	Returns true if the object on the right is greater than that on the left.
>	Returns true if the object on the right is less than that on the left.
<=	Returns true if the object on the right is greater or equal to that on the left.

Here are several peculiarities when testing things that aren't numbers:

- True, often evaluated to 1, is always greater than false, which evaluates to 0.
- A String is less than another String if it occurs lexicographically before it in the dictionary.
- Comparisons on Arrays compare the indexes of both arrays, and *all* values must satisfy the condition.
- Undefined == null returns true, but undefined === null returns false because undefined and null are two different types.

In most cases, using ==, ===, !=, and !=== for types that aren't Strings, Numbers, or Booleans will yield unexpected results, so if we need to test identity (which is whether the two objects point to the same instance) or equality, we'll write our own explicit equals function.

Conditional Loops and Statements

Comparison operators and expressions give us a means to compare objects, and conditional loops and statements give us a way to use that information to execute code. The first we'll cover is the `if-else` statement, which allows us to make a set of comparisons, one by one. Listing 3-4 shows a couple `if` statements in practice.

Listing 3-4   *`if-else`* Statements

```
if (name == "John") {
    if (age < 18)
    console.log("Age is less than 18");
else if (age < 35)
    console.log("Age is somewhere between 18 and 35");
else console.log("Age is greater than 35");
} else {
    console.log("User is not named John");
}
```

In the listing, we first check to see if the value stored in the variable name is equal to John. If not, an appropriate message is printed to the console. If the variable name is equal to John, we execute a series of comparisons to determine the age range, preemptively stopping when the expression evaluates to true. Each subsequent else only executes if the preceding if statement has failed. This switch-case statement is a fancier type of if statement that checks the value of a single variable for equality with a range of values. We could use a bunch of if statements to do the same thing, but switch-case is more concise. Listing 3-5 shows the general form of a switch-case statement.

Listing 3-5   General Form of a **switch-case** Statement

```
switch (<expression>) {
    case value1:
        codeToExecute1();
        break;
    case value2:
        codeToExecute2();
        break;
    default:
        codeToExecute3();
        break;
}
```

The values listed in the case statements can be strings, numbers, or Booleans. The break keyword prevents subsequent case statements from being evaluated and prevents their code from being executed. default provides the code to execute when the expression doesn't match any case.

Controlling Program Flow with Loops

Eventually we will need to run blocks of code over and over again. Although copying and pasting the code blocks over and over again does work, it becomes fairly messy when you have to change that code. And it looks very amateurish. Loops allow you to run specific blocks of code given some pre- or post-conditions.

while Loops

while loops run a specific block of code until some expression is no longer true. For example, we could create the variable count with an initial value of 0, printing the count to the console and incrementing count until it is equal to 10. Listing 3-6 shows the code for that while loop.

Listing 3-6   Sample **while** Loop

```
var count = 0;
while (count < 10) {
    console.log("The count is now:"+count);
```

```
        count++;
}
```

It is useful to note that if the condition tested by the `while` loop evaluates to false on the first attempt, the code block never runs. The `do-while` loop, on the other hand, is a variant of the traditional `while` loop that ensures the code block executes at least once. Listing 3-7 shows a `do-while` loop that executes exactly once due to a nonsense comparison. As opposed to starting the expression with the `while` keyword and expression to evaluate, we start with the `do` keyword and the `while` clause comes at the end.

Listing 3-7   Sample **do-while** Loop

```
do {
    console.log ("This loop executes only once.");
} while (1 != 1);
```

for Loops

`while` and `do-while` loops allow us to test a single condition. `for` loops give us a way to control the flow a bit more. JavaScript `for` loops mirror the form of Java `for` loops, starting with the `for` keyword followed by initialization expression(s), test condition(s), and the looping interval. Listing 3-8 shows the `while` loop shown in Listing 3-7 adapted to a `for` loop.

Listing 3-8   Sample **for** Loop

```
for (var count = 0; count < 10; count++) {
    console.log("The count is now:"+count);
}
```

Each of the expressions in the `for` loop are optional. We could break out the initialization expression as we did in the `while` loop, increment the count in the code block, or omit all three to create an infinite loop. Listing 3-9 shows these variants in code.

Listing 3-9   More **for** Loops

```
/* Loop 1 */
var count = 0;
for ( ; count<10; ) {
    console.log("The count is now:"+count);
    count++;
}
/* Loop 2 */
for ( ; ; ) {
    /* For demonstration purposes only, don't ever do this. */
}
```

Delayed Execution with `setTimeout` and `setInterval`

The fact that JavaScript runs in a single thread drives many design choices in the language. You'll see later in this chapter how various libraries use events to notify applications that something notable has happened. Another means to accommodate this single-threadedness is to use the `setTimeout` function to kick off some arbitrary code sometime in the future. Listing 3-10 shows the code to print the current date and time to the console after a 1,000 milliseconds.

Listing 3-10   Example of `setTimeout`

```
setTimeout(function() {
    console.log(new Date());
    }, 1000
);
```

`setTimeout` executes once and it's done. If we need to repeatedly run the same code over and over again, we can have each `setTimeout` create a new `setTimeout`. However, a more concise way would be to use `setInterval`. Besides using `setInterval` in place of `setTimeout`, the method calls are identical. `setInterval` will attempt to run the code every X milliseconds. JavaScript will make its best effort to honor the requests to execute code. The code within `setInterval` needs to perform reasonably well. Long-running tasks set to a short interval could delay execution of subsequent iterations until the first one is done. `clearTimeout` and `clearInterval` cancel the next execution of `setTimeout` and `setInterval`, respectively. They do not affect the code that might be currently running.

Creating Complex Objects with Inheritance and Polymorphism

As mentioned earlier in the chapter, JavaScript uses functions to expose the concept of object-oriented programming language classes. Another set of features for programming languages that use classes includes the ability to create classes that derive properties and functions from other classes and the ability for objects of multiple classes to respond to the same method signatures. These features are known as **inheritance** and **polymorphism.**

The easy way to decipher inheritance is the "is-a" relationship. Continuing our example from earlier in the chapter, a Toyota *is a* (inherits from) car. JavaScript adds properties or functions to objects using the dot syntax. Using the `prototype` keyword, we can modify all instances of a particular type. Listing 3-11 shows the declaration of two classes: `Car` and `Toyota`. After declaring the `Car` object, we next assign its prototype (its functions and properties) to `Toyota`. Next, the constructor for the `Toyota` type is created and overrides the versions provided by `Car`. If we call `go` on a `Toyota` object, it uses the `Toyota` version instead of the one from `Car`. That is polymorphism at work. As long as the object extends from `Car`, we can be guaranteed that functions and properties created in the base type will have some sort of value. As shown in the last few lines of the listing, we can use the keyword `instanceof` to determine what type of object we have. Given the code we wrote, it will evaluate to true when checked against `Car` and `Toyota`.

Listing 3-11   JavaScript Inheritance

```
function Car() {
    var self = this;
    self.type = "Car"
    self.go = function() {
        console.log("Going...");
    };
};
Toyota = function() {};
Toyota.prototype = new Car();
Toyota.prototype.constructor = function() {
    var self = this;
    self.type = "Toyota";
    self.go = function() {
        console.log("A Toyota car is going...");
    }
};
Toyota.prototype.isJapaneseCar = true;

var t = new Toyota();
console.log(t instanceof Toyota);
console.log(t instanceof Car);
```

Making Inheritance Easier with the Prototype Library

Prototype (www.prototypejs.org) is a library for JavaScript that makes object-oriented programming a little bit easier. The inheritance and polymorphism support it provides isn't all that much different from what you have learned by using the `prototype` keyword directly. Prototype does give us a more concise and readable way of doing inheritance. Using the `Class` object and its function `create` is the principal way we will interact with Prototype. Listing 3-12 revises our inheritance example for use with Prototype. The initialize function is where we put any setup code we would like to execute when the object is instantiated. Even if it will be empty, we must specify one in our classes. When we create the `Toyota` class, we add an extra parameter to the function signature to indicate the class from which the child will inherit.

Listing 3-12   Inheritance with Prototype

```
var Car = Class.create({
    initialize: function() {
        this.type = "Car";
    },
    go: function() {
        console.log("Going...");
    }
});
var Toyota = Class.create(Car, {
initialize: function() {
        this.type = "Toyota";
        this.isJapaneseCar = true;
    },
    go: function() {
        console.log("A Toyota car is going...");
    }
});
```

In neither our raw prototype nor the more spiffy Prototype version can we call the function in the parent that we overloaded in the child. That's because when you modify the prototype, you don't keep a copy of what it used to point to. Although sometimes it might be useful to totally handle the inputs and outputs in the child layer, there are occasions when you might want a parent class to handle some basic common data before sending the rest to the specific child class to finish up. In object-oriented programming languages such as Java and C#, you would use an object named super or base to reference the parent class. In those languages, the reference to the parent class is transparently created for you, and you can use it without any modifications to function signatures. In Prototype, however, for any function that we want to call the parent class, we need to add $super to the beginning of its parameter list. Thankfully, this doesn't change how the function is called by your code. One key change that should be noted is that unlike in the languages that get this capability for free, the $super object is a link to the parent function and not the parent object. A child's go function can only call the parent's go function explicitly; all other parent functions are hidden if they are overloaded. Listing 3-13 shows how we would modify our Toyota class to call the go function of Car before calling its own. Executing the go function on the Toyota class will print "Going..." and then "A Toyota car is going..." to the console.

Listing 3-13   Calling a super Function with Prototype

```
var Toyota = Class.create(Car, {
initialize: function() {
        this.type = "Toyota";
        this.isJapaneseCar = true;
```

```
    },
    go: function($super) {
        $super();
        console.log("A Toyota car is going...");
    }
});
```

Learning JQuery

An important utility in your JavaScript toolset is JQuery (http://jquery.com/) and its variants. That's not to say that a comparable JavaScript framework won't serve our needs, but JQuery boasts a very active development community with a multitude of plugins, some of which, as you will see in Chapter 10, "Developing Mobile Games," are targeted toward mobile development. It is also widely recognized as the most popular JavaScript framework. JQuery uses a global object, $, that exposes functions to inspect and alter the Document Object Model (DOM), handle events, and process AJAX requests. There is even a plugin that exposes a 2D game engine called gameQuery (http://gamequery. onaluf.org/).

One of the most important functions you will learn in JQuery is the `ready` function, which delays execution of the enclosed JavaScript until the document is fully loaded. Listing 3-14 shows the code to print "Hello World!" to the console when the document has finished loading. The `ready` function ensures that we don't try to reference any DOM elements before they are instantiated.

Listing 3-14   JQuery **ready** Function

```
<html>
    <head>
        <script type="text/javascript">
            $(document).ready(function () {
                console.log ("Hello World!");
            });
        </script>
    </head>
    <body></body>
</html>
```

Manipulating the DOM with Selectors

Another important concept of JQuery is selectors. Selectors give us a way to reach deep into the object graph with commands as simple as retrieving all the anchor tags in a document or as complex as retrieving the third `td` element inside a table that is inside a `div`. The selector syntax melds those of CSS and XPath (a language for querying XML documents) with some JQuery-specific syntax. Table 3-2 shows some common selectors.

Table 3-2   Some Common JQuery Selectors

Selector	Description
`#id`	Returns the element that matches the given ID
`element`	Returns all elements of the given type
`.class`	Returns all elements that have the CSS class applied to them
`[attribute="value"]`	Returns all elements that have a matching attribute value.
`:eq(n)`	Returns the element in the set that equals index n (zero-indexed)
`:even`	Returns even-numbered elements in the given set
`:odd`	Returns odd-numbered elements in the given set
`parent descendants`	Returns the descendents of the parent element or selector
`parent > child`	Returns only the first-level children of the parent element or selector
`selector1,selector2, selector3`	Returns a combined list of the results from all the given selectors

Selectors can be chained together, so we could find the `div` element with the `id` "header" by executing the selector for an element and then the selector for an attribute:

```
$("div[id='header']")
```

Alternatively, we could simply execute the following:

```
$(#header)
```

After we have an element or set of elements returned by a selector, we can manipulate them in several ways, including but not limited to the following:

- Adding, removing, or modifying CSS styles and attributes
- Adding or removing child elements
- Adding animated transitions and effects

JQuery Events

Instead of busily waiting for something to happen, JavaScript uses events to notify us of changes. This frees up the application to do other things while there are no events to process and to not lose cycles constantly checking for input. It's more of a "don't call us, we'll call you" model. Because you can't usually predict where or when these events will be fired, the way to be notified of changes is to bind, or attach, a function to be called whenever the event is fired. JQuery has a generalized `bind` function that can generically handle any event type and a set of specific functions for common event types such as click, double-click, key up, and so on. Listing 3-15 shows two equivalent methods of binding (or attaching) a `click` handler to an element with the `id` "menuBar," which might be represented in HTML code as follows:

```
<div id="menuBar">/* Stuff here */</div>
```

We will revisit this concept in Chapter 10.

Listing 3-15   Examples of JQuery Event Binding

```
/* Method 1 */
$("#menuBar").bind("click", function() {
    console.log("Clicked on menu bar.");
});
/* Method 2 */
$("#menuBar").click(function() {
    console.log("Clicked on menu bar.");
});
```

AJAX with JQuery

Eventually every web application is going to need to retrieve assets of some sort that don't reside on the local server. AJAX (Asynchronous JavaScript and XML) allows you to send a request for a document and be notified when the data has been fully retrieved or sent. As was the case with browser events, JQuery has several different forms. For the sake of simplicity, we will assume that there isn't a need for any advanced features such as authentication, headers, and cross-domain requirements. JQuery's API provides options for AJAX requests that rival full-blown server-side frameworks and languages. Listing 3-16 shows a generalized method to execute an AJAX request. In it, we pass off a map of key/value pairs to the `ajax` function indicating the specifics of our AJAX request. There are shortcut methods for common GET (`get`) and POST (`post`) as well as for retrieving data as JSON (`getJSON`) or as a script (`getScript`). JQuery also fires events for the different portions of the AJAX request life cycle.

Listing 3-16   JQuery AJAX: POST and GET

```
$.ajax({
    type: "GET",
    url:"request.html",
    success: function(data) {
        console.log(data);
    }
});
```

Cross-Site Scripting

Generally, websites are prevented from making AJAX calls that didn't originate from the same domain, which is known as the **same-origin policy.** Cross-site scripting is a type of injection attack where a malicious user exploits a flaw in a website's design to inject code that executes as if it came from the same domain. The ability to retrieve assets from other websites and web services becomes extra important when sending and receiving data from them.

JSON: The Other JavaScript Format

JSON, or JavaScript Object Notation, is a data exchange format that is less verbose than XML and as a result is more lightweight and easier to transfer. JSON is more human readable and writeable than XML and less prone to errors. Every JSON object can be composed of five types:

- null
- Number
- String
- Array
- Object (a set of key/value pairs bounded by curly braces)

Table 3-3 shows some sample JSON and its corresponding XML code. You can see that the JSON code reduces the amount of repetition caused by all the greater-than and less-than symbols while keeping a sense of structure.

Table 3-3   Comparing JSON and XML

JSON Code	XML Code

`{`
`    "make":"Chevrolet",`
`    "model":"Cavalier",`
`    "year":2002`
`}`
	`<car>`
	`    <make>Chevrolet</make>`
	`    <model>Cavalier</model>`
	`    <year>2002</year>`
	`</car>`

Although the name of the technology hasn't changed, JSON is a return type or has replaced XML in many AJAX requests. Being a text-based file format, JSON does share some of the drawbacks of XML—namely that it isn't efficient at storing binary data. There are ways to accommodate this particular drawback, such as passing URIs to binary data instead of the data itself or base64-encoding the data, if possible.

JSONP, or JSON with padding, is a workaround for AJAX's same-origin policy. The source field of the `<script>` tag in HTML is one place where the same-origin policy doesn't apply. With JSONP, we construct a URI to retrieve not data, but arbitrary JavaScript for the browser to evaluate. Properly formatted JSON can also be valid JavaScript code. The returned content is generally wrapped in a function call and can contain a mix of JSON and explicit JavaScript code or no JSON at all. Listing 3-17 shows a JSONP request written in HTML code. The `jsonp` portion usually indicates the name of the function call that encapsulates the returned data. The `query` parameter could instead be `callback` or not specified at all. The important thing is that the requesting website has an idea of how the function will be named.

Listing 3-17   JSONP Example

```
<script type="text/javascript"
    src="http://www.example.com/GetTimeLine?UserId=johndoe&jsonp=getData">
</script>
```

JSONP exploits a necessary loophole to the same-origin policy and is itself open to being exploited. Any content could be injected into a site if it uses JSONP, possibly exposing sensitive data.

JavaScript Outside of the Browser

JavaScript began its life as a tool that lived in the confines of browser web pages. In recent years, it has expanded its reach to platforms outside its usual stomping grounds. Let's briefly discuss a few of them.

Mobile Platforms

WebOS, created by Palm for its Pre devices and now led by Hewlett-Packard, has the distinction of being the only mobile device operating system that uses JavaScript as its primary programming language. Titanium Appcelerator, which we will discuss in Chapter 10, uses JavaScript to create native Android and iOS applications.

JavaScript as an Intermediary Language

A new crop of languages and libraries use alternative languages that can be compiled or converted into JavaScript, making it a sort of bytecode or intermediate language for the browser. Some of these tools and languages include CoffeeScript and Google Web Toolkit (GWT), a Ruby/Python inspired scripting language and a web framework for creating

AJAX applications with Java, respectively. Both CoffeeScript and GWT will be covered in Chapter 8, "Creating Games Without JavaScript." Here's a list of some of the languages and tools that won't be covered in this book but I encourage interested developers to check out:

- Cappuccino/Objective-J (http://cappuccino.org)
- Echo3 (http://echo.nextapp.com)
- Vaadin (http://vaadin.com)
- OpenLaszlo (http://www.openlaszlo.org)
- Pyjamas (http://pyjs.org)

JavaScript on the Desktop

Since the creation of the Mozilla Firefox web browser, JavaScript desktop applications have been in mainstream use. They are now primed to make a play for the desktop, as they have already conquered the browser space. In this section, we'll cover some of the notable frameworks from a high level.

XULRunner (https://developer.mozilla.org/en/xulrunner) is a runtime environment created by Mozilla that most notably powers the Firefox web browser and many of Mozilla's suite of applications, including the Mozilla Sunbird (calendar/scheduling) and Mozilla Thunderbird (e-mail). XULRunner uses some C++ code to run the JavaScript engine named SpiderMonkey, but all interaction with the user is conducted via JavaScript. There is also a plugin format called XPI that allows developers to extend the capabilities of their application with packaged JavaScript and assets. XUL and XBL (XML User Interface Language and XML Binding Language, respectively), which determine the layout, look, and interactivity of applications, round out the core features in XULRunner. Several other companies and open-source projects are using XULRunner to package cross-platform applications. Some of the more popular ones are Miro, the Internet TV application, and Songbird, a media library management application whose feature set rivals that of iTunes.

GLUEscript (http://gluescript.sourceforge.net) is a desktop framework that is an evolution of a port of wxWidgets to JavaScript. wxWidgets is a C++-based cross-platform desktop framework that has bindings for many different programming languages. The reasoning is that once you learn the structure of a wxWidgets application in one language, you will be able to use wxWidgets in other languages with less of a learning curve. GLUEscript uses Mozilla's SpiderMonkey engine for its JavaScript layer. Above that layer, all user interface code and logic is in pure JavaScript.

XULJet (http://code.google.com/p/xuljet) is a desktop framework that runs on top of XULRunner. Although the code calls XUL on the backend, developers use a domain-specific language that is based on XUL. This allows developers to co-mingle UI code and logic. Whether that is the most appropriate thing to do—versus having a clear separation of Model–View–Controller—is outside the scope of this book. However, it does make for less-verbose and more-readable user interfaces. Listings 3-18 and 3-19 show equivalent XUL code and XULJet DSL code.

Listing 3-18   XUL Code

```
<vbox>
<toolbox>
     <menubar>
<menu label="File" accesskey="f">
        <menupopup>
             <menuitem label="Close" oncommand="window.close() />
        </menupopup>
</menu>
</menubar>
</toolbox>
<vbox align="center" pack="center", flex-"1">
  <description id="descId" >Press the button</description>
     <button label="OK" oncommand='this["desc"].value = this.message' />
</vbox>
<statusbar>
<statusbarpanel flex=1 label="Ready" />
</statusbar>
</vbox>
```

Listing 3-19   XULJet DSL Code

```
vbox({flex: 1},
    toolbox(
      menubar(
        menu({label: "File", accesskey: "f"},
          menupopup(
            menuitem({label: "Close", oncommand: "window.close()"})))))),
    vbox({align: "center", pack: "center", flex: 1},
      description({bind: "desc"}, "Press the button"),
      button({label: "OK", oncommand: function() {
        this["desc"].value = this.message}})),
    statusbar(
      statusbarpanel({flex: 1, label: 'Ready...'})))
```

Server-Side JavaScript

JavaScript is supported in many browsers, but unlike other programming languages, no single organization steered or shaped it for much of its life. As a result, although many applications claim JavaScript support, their implementations might not always be compatible. Also, as a browser technology, there isn't support for things such as interacting with the file system, package management, and creating desktop applications. The goal is to provide a common set of specifications that developers can implement so that compliant applications and frameworks can interact with each other and share code.

In the past few years, server-side JavaScript (or JavaScript run outside the browser) has become more popular as a means to run web applications. Thanks in part to the Rhino programming language, which is a version of JavaScript built to run on the Java Virtual Machine (JVM), there are many runtimes for server-side JavaScript. Most of these runtimes tap into the web server support in Java and allow the user to call them using JavaScript-like code.

RingoJS is a fairly mature JVM-based runtime that uses Rhino as its main programming language. Node.js is another popular server-side JavaScript runtime that uses Google's V8 JavaScript engine to execute code.

Modules provide a way to encapsulate functionality into a single file or namespace so that it can be used across many applications. Unlike functions written for the browser that attach to the `window` object, RingoJS and Node.js functions attach to the `exports` object. Listing 3-20 shows a simple function to reverse a string. You can see that as far as the declaration of the function is concerned, nothing has changed. We have merely added a line to say that in the `exports` namespace, the function will have the name `reverseString`.

Listing 3-20   Example Module

```
function reverseString(text) {
    var reversed = "";
    for (var i = text.length-1; i>=0; i-) {
        reversed += text[i];
    }
    return reversed;
}
exports.reverseString = reverseString;
```

Summary

In this chapter, we discussed JavaScript and its accompanying ecosystem. No longer is the language relegated to running client scripts in the browser. It is being used as a server-side language, as an intermediary language, and to create mobile applications. The ever-increasing speed of JavaScript engines means that JavaScript will continue to permeate more areas of development. A proper foundation in JavaScript is the key to making HTML5 games. Even if you use an alternate language, that language will compile down to JavaScript. JavaScript is the lingua franca of the Web.

Exercises

1. What keyword allows you to extend objects in JavaScript?
2. What does the `$super` object in Prototype have access to?
3. Explain the difference between == and ===.
4. Write a function that checks every five seconds if it is 12 midnight. Hint: Use `getHours()` and `getMinutes()`.

You can download chapter code and the answers to the chapter exercises at www.informit.com/title/9780321767363.

4

How Games Work

Trying to define exactly what a game is and isn't is much more difficult than it seems. Although we may think of games as being purely for competition or entertainment, they actually encompass a lot more. A simulation that determines whether a building is constructed soundly could be thought of a game, as can trying to predict how people will react to certain stimuli. The best all-inclusive definition I could come up with is that a game is a form of interaction with goals and structure. Building upon the lessons we learned about Prototype and its approach to object-oriented programming, we will be using the Prototype-based Simple Game Framework (SGF) to create the games in this chapter. SGF was chosen because the API is complete yet small, hiding enough low-level details for us to build up easy wins before we delve into more complex topics later in the book. SGF mustn't be thought of as the end-all and be-all of game engines. After all, a quick visit to http://devmaster.com shows that dozens if not hundreds of options are out there.

Designing a Game

One of the most important things you can do before you sit down to code a game is to plan out what it does. For a large game such as *World of Warcraft,* this design document would be many pages long and discuss different areas, worlds, and scenarios. But for our purposes, the design documents will be fairly short. In some cases, they could fit on a sticky note. However, they are nevertheless important to create. With an undefined goal, you never know when you have met it.

Writing a Basic Design Document

The design document is a contract for how your game will work and allows you to have a record for the future of all your thoughts when beginning the project. How else will you remember why the Whosits are green and the Whatsits are blue and how they each respond to power-ups? If you are creating a game that includes characters, you could also include character studies that outline their motivations and back story. At minimum, the design document should contain the following elements:

- The rules of play
- The tagline
- The title or working title of the game

These elements should be prioritized in that order as well. Game play rules form the basis of a good game. A great title and tagline can only go so far to help out a crappy game. The game play rules describe how play begins, how it ends, and how any positive and negative actions are rewarded and penalized, respectively. For the game *Pong,* which will incidentally be the first game we create, the design document might be something like this:

- Two players are represented by rectangular paddles that can move only up and down.
- A ball can be hit between the two paddles and can bounce off the top and bottom walls of the playing area.
- The left and right bounds of the playing area do not make the ball bounce off them as the top and bottom walls do.
- The player must defend his area by hitting the ball into the other player's area.
- A point is scored for the other competitor when a paddle doesn't prevent the ball from moving off the playing area bounds.

A tagline describes your game succinctly for people who have never seen it before. It can also draw upon familiar experiences of the prospective user while also introducing something new—for example, "Soccer in space." Besides some über-rich people, some astronauts, and some cosmonauts, we can't claim to have experienced what it feels like to be outside Earth's atmosphere. But many of us have played soccer (or *football* for the non-U.S. readers). We can understand some of the conditions arising from the familiar experience of soccer played in an unknown setting. There might be the lack of gravity to contend with, possible differences in how the ball moves because of the lack of an atmosphere, or maybe the need for temporary power-ups to counteract the bulkiness of the flight suits.

Deciding on a Game Genre

Games generally fall into a particular genre or type that describes some of its basic characteristics. The video game industry has dozens if not hundreds of genres and subgenres. The games in this book will fall into the casual game genre. Casual games in many cases have less processor-intensive graphics and effects, shorter levels, and a smaller learning curve. The major subgenres of the casual gaming space in the past couple of years have been as follows:

- Puzzle games
- Hidden object games

- Adventure games
- Strategy games (including click/time management, such as *Diner Dash* and *Farmville)*
- Arcade and action games
- Word and trivia games
- Card and board games

The lower processor and graphics thresholds make it easier for a newcomer to break into this area. You don't need a sea of 2D and 3D artists. You can get by on some programming skill, an idea, and a friend who can draw a little.

The Game Loop

Excuse the cliché, but the game loop is where the magic happens. Much of the time the user will spend interacting with your game will be inside the game loop. Each run of the game loop may execute any of the following limited list of actions:

- Retrieving user input, such as pressing buttons or directional keys
- Receiving input from opponents (computer or human)
- Updating player and enemy positions and alive state
- Starting or stopping sound effects and background music
- Drawing the world with the updated positions and states of the players

These actions are often completed many times a second and sometimes at different intervals. The human eye has a limit as to the number of frames it can see, so we might only redraw the screen 30 to 60 times a second, but for we might check for user input 100 times a second. It all depends on the conditions of the game.

Getting Input from the User

User input will usually be transmitted via the keyboard, mouse, or possibly a game controller. Our applications will receive the status as numeric values corresponding the ASCII codes for letters and numbers. JavaScript can also tell us if modifier keys such as Ctrl and Shift were pressed at the same time. In Chapter 3, "Learning JavaScript," we talked briefly about how you can capture these events using JQuery. Because input is very important to them, many game engines and libraries provide some helper functions to encapsulate getting input from the player. You will see this first hand when we create games for this chapter.

Representing Game Objects with Advanced Data Structures

You learned in Chapter 3 that JavaScript provides us with several core object types. We will use all of them, but in many cases they won't be enough. Most importantly, in addition to specific game objects such as Rectangles, Circles, and Sprites, we need more complex structures to hold them. Arrays allow us to hold a list of things, but their functions are pretty basic. What if we wanted a `Set` class that only stores unique objects? What about a class that stores an object graph between different points? For each of these we will have to roll our own.

Making Unique Lists of Data with Sets

Sets are collections that have no duplicate values. The object that holds a single deck of playing cards or a grocery list could be implemented as a set. At the core of our implementation is an **array,** which works behind the scenes to store our objects. Enforcing uniqueness means that if we use types that aren't Strings, Numbers, or Booleans, we should make sure the object we insert into the set implements its own `equals` method. Listing 4-1 shows the code for a `Set` class and for adding an `equals` method to `Number` so that you can use Numbers seamlessly in sets. If you want to use Strings, the same thing would have to be done.

Listing 4-1   JavaScript **Set** Class

```
var Set = Class.create({
 initialize: function () {
   this.rawArray = [];
 },
 add: function (object) {
   if (this.contains(object) == undefined) {
     this.rawArray.push(object);
   }
 },
 get: function (index) {
   return this.rawArray[index];
 },
 remove: function (object) {
   var index = this.contains(object);
   if (index != undefined)
     this.rawArray.remove(index);
 },
 contains: function (obj) {
   for (var i = 0; i < this.rawArray.length; i++) {
     var obj2 = this.rawArray[i];
     if (obj.equals(obj2))
       return i;
```

```
   }
   return undefined;
 }
});
Number.prototype.equals = function (obj) {
 return this == obj;
}
```

Now that we have a way to store unique values, it would be nice to be able to sort them. Trick-based card games, such as Hearts and Spades, are some examples that jump to mind where a sorted set might be desired. JavaScript doesn't allow us to use operations such as <, >, >=, and so on, with our custom types also known as **operator overloading**. We can get around this limitation by using a concept from Java called **Comparator**, which is a contract, or interface, that requires any class implementing it to have a function that takes two objects as parameters and returns a negative number, zero, or a positive number if the first object is less than, equal to, or greater than the other parameterized object. Whereas in Java, the function would have to be named "compare," we don't have that requirement in JavaScript, and the function doesn't even need to be a member of the class. We can see in Listing 4-2 how this might be implemented for a `card` class that's sorted by suit and rank. Like we saw earlier with the `equals` method, primitive types don't have their own compare methods. `primitiveCompare` works for all primitive types (Booleans, Numbers, and Strings).

Listing 4-2   **JavaScript Comparator**

```
primitiveCompare = function (s1, s2) {
 if (s1 == s2)
   return 0;
 else if (s1 < s2)
   return -1;
 else return 1;
}
compare = function (obj, obj2) {
   if (primitiveCompare(obj.getSuit(), obj2.getSuit()) == 0){
     return primitiveCompare(obj.getOrd(), obj2.getOrd());
   } else
     return primitiveCompare(obj.getSuit(), obj2.getSuit())
}
```

With all the components in place, we can now sort our objects. We can sort an array by executing this:

```
set.sort(compare)
```

To sort another object that is backed by an array, simply provide a pass-through method to invoke the sort. The default sort algorithm in most JavaScript engines will

serve your needs well for the amount of data you'll probably be sorting. If you notice
your sort becoming slow, you can always implement your own. Many resources can be
found online that explain the different sort algorithms along with what conditions are the
best for each one.

Creating Object Graphs with Linked Lists

Linked lists are another common advanced data structure consisting of objects that each
contain a reference, or link, to the next one of more objects in list. Singly linked lists will
only link from parent to child, so you have to traverse all the objects (commonly called
"nodes") until you reach the one you want. A node in a doubly linked list contains both a
reference to the preceding and next nodes. Linked lists are useful for objects that have
some sort of implicit hierarchy. For example, you could use a linked list to hold the components of a robotic arm. The upper arm is the parent of the lower arm, just as the lower
arm is the parent of the hand, and so on. Listing 4-3 shows the code to create a singly
linked list.

Listing 4-3   **JavaScript Linked List**

```javascript
var Node = Class.create({
 initialize: function (val) {
   this.value = val;
   this.next = null;
 },
 addChild: function(node) {
   this.next = node;
 }
});
var LinkedList = Class.create({
 initialize: function () {
   this.root = new Node(null);
   this.size = 0;
 },
 add: function (object) {
   obj = this.root
   while (obj.next!= null) {
     obj = obj.next;
   }

   obj.next = new Node(object)
 }
});
```

Linked lists are used extensively for artificial intelligence (AI), which we will discuss
later in this chapter. With a linked list, you can represent all the possible states of a game,

and in evaluating each one, the computer can backtrack and try other paths, eventually coming to the optimal solution.

Understanding the APIs in Simple Game Framework

As mentioned before, SGF builds on the Prototype JavaScript framework to create its game objects. Another interesting feature is that SGF can use the same game logic and assets as well as execute in the browser or on desktop Java. It does this by taking advantage of the Rhino programming language, JavaScript on the Java platform, and a Java backend API mirroring the HTML version. It is able to run anywhere that has a JavaScript engine. One key difference between SGF and the techniques we will examine later in the book is that SGF doesn't use the `Canvas` tag in any way. It instead uses `div` and `img` elements along with CSS styles to create game play. Even though this is a book about HTML5, having backward compatibility is an important consideration, and there will be occasions when you might want to mix techniques. For your convenience, SGF has been bundled with the source code for this chapter, but you can also download a possibly newer version at http://sgfjs.org/. Let's briefly discuss its APIs.

Core API

The Core API is where the magic happens. It manages the interactions between the keyboard, mouse, and our games, renders our frames, and provides an interface for adding new events to subscribe to using the Observer pattern (http://en.wikipedia.org/wiki/Observer_pattern). The classes and namespace are listed here:

- `Game`
- `Input`
- `SGF` (namespace)
- `EventEmitter`
- `Screen`

`Game` and `Input` are the two classes in this area that we will use the most. The `Game` class is a container for all our game objects and manages our game loop by calling the `render` and `update` functions on the objects. We can also set our frames per second, which is the number of times we'd like the game to update its state. The `Game` class also exposes functions to load fonts, other JavaScript files, and sounds.

The `Input` class, as you might guess, gives us a means to get the mouse clicks, mouse movement, and key presses at any given time. `isKeyDown` is the only instance function we need to worry about and is incidentally the only instance function. We can use it with the preset class properties for common keystrokes, such as the mouse and directional keys, or with key codes from other buttons on the keyboard.

The `SGF` namespace provides only two (but very important) functions. The first is the `log` function, which is an alias for the native logging function on the platforms that SGF supports. In the case of JavaScript, it is console.log. The second function the `SGF` name-space provides is `require`, which is a method that only imports the components you need into your application. In a basic SGF game, all classes are hidden by default and you must use `require` to make them available for use. `EventEmitter` and `Screen` won't be used directly in any of this chapter's games, so learning about them will be left as an exercise for the interested reader.

Components API

Whereas the Core API controls how the objects interact with each other, the Components API specifies how they are drawn. Here are the classes in this API:

- `Component`
- `Container`
- `Shape`
- `Rectangle`
- `Sprite`
- `DumbContainer`

`Component` is a class from which all SGF-viewable game objects extend. It can't be instantiated directly but rather represents a contract that the objects must follow. `Component` contains properties to specify an object's dimensions, orientation, depth (z-index), and its own `render` and `update` functions. The `Container` class is a concrete sub-class of `Component`. It implements all of `Component`'s methods and can hold other `Component` objects and their subclasses. `Container` could be used to animate many different objects at once to create interesting simulations. `Shape` is another class that exists only to provide a contract, giving its children access to a `color` property in addition to the ones available in `Component`. `Rectangle` is a child of `Shape`. `Sprite` is a class that represents a single rendered image in a game. These images usually come in what are called **spritesheets,** providing all the images to create an animation—similar to a flipbook. We will talk about the nuts and bolts of sprites in Chapter 5, "Creating Games with the Canvas Tag." Figure 4-1 shows the Components API classes and their descendants.

Resources API and Networking APIs

Games would look rather boring if we were stuck with the default system font and solid colors for objects. SGF's Resources API gives you the ability to load custom fonts and images to use with your games. Because we will be covering much of this content in greater detail in Chapter 5, we will defer talking about this for now.

SGF has the capability to connect to other clients or servers using its built-in `Client` class and either the corresponding `Server` class or another WebSocket server. Mentioned for sake of completeness when talking about SGF, we won't cover any of the networking capabilities in this chapter. The API documentation has some sample code, and it might

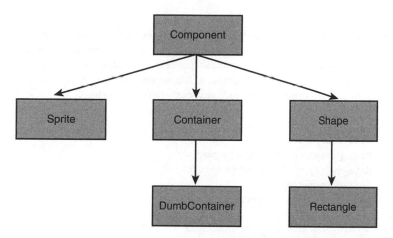

Figure 4-1   Components API classes and descendents

be beneficial to review the networking material in Chapter 9, "Building a Multiplayer Game Server," that specifically deals with `Socket.IO` before trying to make SGF games "network capable."

Building *Pong* with the Simple Game Framework

Pong is often thought of as the game programming version of "Hello, World!" It is a 2D form of ping-pong (table tennis). The game that helped launch the video game industry has a retro look that hides its complexity. In coding *Pong*, we have to manage game state, track scoring, track game components, and perform collision detection and response.

Setting Up the Application

Listing 4-4 shows the scaffolding HTML code we need to embed our application in a web page. The stylesheet designation, the contents of which are shown in Listing 4-5, are extra important. SGF uses HTML `div` elements to draw its graphics. This element has an intrinsic desire to take up as little space as possible. The stylesheet tells the browser to allocate the indicated dimensions for our game, whether we are using it or not. Another notable piece of code is the following in the `script` tag:

`data-screen="screen"`

It tells SGF which `div` will hold the game. If we omit it, the game is added to the body of the page.

Listing 4-4   **Pong HTML Host Page Code**

```
<!DOCTYPE HTML>
<html>
   <head>
```

```
      <title>Pong</title>
      <meta http-equiv="Content-Type" content="text/html; charset=UTF-8">
      <!-- For IE. Force the browser to the most current rendering mode. -->
      <meta http-equiv="X-UA-Compatible" content="IE=edge" >
      <!-- A few basic styles. These are NOT mandatory for SGF... -->
      <link href="styles.css" type="text/css" rel="stylesheet" />

      <script type="text/javascript" src="js/SGF.js"
          data-debug="true"
          data-prototype="lib/prototype.js"
          data-swfobject="lib/swfobject.js"
          data-screen="screen"
          data-game="Pong"></script>
  </head>
  <body>
    <div id="screen"></div>
  </body>
</html>
```

Listing 4-5   **Pong CSS Code**

```
body {
   margin:0 0 0 0;
   width:100%;
   height:100%;
   text-align:center;
}
#screen {
   width:400px;
   height:400px;
   border:Solid 1px #000000;
   margin:0 auto;
}
```

Listing 4-6 shows the beginnings of our game. All SGF games require a main.js file that contains the outermost logic to run the game. In the listing, we can see that we are retrieving several objects from the SGF namespace and are setting up game properties such as the height, width, and input instance. Lastly, we retrieve a script for our Paddle class and draw a paddle on the screen at (0,150). After you understand this bit of code, we can move on to creating our game pieces.

Listing 4-6   **Pong main.js**

```
// Import required classes
var Game = SGF.require("Game");
```

```
var Input = SGF.require("Input");
var Rectangle = SGF.require("Rectangle");
var Label = SGF.require("Label");
// Get a reference to our Game instance
var myGame = Game.getInstance();
// Get a reference to our game's Input instance
var myInput = myGame.input;
var game_height = 400;
var game_width = 400;
myGame.getScript("Paddle.js", function(){
        // left paddle
        myGame.leftPaddle = new Paddle();
        myGame.leftPaddle.setPosition(0, 150);
        myGame.addComponent(myGame.leftPaddle);
});
```

Drawing the Game Pieces

Our easiest game pieces to draw are the paddles. We begin with the `Rectangle` class and extend it with a couple of methods. In our constructor (`initialize`), we set up the width, height, and color of the paddle. We have convenience functions for getting and setting the position, but the real stars are the `checkInput` and `update` functions. `checkInput` looks for key presses of the up- and down-arrow keys from the keyboard. When a key press is detected, it adjusts the paddle's y position by 10 pixels to the north or south. There are conditions to keep the paddle within the bounds of the game board. Finally, our `update` function fires many times every second to see if there has been input from the user. *Pong* is a two-player game, so we created our paddles to respond to the up- and down-arrow keys or the A and Z keys. The code for the full `Paddle` class is shown in Listing 4-7.

Listing 4-7   **Paddle.js**

```
// Paddle.js
var Paddle = Class.create(Rectangle, {
   initialize: function($super){
       $super();
       this.height = 100;
       this.width = 20;
       this.color = "0011FF";
       this.isPlayerOne = true;
   },
   setPosition: function(x, y){
       this.x = x;
       this.y = y;
   },
```

```
        getPosition: function(){
            return {
                'x': this.x,
                'y': this.y
            }
        },
        setIsPlayerOne: function(bool){
            this.isPlayerOne = bool;
        },
        checkInput: function(){
            if (this.isPlayerOne == false) {
                if (myInput.isKeyDown(Input.KEY_UP)) {
                    if (this.y > 0) {
                        this.y = this.y - 10;
                    }
                }
                else
                    if (myInput.isKeyDown(Input.KEY_DOWN)) {
                        // x,y are taken from the left corner
                        if (this.y < game_height - this.height)
                            this.y = this.y + 10;
                    }


            }
            else {
                if (myInput.isKeyDown(65)) { // 'A'
                    if (this.y > 0) {
                        this.y = this.y - 10;
                    }
                }
                else
                    if (myInput.isKeyDown(90)) { // 'Z'
                        // x,y are taken from the left corner
                        if (this.y < game_height - this.height)
                            this.y = this.y + 10;
                    }
            }
        },
        update: function(){
            this.checkInput();
        }
});
```

You might have noticed that our check for the lower bounds does an adjustment for the height of the paddle. That is because, as shown in Figure 4-2, screen coordinates start with (0,0) in the upper-left corner and extend the right and bottom of the screen with positive x and y, respectively.

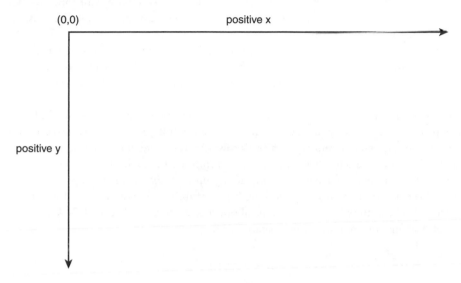

Figure 4-2   Screen coordinate system

Making Worlds Collide with Collision Detection and Response

Before we get to adding our `Ball` object and making it bounce around the screen, let's take a slight detour and talk about what makes it actually work. As you are reading this, even if you sitting relatively still, there are many forces acting upon you. This isn't meant to be an exhaustive discussion but seeks to be just enough to explain the concepts. Isaac Newton—that's right, the falling apple guy—described the laws of universal gravitation and motion that shape our understanding of how objects interact with each other in the physical world.

Understanding Newton's Three Laws

Newton's first law deals with inertia and states that an object at rest will stay at rest and that an object in motion will stay in motion at the same velocity (speed and direction) and direction until an unbalanced force is acted upon it. In the context of our *Pong* game, our ball wants to continue moving and will do so until it encounters a force (for example, a paddle or wall) that is too great to permit the ball from continuing on the intended path.

Newton's second law deals with momentum. Momentum is the product of mass (the matter present in an object) and its velocity. The equation you might have heard of is

F = ma

or Force = mass times acceleration (rate of velocity change over time). Put another way, applying a net force to an object will proportionately affect the object's acceleration. Even though it may be coming at you fast, a soccer ball that you kick with your foot involves applying enough force on the ball to overcome its momentum toward you and cause it to move in the opposite direction.

Newton's third law states that for every action, there is a equal and opposite reaction. There is no such thing as a unidirectional force. If you are pushing a ball, it is exerting the same force upon you, but the momentum (second law) might be different for you and the ball.

You may not have realized it, but the hit game *Angry Birds* uses physics for all of its game play. For the few of you may have not encountered it yet, *Angry Birds* involves using a slingshot to launch different types of birds toward targets and enemies. When you launch a bird, you are putting a net force on it. From the time a bird leaves the slingshot until it hits the target, gravity is constantly acting upon it. Eventually the upward momentum and acceleration imparted by the slingshot succumbs to gravity and the bird begins to descend. The path of its motion is a parabolic arc, as shown in Figure 4-3. When you jump in the air, you are moving in a parabolic arc.

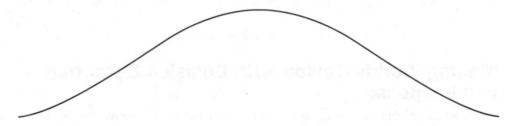

Figure 4-3   Parabolic movement

Some of the *Angry Birds* characters have different characteristics, such as being able to increase velocity mid-flight, thus causing more destruction. Another bird is armed with a fairly heavy egg that, when dropped, causes the bird to soar into the sky (its upward acceleration is affected by the drop in mass).

To keep things simple for our *Pong* game, we won't be doing realistic physics for our collisions. If we chose to do so, we would have to take the preceding laws and some others (such as the Law of Reflection) into account. I don't know about you, but making a 100% realistic *Pong* game is effort I'd rather conserve for a cooler idea. However, the lack of real physics doesn't mean that we won't make a fun game.

Making the Ball Move

Our ball is constrained to four diagonal directions: NW, NE, SW, and SE. In the `Direction` class, we have a map of the directions the ball can move, one pixel either north or south and one pixel either east or west, as shown in Listing 4-8. Our game updates itself 30 times per second, so we can think of our velocity as 30 pixels/sec in one of the four directions.

Listing 4-8   **Ball Directions**

```
this.directions = [
    {code:'SE','x':-1,'y':-1},
    {code:'SW','x':1,'y':-1},
    {code:'NE','x':-1,'y':1},
    {code:'NW','x':1,'y':1},
]
```

The Ball class uses the "velocities" in that map to move the object on the screen, as shown in Listing 4-9. Using a multiplier for the x or y displacement allows us to simulate a greater range of motion and dynamism with the ball's movement.

Listing 4-9   **Ball Class update Function**

```
update: function(){
    this.checkCollisions();
    pos = this.getPosition()

    this.setPosition(pos.x - 2 * this.direction.getX(),
        pos.y - 3 * this.direction.getY())
    if (this.x < 0) {
        myGame.ScoreBoard.scoreRight.incrementScore();
        this.resetBall();
    }
    else if (this.x > game_width) {
        myGame.ScoreBoard.scoreLeft.incrementScore()
        this.resetBall();
    }
}
```

To simulate the ball bouncing off a wall or paddle, we check the Ball's x and y positions relative to other objects in space. If a collision is detected, the appropriate vector is reversed. We are giving up a little bit of the precision to make the code simpler. Therefore, when the conditions are just right, collisions may fail to fire. This mainly occurs around the other edges of the paddles, but is rare. The collision-detection code for the game is shown in Listing 4-10.

Listing 4-10   **Ball Collision Detection**

```
checkCollisions: function(){
    // Collisions with paddles
    //check left
```

```
    var leftPaddleX =  myGame.leftPaddle.getPosition().x;
    var leftPaddleY =  myGame.leftPaddle.getPosition().y;
    var rightPaddleX =  myGame.rightPaddle.getPosition().x;
    var rightPaddleY =  myGame.rightPaddle.getPosition().y;
    if (this.y >= leftPaddleY && this.y <= leftPaddleY +
➡myGame.leftPaddle.height)
        if (this.x == leftPaddleX + myGame.leftPaddle.width)
            this.direction.flipEastWest();
    // check right
    if (this.y >= rightPaddleY && this.y <= rightPaddleY +
➡myGame.leftPaddle.height)
        if (this.x == rightPaddleX - myGame.rightPaddle.width)
            this.direction.flipEastWest();
    // Collisions with walls
     if (this.y <= 0 || this.y >= game_height - 20)
        this.direction.flipNorthSouth()
}
```

Advanced Collision Detection and Particle Systems with Asteroids

Particle systems are a type of simulation that animates many objects based on forces in nature. Explosions, confetti cannons, and pellets from a shotgun are all particle systems at work. They can also use some of the advanced data structures we discussed earlier in the chapter. World forces can act on the particles individually or as a group. Let's begin by looking at a particle system inspired by something from everyday life—a water faucet. We learned in Chemistry class that the smallest thing we can label as water is a molecule of two hydrogen atoms and one oxygen atom. When you turn on the faucet, hundreds of thousands of water molecules, which are under pressure (thus giving them enough energy to make it to your home), rush into your sink. Once in the sink, they might move up the sides or spill over onto the floor. We can ignore or highlight forces in particle systems as we please.

Asteroids is an arcade game where the player controls a spaceship floating out in space in an asteroid field. The player must use his rockets to break up and destroy asteroids hurtling toward him. This gives us a great opportunity to make some limited particle systems. After the first hit, our larger asteroids split into three smaller pieces. A further hit to those asteroids yields two more of the smallest asteroids. The smallest asteroids disappear from the game after being hit. Listing 4-11 shows the code to spawn or destroy asteroids when they are hit. To increase code reuse, we encapsulated the creation of each generation of asteroids into a separate function. Not shown in the snippet is the `pickSpeedAndDirection` function. It picks a random change in x and y to be applied for the lifetime of the asteroid.

Listing 4-11   **Spawning New Asteroids**

```
explodeOrDestroy: function() {
  if (this.generation == 0) {
    // remove this asteroid and create 3 smaller ones
    this.spawnAsteroids(1, 75, 3);
    myGame.removeComponent(this);
  } else if (this.generation == 1) {
    // remove this asteroid and create 2 smaller ones
    this.spawnAsteroids(2, 50, 2);
    myGame.removeComponent(this);
  } else myGame.removeComponent(this);
}
spawnAsteroids: function (generation, size, num) {
  for (var i = 0; i<num; i++) {
      var asteroid = new Asteroid();
      asteroid.width = size;
      asteroid.height = size;
      asteroid.x = this.x;
      asteroid.y = this.y
      asteroid.generation = generation;
      asteroid.pickSpeedAndDirection();
      myGame.addComponent(asteroid);
  }
}
```

Creating Competitive Opponents with Artificial Intelligence

Artificial intelligence (AI), as it pertains to gaming, is the ability for applications to simulate sentience by using code to interact and possibly analyze surroundings and competitors. Whether you have realized it or not, you've encountered a bit of AI in even the most ancient games. Take, for instance, the *Super Mario* franchise. In the original *Super Mario* game, Goombas were about as dumb as you could get; they make their way from point A to point B, reversing course if they bumped into another object or enemy that wasn't Mario or Luigi. Left to their own devices, they would walk off cliffs into the great abyss. A little bit higher on the AI food chain are level bosses, such as Bowser, at the end of the castle levels. He can do rudimentary tracking of your position and attempt to attack you. One of the most intelligent enemies in the *Super Mario* franchise are Boos. Boos are ghost-like creatures that can chase and attack you when your back is turned and, in some cases, can evade you.

Adding AI to Pong

For our simple *Pong* game, we can create AI opponents with multiple levels of complexity pretty quickly. We can do that by giving the computer player periodic access to the ball's position or by giving it a range of values, and it has to guess where the ball might be. Listing 4-12 shows some code that allows the computer player to "sense" the ball's position. In it, we retrieve the ball's current y position and calculate a target y position by subtracting half the height of the paddle. This is an attempt to make the ball strike the middle of the paddle. Remember that coordinates are computed from the top left, so we need this adjustment to avoid a mis-hit. To make the computer movement smoother, the increments are reduced from 10 to 3. Given that the computer player gets the ball's position 30 times a second, it can easily defend its area.

Listing 4-12   **Pong Computer AI**

```
update: function() {
    if (this.isPlayerOne == true) {
      var y = myGame.ball.y;
      var currentY = this.y

      targetY = y - this.height/2

      if (targetY > this.y)
        this.y = this.y + 3;
      else if (targetY < this.y)
        this.y = this.y - 3;
    } else this.checkInput();
  }
```

Advanced Computer AI with Tic-Tac-Toe

To avoid having to use images or fancy CSS effects to represent the X's and O's in a game of tic-tac-toe, we are going to use solid colors: red for O's (the lighter hue in the figure) and blue for X's. Figure 4-4 shows a game board where a player has just won.

One thing that tic-tac-toe has in common with some other two-player games, such as chess, Othello, and checkers, is that they are all zero-sum finite deterministic games. That's a really spiffy way to say the following:

- For any move, what benefits Player A will come at some cost to Player B.
- All possible game states are known to both players.
- There is a limited number of game states/decisions/moves to be made and they can be enumerated.
- There are no variables that introduce randomness to the game.

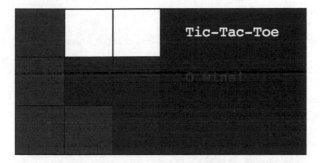

Figure 4-4   Tic-tac-toe winning game

Given the processing power to do so, a computer can calculate all possible moves that a player might take (like the Deep Blue chess-playing computer that beat a chess grandmaster). This method is known as "brute force." It's similar to trying to crack someone's password by trying every word in the dictionary. It is very effective but also time consuming.

Knowing the moves a player might take means nothing if you can't evaluate them. The AI algorithm for these types of games calculates several (up to thousands of) combinations of moves that the computer and player could make. It gives each move a score based on whether it helps it to win or lose. When choosing a possible move for the opponent, it assumes that the opponent will always choose the best move. This algorithm is known as **Minimax**. Without any constraints on it, a Minimax algorithm will try to brute force its way to a solution—and JavaScript doesn't like it. When trying to evaluate a game with few moves, it can easily use up all the space that the browser gave it to run. One method to combat this is to set a depth limit. After some testing, I settled on 200. This gives the algorithm a chance to evaluate a bunch of boards but doesn't have a perceptible lag. Because it can't evaluate all boards, sometimes it makes suboptimal moves.

Our `miniMax` function begins by seeing if we can evaluate the current board for a score. We have three designated scores: 1 for a win by the current player, -1 for an opponent win, and 0 for either no perceptible best move or `depthLimit` is reached. If we can't decide on a score and haven't reached the `depthLimit`, we make a copy of the game board and find the possible moves. Next, we iterate over that list of moves and recursively call `miniMax` again, this time from the opponent's viewpoint. When we receive a score, we compare it to the best score, saving it if need be. When the function has completed, the computer player will play the best move for it to take from all the possibilities it has attempted. The code for the Minimax algorithm is shown in Listing 4-13. Although we leave it in the main code file, the `miniMax` function would be a great candidate for a Worker.

Listing 4-13   **Minimax Algorithm**

```
miniMax: function(board, currentPlayer) {
    if (this.currentDepth == this.depthLimit)
        return 0;
```

```
    if (TTT.checkForWin(board) == currentPlayer)
        return 1;
    if (TTT.checkForWin(board) == this.getOtherPlayer(currentPlayer))
        return -1;
    this.currentDepth++;
    var best = -10;
    var bestMove = null;
    var clone = TTT.cloneGameBoard(board);
    var moves = TTT.generateMovesFromBoard(clone, currentPlayer);

    for (var i = 0; i<moves.length; i++) {
        var m = moves[i]
        clone[m[0]][m[1]] = currentPlayer;
        var value = -this.miniMax(clone, this.getOtherPlayer(currentPlayer));
        //reset board
        clone[m[0]][m[1]] = "";
        if (value > best) {
            best = value;
            bestMove = m;
        }
    }
    if (best == -10)
        return 0
    return bestMove;
}
```

Summary

In this chapter, we created our first game using the Simple Game Framework. We also dove into the fundamentals of what makes games tick, touching on the process of planning our games. The lessons learned in this chapter will serve us well for the duration of the book.

Exercises

1. Why are 2D games easier to code than 3D?
2. How is a game of checkers or tic-tac-toe different from a game of poker?
3. Are leaves on a tree a particle system? Explain why or why not.

You can download chapter code and answers to the chapter exercises at www.informit.com/title/9780321767363.

5

Creating Games with the Canvas Tag

The Canvas (that is, the `canvas` tag) is what many think about when HTML5 is mentioned. Instead of creating a bunch of `div` elements with contained images with CSS to simulate movement and game play, you can use `canvas` to provide a surface to draw objects on the screen. Neither method is easier or harder, but each has different considerations. The Canvas has some built-in translation, rotation, scaling, and clipping, whereas with `div`s you have to handle transformations yourself. However, one advantage that games using `div` and CSS have over the Canvas is that older browsers, such as Internet Explorer 6, are supported. Hopefully, as more browsers become HTML5 compliant, this will become less of an issue.

Getting Started with the Canvas

Unlike with some other technologies, you don't need to include any extra libraries to use the Canvas. As long as you have an HTML5-compliant browser and a text editor, you have all you need to get up and running. As mentioned before, the Canvas is a drawing area on a web page. The first thing that we need to do is to create that area. We can do that by creating a `canvas` tag and setting the height, width, and (optionally) the ID:

```
<canvas id="c" height="400" width="400"></canvas>
```

As you probably have guessed, this line of code draws a 400-pixel-by-400-pixel square Canvas with an ID of "c." Your next guess might be that we could start using the Canvas by running something like

```
var canvas = document.getElementById("c");
```

and then drawing with the `canvas` object. Close, but not quite. What is not apparent at first glance is that the Canvas acts as a container for drawing APIs, which we will actually use directly. WebGL, which we discuss in Chapter 7, "Creating Games with WebGL and Three.js," uses the same HTML tag but a different drawing API. Continuing with our code example, to retrieve the 2D context (or the interface for drawing), we need to call `getContext` on the Canvas:

```
var context = canvas.getContext("2d");
```

Now we can begin drawing graphics.

Not all of the world's graphics are driven by rectangles. No matter how little artistic ability you have, you will eventually need a way to create complex shapes. Paths are how we can create shapes using lines and arcs. The concept of paths pops up several times in the different technologies in this book. Let's take the time to learn about them with a simple example, and the next occasions with be total child's play.

Although they can be as simple as a straight line, paths form complex shapes by accumulating instructions one after another until the final shape is drawn. Any path consists of three primitive types:

- Lines
- Arcs
- Curves

If you think about objects in real life, they are composed of these three types. As I'm writing this chapter, I'm looking out the window at a street lamp and some tree planters. If you take a cross-section of these items, you will see those primitive path components, which can be spun around a center point or repeatedly drawn along a path to create a three-dimensional shape. Engineers using Computer Aided Design (CAD) employ these primitives to prototype the parts for the car you drive or the bike you ride.

Drawing Your First Paths

After creating a `canvas` object and retrieving the context, the first thing we need to do to draw a path is to call the aptly named `beginPath()` function, which clears the stack of any other paths we might have been drawing. This is important to do because path instructions are cumulative, and all paths for a given `canvas` tag draw using the same context. The next thing we need to do is to move to the point where we would like to begin drawing. Calling `moveTo()` with an x position and y position does just that. You can think of this as picking up the pen from the paper in order to draw another shape. Once the "pen" is in place, calling `lineTo()` with x and y positions places the pen down on the paper and draws a line to that point. The last thing we need to do is to stroke the lines we have drawn. You can think of the `moveTo` and `lineTo` instructions as tracings on the paper, and the stroke instruction is for going back and filling in the lines now that we know where we want them. We can use this knowledge to draw our game board for the tic-tac-toe game, as shown in Listing 5-1. It consists of two parallel vertical lines and two parallel horizontal lines to form a grid of nine spaces.

Listing 5-1   **Drawing the Game Board for Tic-Tac-Toe**

```
self.drawGameBoard = function() {
    var ctx = self.context;

    ctx.beginPath();

    ctx.moveTo(200,0);
    ctx.lineTo(200,600);

    ctx.moveTo(400,0);
    ctx.lineTo(400,600);

    ctx.moveTo(0,200);
    ctx.lineTo(600,200);

    ctx.moveTo(0,400);
    ctx.lineTo(600,400);

    ctx.stroke();
}
```

Drawing Game Sprites for Tic-Tac-Toe

Now that the game board is squared away, we need to draw the sprites to play the game. Let's start with the X's.

We can again use paths for X's. They are drawn by starting at a point, drawing a line indicated by an offset to the right and down, picking up the "pen," moving up by that same number of units, and then drawing a line that is down and to the left this time.

To make things simple for our game sprites, the game board was set at 600 by 600 pixels. That gives us a 200-pixel square for each space. We don't want to the sprites to touch the dividing lines, so all the lines are drawn just short of the edges. Listing 5-2 shows the code to draw an X on the canvas.

Listing 5-2   **Drawing an X for Tic-Tac-Toe**

```
ctx.lineWidth = 2;
ctx.beginPath();

ctx.moveTo(10,10);
ctx.lineTo(190,190);
ctx.moveTo(190,10);
ctx.lineTo(10,190);
ctx.stroke();
```

Drawing our O's requires using arcs. The most simple arc is a shape that we see every day—a circle. A circle is defined by a center point and a given distance (or radius) from that center point; the line that is drawn about that center point keeps the same radial distance. The `arc` function can draw a segment of a circle as well as a full circle, so we have to indicate the starting and ending angles along with an optional clockwise or counter-clockwise flag.

You might have learned in Geometry class a little of the math used to calculate the surface area of shapes, the area and circumference of circles, and things like that. If you've forgotten it all, rest assured. We will only be using the fundamentals for now. One important concept from Geometry class is the calculation of angles. Instead of using degrees, we use radians. So for a full revolution about a point, we say that we are rotating 2π (or 2 times pi) as opposed to 360 degrees. Pi is a mathematical constant representing the ratio of any circle's circumference, or the distance of the line around a circle's edge to its diameter, which is twice the distance from any point on the edge to the center point. Pi, which equals roughly 3.14159... can't be represented cleanly as a decimal number, so it is much simpler to denote the approximation by using the symbol. Table 5-1 shows some common angles in both their degree and radian representations.

Table 5-1   **Common Angles in Degrees and Radians**

Number of Degrees	Representation in Radians
0°	0
45°	$\pi/4$
90°	$\pi/2$
180°	π
270°	$3\pi/2$
360°	2π

If you need an angle that isn't listed in the chart, you can convert from degrees to radians by using the following formula. You don't have to worry about remembering pi because JavaScript stores the value in the `Math.PI`.

angle in radians = (angle in degrees) * (pi / 180)

The following snippet shows the code needed to draw our O's. The circle is drawn by selecting a center point and radius and drawing from 0 to 2*π radians. In keeping with the size of our X's and game board, the radius is 90 pixels, giving a diameter of 180 pixels. It looks nicer than 190 pixels, and that's what programming is about. In other words, sometimes the mathematically correct solution isn't always the most pleasing.

```
ctx.lineWidth = 2;
ctx.beginPath();

ctx.arc(100,100, 90, 0, 2*Math.PI);
ctx.stroke();
```

Drawing Objects on the Canvas with Transformations

On a traditional Tic-Tac-Toe game board, there are nine possible spots where an X or an O could go. We could just create functions that explicitly draw the objects in each spot, but that wouldn't be efficient. Instead, we can use translation to move the entire drawing plane from the origin to our desired point, draw our object, and then move the drawing plane back. This allows us to reuse the same code if we decided to make a 4×4 grid instead of a 3×3 grid.

A **matrix** is a collection of rows and columns of numbers that define the location, scale, and orientation of an object in space. For anything but translation, we would use a 2×2 matrix to represent transformations. But before we get to the more complex examples, let's start out with translation.

To translate an object currently located at (x,y) by (xr, yr) relative units, we would add two 2×1 matrices together, as shown in Figure 5-1. In this figure, we have a point located at (0,5) that we want to move 5 units to the left and 5 units down.

$$\begin{bmatrix} 0 \\ 5 \end{bmatrix} + \begin{bmatrix} -5 \\ 5 \end{bmatrix} = \begin{bmatrix} -5 \\ 10 \end{bmatrix}$$

Figure 5-1   Translation of an object

For scaling, shearing, and rotation, we have to multiply matrices. This is also where our 2×2 matrices come into play. Figure 5-2 shows the role of each position in the matrix.

$$\begin{bmatrix} \text{scale-x} & \text{skew-y} \\ \text{skew-x} & \text{scale-y} \end{bmatrix}$$

Figure 5-2   Definitions of the positions in
a 2×2 matrix

The most basic matrix we could use is the Identity matrix, as shown in Figure 5-3. The interesting property about the Identity matrix is that for any other matrix, multiplying it by the identity will return the original matrix. We can see from the figure that it represents a scale of 1 on the x and y axes with no skewing.

$$\begin{bmatrix} 1 & 0 \\ 0 & 1 \end{bmatrix}$$

Figure 5-3   Identity matrix

Let's put the Identity matrix to the test by demonstrating multiplication. To multiply a 2×2 matrix by a 2×1 matrix, we would follow the order indicated in Figure 5-4. You can also see in this figure that the Identity matrix's property holds true.

$$\begin{bmatrix} A & B \\ C & D \end{bmatrix} \begin{bmatrix} E \\ F \end{bmatrix} = \begin{bmatrix} AE + BF \\ CE + DF \end{bmatrix}$$

Figure 5-4   Matrix multiplication

Looking again at Figure 5-2, we can easily discern how to do scaling or skewing by placing our scale or skew constants in the proper slots. Rotation, however, is a bit more complicated.

Figures 5-5 and 5-6 show the matrixes needed to multiply by the vector representing some point to rotate it theta degrees about its center.

$$\begin{bmatrix} \cos \theta & \sin \theta \\ -\sin \theta & \cos \theta \end{bmatrix}$$

Figure 5-5   Counterclockwise rotation

$$\begin{bmatrix} \cos \theta & -\sin \theta \\ \sin \theta & \cos \theta \end{bmatrix}$$

Figure 5-6   Clockwise rotation

Ordering Your Transformations

Similar to the order of operations mnemonic device "Please Excuse My Dear Aunt Sally" (which represents parentheses, exponents, multiplication, division, addition, and subtraction), transformations have to be applied in a specific order; otherwise, unexpected results will occur. The issue at hand is that each subsequent matrix that is multiplied builds upon and distorts the result of the final position. The general order is scaling, rotation, and then translation.

For example, let's say you want to draw a box at location (10,10) and you want to rotate it 2 radians around its center. The current matrix is located at (0,0), as is the box's center. You would rotate the box using the desired amount and then translate it to (10,10). To move it a further 3 radians, you use the inverse order, translating the object back to the origin and applying the rotation before translating it to its desired location.

When a person does a back flip in real life, he is rotating about his current position. To account for this in a game, we must move the object to the origin, do the rotation, and then translate the object back to its original position.

The Canvas allows us to set the transformation matrix directly by calling `setTransform` and `transform`. `setTransform` sets the matrix to the identity before setting the transformation, whereas `transform` creates a product of the current matrix and the developer-provided matrix. Luckily for us, `canvas` has first-class support for translation, rotation, and scaling using `translate`, `rotate`, and `scale`. Both `translate` and `scale` take x and y parameters, whereas `rotate` takes an angle to rotate the matrix in radians.

Saving and Restoring the Canvas Drawing State

The last thing we need to properly transform objects is a way save and restore the Canvas state. We need to save and restore the transformation matrix so that we properly isolate transformations from one object affecting those that are drawn after it. `save` and `restore` do just that. Their combined functionality is similar to hitting a save point in a game, going down a fork in the road to retrieve some sort of power-up, being able to restore the state to return to the fork, *and* keep the power-up.

These functions save and restore not only the current transformation matrix but also the clipping region and several properties, including `strokeStyle`, `fillStyle`, `globalAlpha`, `lineWidth`, `lineCap`, `lineJoin`, `miterLimit`, `shadowOffsetX`, `shadowOffsetY`, `shadowBlur`, `shadowColor`, `font`, `textAlign`, `globalCompositeOperation`, and `textBaseline`. Listing 5-3 shows our updated function for drawing O sprites and properly handling translation.

Listing 5-3   **Drawing Several O's**

```
self.drawOSprite = function(x, y) {
var ctx = self.context;

    // Save the canvas state and translate
    ctx.save();
    ctx.translate(x,y);

    ctx.lineWidth = 2;
    ctx.beginPath();

    ctx.arc(100,100, 90, 0, 2*Math.PI);
    ctx.stroke();

    // Restore canvas state
    ctx.restore();
}
```

Using Images with the Canvas

For every image your game uses, another hit is incurred against the server to retrieve it. We already know from basic HTML how to use the `img` tag. In this section, we look at a couple more ways to use images in our applications.

Serving Images with Data URLs

Data URIs provide a way to include the data for a file inline in HTML code. The contents of the file then get retrieved when the HTML is downloaded, thus reducing the number of hits to the server and theoretically the wait time. The general format is as follows:

```
data:[<mime type>][;charset=<charset>][;base64],<encoded data>
```

Here is a simple data URI inside an image tag:

```
<img src= "data:image/gif;base64,R0lGOD1hDwAOAIAAAP///
    wAAACwAAAAAD wAOAAACGISPCaG9rhhEcppq8dSQO9+AUUCWpoVOBQA" />
```

Let's examine this URI. The original file is a GIF, so `mime type` is set to `image/gif`. The MIME type would be `image/png`, for example, to reflect that the source file is PNG. `charset` refers to the character set of the file if the source is a text file. The source file isn't text, in this case, so we omit `charset`. If both the MIME type and character set are omitted, the default values will be `text/plain` for the MIME type and `US-ASCII` for the character set. The next component, `;base64`, indicates whether the data is Base64 encoded. Base64 is used when you need to transmit binary data over a medium that is more tailored to transmitting text. It is also used sometimes to do basic password encoding for web services. Base64 encoding formats data using A–Z, a–z, and 0–9, plus two additional printable characters, generally + and /. Many tools on the Web will convert image files to data URIs. The website www.sveinbjorn.org/dataurlmaker offers a web-based application along with links to desktop applications.

Serving Images with Spritesheets

Trying to load a bunch of image files, even if they are small in size, can be very taxing on a server and cause your users to wait a really long time. Spritesheets solve this by packaging the images for many files into one. They are generally used for a large number of small images of a similar size. Images are padded to have uniform dimensions and can be retrieved using the images' calculated coordinates. Image-editing applications such as GIMP, ImageMagick, and Photoshop can create them for you, and certain web services can create them as well. Spritesheets can be combined with data URIs.

Drawing Images on the Canvas

Now that we have our images loaded, we need a way to draw them. The Canvas has a function appropriately named `drawImage` with several variants. All our examples assume we have retrieved an image from an image tag using `document.getElementById`, pulled it from the `document.images` collection, or created the image directly in JavaScript using `Image()` and adding a `src` URI to it.

The simplest variant is

```
drawImage(image, x, y)
```

which draws the image in its entirety with its current size with its left-upper corner at (x,y).

The second variant is

```
drawImage(image, x, y, width, height)
```

which, like the first variant, draws the entire image. The last two parameters scale the drawn image in the Canvas.

The last variant is the most powerful and has the most parameters:

```
drawImage(image, sx, sy, sWidth, sHeight, dx, dy, dWidth, dHeight)
```

This one allows you to use only parts of the source image and do scaling on the Canvas. sx and sy refer to the left-upper corner of the image slice. All data in the bounds of (sx,sy) and (sx+sWidth, sy+sHeight) is drawn. On the Canvas, the image is drawn in the area of (dx,dy) and (dx+dWidth, dy+dHeight).

Animating Objects with Trident.js

Trident.js (https://github.com/kirillcool/trident-js) is an animation library for JavaScript created by Kirill Grouchnikov that was ported from his Java library of the same name. The main focus of the library comes from the timeline, not that much unlike one in a video-editing program, allowing us to transition between different states with keyframes. Easing functions allow objects to move in a more life-like manner. Many timelines with different functions can operate simultaneously or in a specific order, one at a time. This is the main reason Trident.js was selected over the myriad of possibilities when it comes to JavaScript animation libraries.

Trident, at present, uses `setTimeout` instead of `requestAnimationFrame`. `requestAnimationFrame` determines whether to draw an object based on if the browser window is obscured of if the page is currently rendering, and it caps the refresh rate to 60Hz. `setTimeout` does none of this. It tries to render as much as possible even if the app is still rendering or not in view. Trident is a multipurpose animation library. `setTimeout` can be applicable to both DOM- and Canvas-based animation. `requestAnimationFrame` cannot. It might seem that the use of `setTimeout` disqualifies Trident before it even gets out of the gate. The feature that redeems it is the ability to pause a timeline. This, along with the other features, temper the disadvantages of using `setTimeout`.

Creating Timelines

The most basic timeline in Trident.js has a duration over which it will run and an object and property to interpolate. The interpolator tells Trident.js how to make intermediary values and optional starting and ending values. Timelines work by periodically waking up, or pulsing, to check how much time has passed and adjusting values appropriately. Although there is no guarantee on the frequency or time period of timeline pulses, for most applications, they perform reasonably well and regularly. These attributes are affected by the load on the client machine and what is being run on each pulse. Listing 5-4 shows some code to create a timeline.

Listing 5-4   **A Timeline to Interpolate Text Size**

```
var rolloverTimeline = new Timeline(myspan.style);
  rolloverTimeline.addPropertiesToInterpolate([
    { property: "font-size", from:16, to: 36,
      interpolator: new IntPropertyInterpolator()}
  ]);
  rolloverTimeline.duration = 2000;
```

First, we instantiate a timeline, assigning the element and property that will be modified. In this case, it is the style field of an element with the ID "myspan." Next, we added the properties that will be modified. In the code, we state that the font size will range from 16 to 36 units and to interpolate the values as integers. Lastly, we set the duration of the animation to be 2 seconds (in milliseconds).

As opposed to constantly monitoring the state of the interpolated properties, which could cause the page to become unresponsive anyways, Trident.js fires a timeline pulse or an instant in time in which wakes up, checks the state, and modifies it as needed. Unlike the Java version of Trident, which has a pulse rate of once every 40 ms, the pulse rate of Trident.js depends on the system load and the runtime environment. That being said, JavaScript engines in browsers are getting faster and faster with every iteration. Given the proper load, I wouldn't expect it to get too bogged down. We can also use a timeline to control our game loop. You can see this in action in this chapter's *Copy Me* game source code.

The last thing we need to do is to add a way to start our animation. I decided to put the start and reverse functions on onmouseover and onmouseout in a span element, as shown in Listing 5-5. Thanks to timeline pulses, the reverse action starts relatively quickly after onmouseout is fired. In addition to play and playReverse, there is also a replay function we could use as well to interact with the timeline.

Listing 5-5   **Starting and Reversing a Timeline**

```
<span id="myspan"
  onmouseover="rolloverTimeline.play();"
  onmouseout="rolloverTimeline.playReverse();">Some text</span>
```

In addition to integers, we could also interpolate over floating-point numbers or even RGB color values. We just need to set the appropriate "from" and "to" values with a different interpolator: `IntPropertyInterpolator`, `FloatPropertyInterpolator`, or `RGBPropertyInterpolator`, respectively. We aren't limited to HTML elements. Trident can also interpolate properties on JavaScript objects.

Animating with Keyframes

Normal timelines transitions between the beginning and ending points without any control over any intermediary value. Keyframes provide a way to indicate what a value should be at a given point on the timeline. A new field called `goingThrough` is where you would specify the values on the range from 0 (beginning of timeline) to 1 (end of timeline). You can see keyframes in action in Listing 5-6.

Listing 5-6   **Animating a Timeline with Keyframes**

```
var keyframeTimeline = new Timeline(keyframespan.style);
  keyframeTimeline.addPropertiesToInterpolate([
     {   property: "font-size", from:16, to:36,
         interpolator: new IntPropertyInterpolator()
     },
     {   property:"color",
         goingThrough: {
             0: "rgb(0,0,0)",
             0.4:"rgb(0,255,0)",
             1:"rgb(200,140,140)"
         },
         interpolator: new RGBPropertyInterpolator()
     }
  ]);
keyframeTimeline.duration = 3000;
```

Creating Nonlinear Timelines with Easing

By default in Trident.js, object and transitions happen at an equal rate of speed from start to finish. This is not what we usually see in real life. Friction, inertia, and other forces are in play that will cause an object to accelerate, decelerate, or bounce. Although doing precise physics calculations is outside the scope of this chapter, we can use easing functions to bring our animations somewhat close to what is expected. Given a ball that moves up and down on the y-axis, Figure 5-7 shows regular linear motion where every unit of time passed corresponds to one unit of movement on the y-axis. Figure 5-8 shows a bounce effect. We can see a couple of rebounds along the y-axis. Also notice the sharp decline on some of the segments, which corresponds to a faster speed.

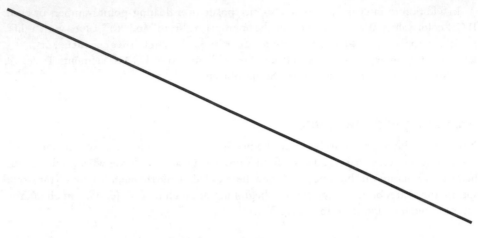

Figure 5-7   Graph of linear motion

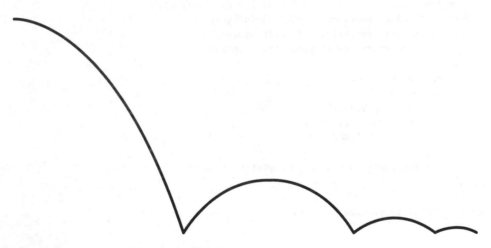

Figure 5-8   Graph of a bounce easing function

Trident.js, at the time of this writing, has 31 easing functions. Rather than list them here, I encourage you to download the source and try out the testBallLoop page for yourself. We will cover easing functions again when we discuss SVG in Chapter 6, "Creating Games with SVG and RaphaëlJS."

Animating Game Objects with Spritesheets

After learning how to slice and dice our images to draw on the Canvas, we can use some Trident.js timelines to create animations. The sprites for this demo were sourced from OpenGameArt (http://opengameart.org). All of the game assets listed on the site have very permissive licenses and are free to use in games. The spritesheet I selected for the demo is of a walking zombie that is subsequently shot in the head. All of the individual frames are 128 pixels by 128 pixels. Let's begin by setting up our timeline to control the animation. Given a JavaScript function named `sprites`, Listing 5-7 shows the code from the initialization function that sets up the timeline.

Listing 5-7   **Setting Up the Timeline for an Animation**

```
self.init = function() {
// Truncated for brevity
    var self = this;
self.current = 0;
self.spriteTimeline = new Timeline(this);
    self.spriteTimeline.addPropertiesToInterpolate([
        { property: "current", from:0, to: 36,
            interpolator: new IntPropertyInterpolator()}
    ]);

    self.spriteTimeline.duration = 5000;
    self.spriteTimeline.addEventListener("onpulse",
      function (timeline, durationFraction, timelinePosition) {
        self.drawSprite();
    });
    self.spriteTimeline.play();
}
```

One notable difference between this and the other examples so far is that the parameter for a new timeline is `this`, referring to the current object. The other difference is how we handle drawing on the Canvas. Unlike with CSS properties, which are automatically propagated to HTML elements, we have to make the changes in two steps. First, we set up a listener to fire every time the timeline position is updated. When the timeline is played, it modifies the current property, which is used by `drawSprite` function to calculate the proper slice to draw. Listing 5-8 shows the code to draw an individual sprite.

Listing 5-8   **Drawing an Individual Sprite**

```
self.drawSprite = function() {
    var ctx = self.context;
    var row = 3;
    ctx.clearRect(0, 0, 128, 128);
    ctx.drawImage(self.sheet, self.current *128,
      row*128, 128, 128, 0, 0, 128, 128);
}
```

Simulating 3D in 2D Space

Starting back in the arcade and early console days, the ability to simulate three dimensions in 2D space made for a more pleasing game experience. At that time, real 3D wasn't possible, and simulated 3D (called 2.5D) was the only option. In a way, the more things change, the more they stay the same. At this time of writing, the 2D Canvas API was more widely supported, with WebGL being regulated to experimental status. As a result, a 2.5D game in Canvas will have more potential users that one in WebGL. Another advantage of 2.5D is that it can potentially take less computing power than a true 3D game. In this section, we discuss some of the options to create a 2.5D experience.

Perspective Projection

Perspective projection seeks to mimic how the human eye sees objects. What our eyes see is a 2D projection of a scene in 3D. Several things are happening in concert that give us a perception of depth. For example, distant objects appear smaller and with less detail than closer objects. The simplest form and most appropriate for 2D games is one-point perspective. This point is known as the vanishing point, and it is the point where parallel lines appear to converge. Figure 5-9 shows an example of this in action with a graphic created in the 3D modeling application Blender. Orthographic projection is a way to represent a 3D object in 2D space. Images are created for the top, bottom, left, right, front, and back of the object. Often, just the information from the front, top, and right views are enough to recreate the object. The views on the right side of the figure are the top and side views, respectively. In the perspective view on the left, we can see the edges of the rectangles appear to be slowly converging toward a point on the horizon. We could heighten the effect by texturing closer objects in more detail than distant object.

Figure 5-9   Perspective projection rendered in Blender

Parallaxing

One technique that is often used in side-scrolling video games such as *Super Mario Brothers* and *Sonic the Hedgehog* to simulate three dimensions and create a more immersive experience is parallaxing. We can create the effect by making different components of the background exist as separate, independently movable layers that move at different speeds. It is similar to what you would experience if you were a passenger in a car riding across a bridge. The cars and barriers around you would move relatively fast compared to a city skyline you might see far in the distance. Let's dig a little deeper by creating a parallax effect ourselves.

Creating a Parallax Effect with JavaScript

For this demo, I have created some rudimentary graphics, including a sky dome layer representing the sky and clouds, a mountain range layer, and a layer showing the ground and other near objects. These are PNGs, but any image format that allows transparency will do. Each is like a sheet of paper with cutouts that let you see through to the sheet below it. This concept is known as z-ordering.

To keep things simple, our animation will continuously move. However, in a real side-scrolling game, motion would respond to player input such as a key press or move of the mouse. Besides the backmost layer, which is usually stationary, each layer moves at a rate 100% faster than the one behind it. We can start by setting up our timeline as shown in Listing 5-9. Because we'll be using multiple layers of images, we will use the `timelinePosition` value directly and draw our layers every time there is a pulse.

Listing 5-9   **Setting Up the Parallax Timeline**

```
self.setupTimeline = function() {
    self.parallaxTimeline = new Timeline(this);

    self.parallaxTimeline.duration = 5000;
    self.parallaxTimeline.addEventListener("onpulse",
        function (timeline, durationFraction, timelinePosition) {
          var ctx = self.context;
          ctx.clearRect(0, 0, 320, 200);
          // background layer is stationary
          ctx.drawImage(document.images[0], 0, 0);

          self.drawLayer(timelinePosition, document.images[1]);
          self.drawLayer(timelinePosition, document.images[2]);
          self.drawLayer(timelinePosition, document.images[3]);
    });
    self.parallaxTimeline.playInfiniteLoop(RepeatBehavior.LOOP);
}
```

We begin by clearing the Canvas and drawing our background. We are drawing it whole with no transformations, so we can use the simplest `drawImage` function. Its size is 320 pixels by 200 pixels. Each of our other layers will have a width that is some multiple of 320 pixels. Doing so frees us from having to perform much calculation for the speed of the layers. Layer 1 has a width of 320 pixels, so a full cycle of the timeline will only move it that far. However, layers 2 and 3, which are 640 pixels wide and 960 pixels wide, respectively, have to cover a greater distance in the same amount of time.

You won't be able to escape a little bit of math. The scrolling effect doesn't come for free, but luckily it requires only a minimal amount of arithmetic. Listing 5-10 shows our function for drawing a layer given a position in the timeline.

Listing 5-10   **Drawing a Layer**

```
self.drawLayer = function(position, image) {
    var ctx = self.context;

    var startX = position*image.width;
    var pixelsLeft = image.width - startX;
    var pixelsToDraw;
```

```
    ctx.drawImage(image, startX, 0, pixelsLeft, 200, 0, 0, pixelsLeft, 200);
    if(pixelsLeft < 320) {
        pixelsToDraw = image.width - pixelsLeft;
        ctx.drawImage(image, 0, 0, pixelsToDraw, 200,
            pixelsLeft-1, 0, pixelsToDraw, 200);
    }
}
```

Based on the timeline position, we can calculate where in the source image to start retrieving pixels to draw. If there aren't enough pixels to fill the viewport, we calculate how many pixels we need to draw (`pixelsToDraw`) and we draw a portion from the beginning of the source image to fill that space. To avoid having a 1-pixel gap between the seams of the image, we decrement the destination x position in the Canvas by 1 to cleanly stitch everything together.

Creating *Copy Me*

To put some more of what you've learned so far into practice, we will create a clone of the old electronic memory game *Simon* called *Copy Me*. The game's name is a play on children's game Simon Says, where the players must do everything that Simon says to do. In the game *Simon*, the computer creates a sequence of tones for the player to mimic. As each tone is played, a corresponding light—either red, green, blue, or yellow—illuminates. With each passing round, the sequence is increased by one. Game play continues until the player makes a mistake.

Drawing Our Game Objects

Instead of making our game look just like the traditional *Simon* game, we will instead use rectangles and drop shadows, thus taking advantage of some other features of the Canvas Path API. Listing 5-11 shows the code to create one of the rectangles.

Listing 5-11   **Drawing a Rectangle with a Shadow**

```
ctx.save();
ctx.fillStyle = "rgb(150,150,0)";
ctx.shadowOffsetX = yellowOffset.x;
ctx.shadowOffsetY = yellowOffset.y;
ctx.beginPath();
ctx.rect(400,200, 200,200);
ctx.fill();
ctx.restore();
```

The rect function takes the x and y coordinates of the left corner—in this case (400,200)—followed by the width and height. Creating drop shadows is easy as well. It is important to note that the shadowColor needs to be set on the context before a shadow can be drawn. Figure 5-10 shows the completed game board.

Figure 5-10   The *Copy Me* game board

Making the Game Tones

When I think of a game from the 1970s, I immediately think of the 8-bit sound board that was melodic yet electronic. To duplicate that effect, we could try to find tones or we could create them ourselves using MIDI, the Musical Instrument Digital Interface. The advantage that MIDI gives us is that software packages are available that allow use to create our tones using a text file. MIDI also gives us the flexibility of using the files as is, depending on the instruments available on the client machine, or converting to WAV or MP3 to bring obscure and unique instruments to our games. We only need four tones, so this is very manageable for our needs. Convention states that tones be organized as follows:

- Red button: An A note
- Green button: An A note one octave up from the red button
- Blue button: A D note, a fourth above the green button
- Yellow button: A G note, a fourth above the blue button

Several software projects are available that can generate MIDI files (GarageBand, for instance) and several can even use text files to do it. Because I didn't have a musical keyboard handy, I went the text route. Two of the more popular text-to-MIDI applications are Lilypond and ABC notation. However, both are more suited to creating long-form compositions and are overkill for our four-note "score." What's more, their notation styles are a bit complicated. I instead went with JFugue, a Java API for programming sequences without the complexity of MIDI. With about ten lines of code, I was able to hear all the tones together to determine whether they sounded right. It's not JavaScript, but you can't really argue with concise code. After creating the MIDI file with Java, we can use a MIDI editor/sequencer such as GarageBand to chop up the "score" into one-note pieces and convert them to WAV or MP3 files.

Listing 5-12 shows our tones, starting at the fourth octave, with a half-note duration and played as a harpsichord. Include just a single note after the instrument designation, and we have a single-note MIDI file. Easy peasy.

Listing 5-12   **Generating MIDI Tones with JFugue**

```
import org.jfugue.Player;
public class TestMidi {
    public static void main(String [] args) {
        Player player = new Player();
        String musicString ="I[Harpsichord] A4h A5h D5h G5h";
        player.play(musicString);
        player.saveMidi(musicString,
            new File("/Users/jwill/Desktop/test.mid"));
    }
}
```

Playing MIDI Files in the Browser

Now that we   have our MIDI files, we have a slight problem. We don't have a means to play them. Some browsers do have plug-ins to play .mid files, but they don't give us the programmatic control we need for our game. Lucky for us, the jasmid (https://github.com/gasman/jasmid) project fills that need. It can parse and play MIDI files using the HTML5 Audio API with a fallback to Flash. At runtime, the .wav files are generated and piped to the Audio API. A fair bit of work is involved in retrieving the file and assigning an instrument, so it will be an exercise for the intrepid to venture down that path. I fully expect browsers to eventually have native MIDI support as they currently support other sound file formats. In the meantime, some of the effort can be cut by preprocessing MIDI into another sound format such as WAV, MP3, or OGG. The open-source project Audacity does a fairly good job of this task, along with fulfilling other audio-editing needs.

Playing Multiple Sounds at Once

You saw in Chapter 1, "Introducing HTML5," how we could use the Audio API to write HTML or JavaScript code to play sound. One thing that we didn't cover in that chapter was playing multiple sounds at once. It's a bit more complicated than just piping multiple sounds at once to an `Audio` object and executing `play()`.

Each `Audio` object can only do a single thing at once. When you call `play` on something that is already playing, it silently ignores the request. If you wait until slightly after it has finished playing to try and play it again, it will probably work. If your sounds sometimes don't play, it could ruin the game experience and make people think your game is wonky. The way we can solve this is instead of creating a `Audio` object for each sound, we create a pool of `Audio` objects that we can iterate through, looking for one that isn't currently playing. We can check the status by comparing the `duration` and the `currentTime`. If they are equal, the sound has finished playing and we can use the channel. If not, the sound is either playing or cueing up to play. You can see this code in action in Listing 5-13.

Listing 5-13   **Playing Multiple Sounds**

```
var numChannels = 10;
channels = new Array();
for (var i = 0; i<numChannels; i++) {
    channels[i] = new Audio();
}
var play_multi_channel = function(id) {
for (var i = 0; i<channels.length; i++) {
        if (isNaN(channels[i].duration) ||
          channels[i].duration == channels[i].currentTime) {
            channels[i].src = document.getElementById(id).src;
            channels[i].load();
            channels[i].play();
            console.log("Playing on Channel: "+i);
            break;
        }
    }
}
```

This code assumes that the sounds will be enclosed in audio tags, but we could just as easily pass in the URLs to the files.

Playing Sounds Sequentially

Although the method described in   the previous section would be great for a side-scroller, it doesn't serve us that well for the *Copy Me* game. One sound shouldn't play until the other one has finished playing. We can do this by registering listeners for the `ended` event on `Audio` objects. We need an array of objects, `self.audios`, to which we have added objects containing an Audio object and a timeline like in the following snippet:

```
self.audios.push(
{audio: new Audio(self.sounds.red), timeline: self.timelines.red});
```

When the audio plays, the timeline will also be executed to simulate a color pulse. On every `Audio` element except the last on in the sequence, we need to execute

```
self.audios[i].audio.addEventListener('ended', self.playNext, false);
```

`self.playNext` very simply increments the counter, noting the current position, plays the sound, and starts the timeline to blink the proper rectangle, as shown in Listing 5-14.

Listing 5-14   **Playing the Next Sound**

```
self.playNext = function() {
    var j = self.currentPosition++;
    self.audios[j].audio.play();
    self.audios[j].timeline.play();
}
```

Drawing Our Game Text

The Canvas 2D contex gives us some basic functions to draw text. We can draw filled or stroked (outlined) text, set font attributes, and set text alignment. Listing 5-15 shows the code to draw a couple strings in our game. The `fillText` and `strokeText` functions take as parameters the text string to draw and x and y coordinates from which to start drawing text. An optional parameter, `maxWidth`, scales the font size to fit in that width. Our font string is composed of the attributes we specify, such as the weight (bold or italic), the font size, and the desired font with fallback options.

Listing 5-15   **Drawing the *Copy Me* Game Text**

```
var ctx = self.context;
ctx.font="bold 24px Arial, sans-serif";
ctx.fillText("Copy Me", 250,250);
ctx.fillText("Round " + self.currentRound, 250,300);
```

Styling Text with CSS Fonts

Although we can relatively guarantee that some fonts with be available on most operating systems, such as Arial, Georgia, and Times New Roman, sometimes you might want a font that isn't included by default on the client's machine. With CSS fonts, we can bundle them with our games. Whereas for a regular website, it might be appropriate to use a font loader that pulls from the Web, this doesn't work well with the Canvas unless we can ensure that the fonts are loaded before the Canvas is drawn. Otherwise, we have a big empty space where our text should go or text in the default font.

Listing 5-16 shows the code in a fonts.css file. In it, we have listed the font family of the included TrueType font file and the format of the font file, generally either TrueType or OpenType. This code loads the ReenieBeanie font asynchronously. We can ensure it's loaded in a rudimentary way by calling `setTimeout` with an interval of 3 to 5 seconds, depending on the number of fonts we are loading. A more elegant means is to employ a loading screen that waits for user input before starting the game or directly embedding the fonts using data URIs.

Listing 5-16   CSS File Demonstrating the Use of `font-face`

```
@font-face {
    font-family:'ReenieBeanie';
    src: url('../ttf/ReenieBeanie.ttf') format("TrueType");
}
```

We now just need to include that CSS file in the HTML page hosting our Canvas:

```
<link href='css/fonts.css' rel='stylesheet' type='text/css'>
```

Now we're all set. ReenieBeanie is downloaded from the Google Font Directory (http://code.google.com/webfonts), which has very permissive licenses for the all the listed fonts. Another great resource is the Open Font Library (http://openfontlibrary.org/). Be sure to verify the license terms of any font you include with your games.

Summary

In this chapter, through the development of several games and game-related examples, we dove deep into the Canvas 2D context. You learned how to animate images on a canvas, draw primitives, and create text. In the later examples, we wove together MIDI sounds and bundled fonts into our game.

Exercises

1. Convert 290 degrees to radians.
2. How would you play a theme song for your game level and then play sounds for actions such as jumping and kicking without interrupting the theme song?
3. Despite the small file size, why might you not use MIDI directly for game sounds?

You can download chapter code and answers to the chapter exercises at www.informit.com/title/9780321767363.

6

Creating Games with SVG and RaphaëlJS

One of the problems we saw when creating games with Canvas was that we had to independently track mouse interactions and locations of the drawn objects after rendering was complete. Scalable Vector Graphics (SVG) addresses these concerns by giving us a means to draw objects while retaining their locations as well as to receive events and modify them. In this chapter, you learn the essentials of SVG to get started in creating games. We also discuss how it compares to Canvas in regard to rendering capabilities and the subset of SVG that most clients implement.

Introduction to SVG

Compared to other elements of HTML5, SVG is a relatively mature component, first released in 2001, with its most recent release in December 2008. Unlike Canvas, it uses an XML-based format that stores instructions to draw components. As a result, an object drawn in pure SVG can be scaled up with no loss in quality. Figure 6-1 shows a raster (Canvas) image that's scaled to quadruple its size. An SVG image wouldn't have the blurring and jagginess.

One area where Canvas and SVG are similar is in the primitives they offer for drawing. Both offer the following primitives and effects:

- Circles or arcs
- Lines or paths
- Polygons
- Strokes
- Text
- Gradients
- Embedding of images
- Clipping, masking, and compositing

Figure 6-1   Scaled raster image using Canvas

Both are largely unsupported by versions of Internet Explorer previous to Internet Explorer 9, which will support both Canvas and SVG. Beyond the purely drawing-based functions, SVG objects can be scripted with JavaScript and can respond to the following events:

- `click`
- `doubleclick`
- `hover`
- `mouseover`
- `mouseout`
- `mouseup`
- `mousedown`
- `mousemove`

In some implementations, SVG supports `keystroke`, `mousewheel`, and `textinput` events as well. In the browser, `keystroke` events are a point of overlap with the native capabilities of most modern web browsers. Modern browsers can also directly embed SVG objects, enabling them to be used to render complete web pages as is done with Flash.

Chapter 8, "Creating Games Without JavaScript," introduces another means to create SVG assets using the Java programming language, but the current chapter will use two more widely methods: RaphaëlJS, a JavaScript library with capabilities to render in browsers earlier than IE9 for dynamic assets, and Inkscape, an open-source vector graphics application similar to Adobe Illustrator for more complex static assets. If you haven't installed Inkscape (http://inkscape.org/) or your preferred vector graphics application, take a moment and do so.

First Steps with RaphaëlJS

For our first experience with RaphaëlJS (http://raphaeljs.com/), we will be creating a simple card match game. This will allow us to keep the focus mostly on SVG and not the game logic. Our game will display several rows of cards on the game board and include a timer and a counter for how many moves have been completed. Figure 6-2 shows a frame from our completed game.

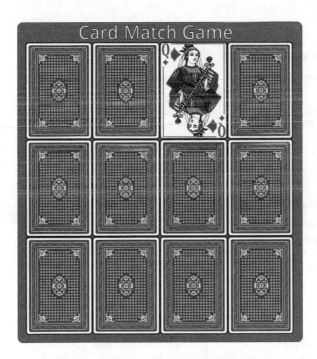

Figure 6-2   Screenshot from card match game

Setting Up Our Development Environment

Some web browsers are more stringent that others in allowing you to reference JavaScript files from your local machine and require you to host your JavaScript on a server. This can be unwieldy and prone to latency if your web server is far away from your present location. The flow of editing a file, uploading it, and checking the updated result gets old really fast. That is, of course, if you aren't editing files directly on your server. And you're not doing that, are you?

Luckily for us, Java has a lightweight server called Jetty that we can use locally to simulate a running server. Don't worry, you won't actually have to write any Java code, but you will have to work a little command-line mojo to get the server started. In the code directory for this chapter is a directory called webserver. Copy it to your working directory (or somewhere higher if you want to access multiple directories). Provided that you have Java installed, in a command prompt, enter the following:

```
java -jar webserver/webserver.jar
```

This command starts a Jetty server listening on localhost port 8080. If you don't like Java, feel free to substitute a local instance using your preferred technology, such as Django, Node.js, or Rails. Now that we can test our game locally, just like it were live on a server, let's create the game board.

Drawing the Game Board

The area where a SVG drawing is displayed in a web page is often called a "canvas." But to reduce confusion with the HTML5 Canvas, we will be using the Raphaël term "paper." We first need to create a paper to draw our game. Raphaël has several overloaded constructors to create a paper, but we will use the version that takes a DOMElement name, a width, and a height. After creating the paper, which is transparent by default, we need to create a rectangle background for our game board. Listing 6-1 shows the code to create these elements.

Listing 6-1   **Initializing the Game Board**

```
<script src="raphael.js" type="text/javascript"/>
<script type="text/javascript">
    var paper = Raphael("gameBoard", 800, 600);
    /* Draw at 0,0 with a 800px width and 600px height
        and rounded corners [optional param].
    */
    var rect = paper.rect(0, 0, 800, 600, 15);
    rect.attr({
        fill:'#090',          /* fill with a greenish color */
        stroke:'#000'    /* draw a black border */
    });
</script>
<body>
    <div id="gameBoard"/>
</body>
```

In Listing 6-1, we draw a rectangle and apply a fill and a stroke to it. We aren't limited to those attributes, however. Table 6-1 shows the other attributes we can apply to most objects.

Table 6-1   **Drawing Attributes**

Attribute Name	Description
cursor	Sets the cursor to display.
fill	The color to fill in a closed object or path.
fill-opacity	The opacity of the color fill.
stroke	The color of the line outlining a path or closed object.
stroke-width	The thickness of the line outlining a path or closed object.
opacity	The global translucency of the object.
path	A set of coordinates and instructions to draw complex objects. (This attribute is discussed in detail later in this chapter.)

Next, we need to draw the text for our title.

Drawing Game Text

Raphaël gives us several options to draw text, and we can even alter attributes on the text such as the color and fill values after they are drawn. We can draw text in the default browser font and with a white fill by executing code like the following, where the first two parameters specify the x and y positions, followed by the text string to print. Including \n inserts carriage returns in the output text:

```
var text = paper.text(600, 50, "Timer");
```

As you saw in Listing 6-2, objects can have attributes applied to them as a JSON map or as a single pair in the form obj.attr("attribute","value"). Attributes that are not applicable to the current object are ignored silently. Table 6-2 shows a list of the attributes we can attach to a text string.

Table 6-2   **Font Attributes**

Attribute Name	Description
font	The name of a font to be used
font-family	A set of fonts with the same general style but having different font sizes, weights, and styles
font-size	The size of the specified font's text
font-weight	The style of the text (bold, plain, or italic)

Custom Fonts

Sometimes, the basic fonts won't do. Why should your games be limited to the same hand-ful of fonts guaranteed to be present on all computers, thus limiting your creativity and style? Well, the good news is that, thanks to Cufón, they don't have to.

Cufón is a tool that allows you to take proprietary fonts and convert them to a JavaScript format that can be used to style text. So if the graphic designers of the world unite and succeed with getting Comic Sans stricken from all the world's browsers, rest assured you can include it in your games if you so choose. One of the other benefits of Cufón is the reduction in size versus native font formats such as TTF and OTF. The proj-ect claims a reduction of 60% to 80% in file size. You can have the best of both worlds by not needing a plug-in like Flash and not needing to embed large font files and thus slow down loading time.

It's fairly easy to convert a font using Cufón. Navigate to http://cufon.shoqolate.com/ generate/ to convert fonts online or download the code to run the conversion tool on your own server. The Cufón generator allows you to specify fonts for the default weights beyond the regular weight, including bold, italic, and bold italic. You can also modify the given `font-family` identifier. Figure 6-3 shows these options.

Figure 6-3   Selecting font typefaces to convert

Figure 6-4 shows the different combinations of glyphs you can output in the gener-ated font. This is an area where we can further reduce the size of the output font. The default selection is Basic Latin, which includes the uppercase and lowercase alphabet, dig-its, and punctuation. Options such as Latin Extended-A and B, Cyrillic, Russian, and Greek depend on the underlying capabilities of the font. Those extended character sets might not be available, so use caution to verify they are there if you need to use them.

Cufón gives us some other option for restricting a font to a certain domain and mak-ing the output file even smaller. However, the option I'm most interested in is shown in Figure 6-5. On the right side is a teeny-tiny Raphaël symbol that formats the font for use in Raphaël. If you forget to tick it, or find a Cufón file you'd like to use, don't fret. You can convert a Cufón file for use with Raphaël by performing a Find operation on Cufón and replacing instances with Raphaël. This is the part of the book where I tell you to not steal. All fonts aren't created equal, and many of them have field of use restrictions. Make sure you investigate what licenses the fonts you want to use have. Conversely, you could stick to open-source and royalty-free fonts, which are freely available on the Internet.

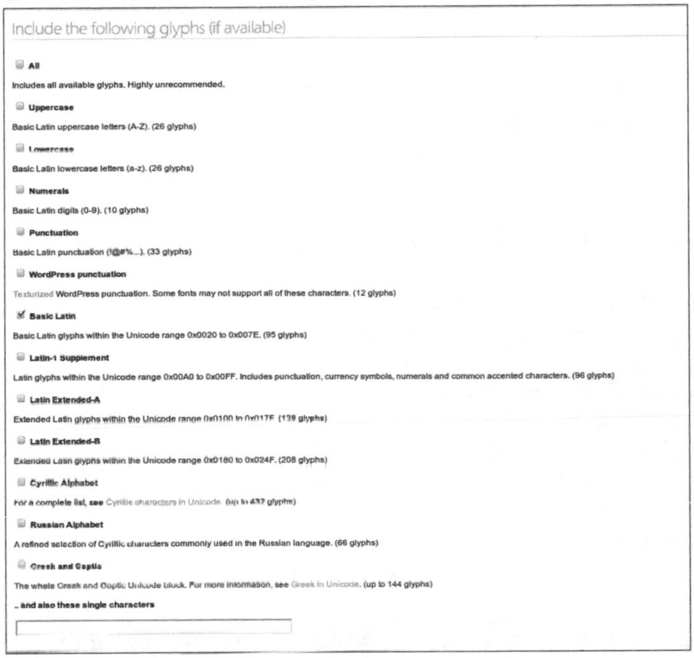

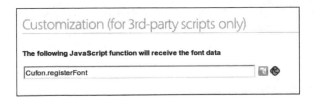

Figure 6-4   Selecting glyphs to convert

Figure 6-5   Font customization

Unlike the
```
text(...)
```
function we used before, there is another function, called
```
print(...)
```
in Raphaël that gives us a great deal of granular control over characters. Whereas attributes on a string created with `text(...)` apply for all characters, strings created with `print(...)` can be applied on a character-by-character basis. The same is true with animations.

SVG and the attributes Raphaël exposes allow us to truly interact with the Web and link to other SVG documents or web pages, and thanks to search engine mojo, those links are discoverable. Listing 6-2 shows several rectangles and a circle that navigate different websites.

Listing 6-2   **Linking to an External Document**

```
var paper = Raphael(0, 0, 300, 300);
var circle = paper.circle(50, 50, 40);
circle.attr({fill:'#F00'});
circle.node.onclick = function () {
    document.location = "http://facebook.com";
};
circle.node.onmouseover = function () {
    console.log("over at "+ new Date());
};
var r = paper.rect(200,100, 40, 40);
r.attr("fill", "#00C");
r.click(function () {
    document.location = "http://amazon.com";
});
var rect = paper.rect(150,200, 80, 80);
rect.attr({fill:"#0F0", href:"http://google.com"});
```

Listing 6-2 demonstrates several things. First, we see the first use of the `node` keyword, which specifies that you want to access and manipulate the underlying DOMElement. Alternatively, for the most common event types, we can attach the listener function directly to the element like we did with the blue rectangle. Although all three will forward the browser to a different page, it is important to note that only the last element with the `href` attribute acts like a conventional link, changing the cursor to a "clicky hand." Table 6-3 shows some other attributes that an SVG object can use to link documents.

Table 6-3   **Linking Attributes**

Attribute Name	Description
href	Turns the associated object into a hyperlink
target	A sub-element on a `href` page to link to

We'd like to have our game text use a font that will most likely be present on users' machines, so along side the font size, we will specify a list of fonts to attempt. If none of them are present, Raphaël will fail back to a sans serif font. Listing 6-3 shows how we can make it this happen.

Listing 6-3   **Setting Attributes on Text Blocks**

```
var attrList = {fill:"#FFF", stroke: 2};
var gameTitle = paper.print(150,30,
    "Card Match Game", paper.getFont("Droid Sans", "bold"), 48
)
gameTitle.attr(attrList)
```

Specifying Color

In the earlier examples, we indicated color by using a simple three-character hexadecimal representation for the red, green, and blue values. Raphaël provides many different ways to specify color. In addition to the shortened RGB hexadecimal format, we can specify colors using the identifiers shown in Table 6-4.

Table 6-4   **Methods to Specify Color**

Method	Description
Color name	A string specifying one of the 147 colors defined in HTML and CSS.
	Examples: `"yellow"`, `"green"`, `"pink"`
Color channel	Specifies the values of red, green, and blue as values from 0 to 255 or as percentages from 0% to 100%. Optionally, an alpha channel can be specified using the same methods.
	Example: `rgb(140,200,10)`, `rgba(100%, 5%, 20%, 90%)`
Hexadecimal	Represents a color using hexadecimal format. Both the shortened (#RGB) and long forms (#RRGGBB) are supported.
Hue, Saturation, Brightness, (Alpha)	Represents a color using hue, saturation, and brightness values between 0.0 and 1.0, inclusive. Alternatively, percentages can be used and opacity can be specified.

SVG also supports gradients, which allow you to smoothly transition between colors at given intervals. They take a little bit more work to specify. Gradients fall into two major categories: linear and radial. Linear gradients assume one dimension of influence, with a vector extending into space and some angle of incidence and with the resulting gradient matching the vector. Linear gradients take the general form

```
angle-color[-color[:offset]]*-color
```

where `angle` is the angle of incidence/depart, followed by a hyphen and a color. After the initial color, any number of optional transition stops can be specified. They are demarked by a hyphen, a color, a colon, and an optional percentage of the offset from the origin of the vector. If the offset isn't specified, the transitions will be equally divided between all the colors. Finally, a terminal color is listed. Note that any of the methods for indicating a color can be mixed and matched in gradients. So even though something like

```
10-blue-rgb(0%,100%,0)-rgba(255,0,0,255)-hsb(0.5, 1.0, 1)
```

is totally valid, it is a really bad idea to use when it comes to quickly discerning the transitions because mixing and matching affect readability.

Radial gradients, on the other hand, work in two dimensions. The gradient effect extends in all directions from a focal point somewhere inside the object. Radial gradients can only be applied to ellipses (including circles). This is only a compatibility issue, because SVG supports assigning radial gradients to any object.

Radial gradients take the following form:

```
r[(fx, fy)]color[-color[:offset]]*-color
```

Besides the focal point, generally you can easily convert a linear gradient to a radial gradient by dropping the angle, which no longer applies, and adding an *r*. For example, our ill-fated example from before becomes this:

```
rblue-rgb(0%,100%,0)-rgba(255,0,0,255)-hsb(0.5, 1.0, 1)
```

The focal point for a radial gradient is composed of two values, from 0 to 1, inclusive. The default value is "0.5, 0.5", which creates concentric color circles. Changing the focal point values moves that point into one of the four quadrants.

Loading Game Assets

Although it would be interesting to try and draw our own assets for playing cards, the DRY (Don't Repeat Yourself) principle applies here. Instead of wasting time on that, we can use assets from the open-source project SVG-cards (http://svg-cards.sourceforge. net/) for our card fronts and backs. Figure 6-6 shows the default card designs from SVG-cards. If we instead choose to be creative, we could substitute a custom card back.

Figure 6-6   Front and back examples
from SVG-cards

The way that Raphaël stores SVG is a subset of the SVG specification, so we can't just take any SVG file and manipulate it in Raphaël. Several parsers are available on the Internet that can take a raw SVG file and create Raphaël code to render it. Our other option is to render the complex portions of the object to a bitmap file and use it to skin a simpler object in Raphaël. The latter option is the best for our simple game. If we had rendered the cards as vector objects, the renderer would have to redraw intricate designs such as face cards over and over again, thus slowing the interactivity of the game. Luckily for us, in addition to being able to read and create SVG files, Inkscape can also convert them to PNG, PDF, Postscript, and several other file formats.

Converting SVG Files to Bitmap Images

In SVG-cards, each card is stored in a group with the name of the card and suit in the following format:

```
{1,2,3,4,5,6,7,8,9,10,jack,queen,king}_{club, diamond, spade, heart}
{red,black}_joker
```

To convert, say, the two of clubs, we would open an Inkscape shell by typing this:

```
inkscape -shell
```

The interactive shell allows us to run several commands in succession without spawning a bunch of Inkscape processes. We then need to specify the parameters for the request:

```
> svg-cards.svg -i 2_club -e 2_club.png
```

The code samples directory for this chapter contains the required converted assets for this project. Now that we have our card images and card backs as a bitmap file, we just need to create our classes for the interaction.

Creating Our Game Classes

The first classes we should create are the Card and Deck classes. Our Deck class will allow us to specify a number of decks, shuffle them, and deal cards. Our Card class contains properties for storing the ordinal and suit values with paths to the card back and front. The path for the image showing on the front of the card is constructed from the ordinal and suit. The card also knows how to draw itself at a given position with a paper object. The Deck class contains a collection of cards and has a notion of shuffling and dealing cards. Listings 6-4 and 6-5 display the basic framework for our Card and Deck classes, respectively.

Listing 6-4 **Card Class Source Code**

```
/*
    Defines the Card object.
    @author jwill
*/
function Card(ordinal, suit) {
```

```
        if ( !(this instanceof arguments.callee) ) {
            return new arguments.callee(arguments);
        }
    var ord;
    var suit;
    var cardBackPath = "";
    var cardFrontPath = "";
    var self = this;
    self.init = function() {
            var paper = Raphael($("#gameboard")0, 800,600);
            self.ord = ordinal;
            self.suit = suit
    };
    self.createCard = function(ordinal, suit)  {   };
    self.init();
}
```

Listing 6-5   **Deck Class Source Code**

```
/*
    Defines the Deck object.
    @author jwill
*/
function Deck(numDecks) {
    if ( !(this instanceof arguments.callee) ) {
        return new arguments.callee(arguments);
    }
    var cards;
    var self = this;
    self.init = function() {
        var paper = Raphael($("#gameboard")[0], 800,600);
        self.cards = new Array(52 * numDecks);
        self.initCards();
    }
    self.initCards = function() {
        // Initialize the cards
        var ordinals = ['1','2','3','4','5','6', '7', '8', '9', '10', 'jack',
➥'queen', 'king',];
        var suits = ['club', 'spade', 'heart','diamond'];
        // Populate card array
        for (var k = 0; k<numDecks; k++) {
            for (var j = 0; j < suits.length; j++) {
                for (var i = 0; i < ordinals.length; i++) {
                    var index = (i + (j*13) + (k*52));
                    self.cards[ index ] = new Card(ordinals[i],suits[j]);
                }
```

```
            }
      }        // Shuffle the decks
      self.shuffleDecks();
   }            self.init();
}
```

Shuffling Cards

As with a normal deck of cards you could buy in a store, our deck is in sorted order
when we initialize it. To shuffle the cards, we can use a randomizing algorithm popular-
ized by Donald Knuth in which we start at the next-to-last card in the array, moving
backward, and pick a random number between zero and the current position. We then
swap the cards referenced in these indexes and repeat the process until we're done. To
really scramble the cards, the algorithm repeats this process one time for each deck that is
present. Listing 6-6 shows the code performing card shuffling.

Listing 6-6   Shuffling Cards

```
self.shuffleDecks = function () {
      var rand = function(max) {
            return Math.floor(Math.random()*max);
      }
      var swap = function(i,j) {
            var temp = self.cards[j];
            self.cards[j] = self.cards[i];
            self.cards[i] = temp;
      }        for(var j = 0; j<numDecks; j++) {
            for(var i = (numDecks * 51); i>=0; i--) {
                  var r = rand(i);
                  swap(i,r);
            }
      }
   }
}
```

Drawing and Animating Cards

Although it would be perfectly acceptable to have no transitions between card states,
doing so adds a little bit more polish to the game and makes game play a bit more enjoy-
able. Tables 6-5 and 6-6 introduce the last of the most commonly used attributes in
Raphaël, those needed to position and transform objects.

Table 6-5   **Position Attributes**

Attribute Name	Description
cx	The x position for the center
cy	The y position for the center
r	The uniform radius of the object
rx	The horizontal radius of the object
ry	The vertical radius of the object
height	The height of the object
width	The width of the object
x	The x position of the object
y	The y position of the object

Table 6-6   **Transformation Attributes**

Attribute Name	Description
rotation	Spins an object about a center point
scale	Increases or decreases the size of the object
translation	Moves an object on the screen

Our requirement for graphic effects is pretty low in this game, but we will need a couple of transitions to enhance the game play. We need to come up with a transition to flip cards, to make them disappear when we have found a match, and transitions to start and end the game. Let's begin with animating the cards.

As you saw earlier, we can wire up the cards like any other DOMElement to respond to events such as button clicks. Because we are working in only two dimensions, we will "flip" cards by transitioning one side of the card to zero, making it transparent, while gradually making the other side of the card opaque. Listing 6-7 shows our `flipCard` function, which reads whether or not the front of the card is showing, inverts the value, and executes the transition.

Listing 6-7   **Flipping Cards**

```
    self.flipCard = function(frontShown) {
        if (self.meta['hidden'] == true)
            return
      self.frontShown = !self.frontShown;
        if (self.frontShown) {
            self.cardBack.animate({opacity:0.0}, 1000)
            self.cardFront.animate({opacity:1}, 1000)
            game.selectedCards.add(self);
        } else {
```

```
        self.cardFront.animate({opacity:0.0}, 1000)
        self.cardBack.animate({opacity:1}, 1000)
        game.selectedCards.remove(self);
    }                    console.log(game.selectedCards);
}
```

These lines specify that we should animate the opacity of the object from the current value to 0.0 or 1.0 and to animate over a duration of 1000 milliseconds (1 second). We don't have to stick to just the opacity; most of the events that have numeric values can be animated. Table 6-7 shows a list of them; many will be familiar from our earlier discussion of attributes.

Table 6-7 **Animateable Attributes**

clip-rect	cx	cy
fill	fill-opacity	font-size
height	opacity	path
r	rotation	rx
ry	scale	stroke
stroke-opacity	stroke-width	translation
width	x	y

In addition to a smooth transition from start to end, Raphaël allows us to add other modifiers to an animation. Easing allows a developer or designer to modify the animation path to mimic conditions we see in real life. For example, when there is a key press to indicate an abrupt stop, you could make a car object slightly recoil as if someone slammed on the brakes at a low speed. We could also apply functions to imitate acceleration and deceleration. Or maybe an elastic effect or a bounce effect, where each rebound is slightly lower that the previous one, until the object comes to a stop. You can provide your our easing function or use one of the presets listed in Table 6-8.

Table 6-8 **Preset Easing Functions**

Value	Description
>	Simple deceleration
<	Simple acceleration
<>	Accelerate then decelerate
backIn	Move backward then move to destination
backOut	Move to destination, slightly past it, then to proper position
bounce	Move to destination and lightly bounce the object
elastic	Combination of backIn, backOut, and bounce

Although we won't cover them in this chapter, you can also specify keyframes encapsulating the animation to say, for example, that from 0% to 20% into the animation, I want the acceleration to be very slow. When a player finds a match, we apply an animation to fade the cards to transparent with a bounce effect to approximate a blink. This can simply be done with a single line of code:

```
self.cardFront.animate({opacity:0.0}, 1000, "bounce")
```

The next line in the source

```
self.meta['hidden'] = true;
```

corresponds to a conditional statement in `flipCard` that short-circuits any animations taking place on that card if it is supposed to be hidden.

Creating Advanced Animations

The last bit of animation we have to complete is the animation for signaling the end of the game. No one can lose our friendly game, so let's make it extra special by showing an animated "You win!" message. Before we dive into animating the message, let's take a step back and talk about a concept that we haven't yet covered in SVG: paths.

Paths

Paths provide a means to create complex shapes. By themselves, they don't have a visible representation. There are an abstract set of lines for drawing. If we give them a color fill, a solid object will be drawn. If we add a stroke, they will resemble a set of lines. We can also take a shape and draw it multiple times along a path to create a extruded shape with a 3D effect. In Raphaël, we can also use paths to determine how an object will be animated.

Paths are useful because they allow us to mix and match lines and curves. Any primitive object, such as a circle, rectangle, or even text, can be represented by path components with the proper stroke and fill properties. A path can be represented by a sequence of segments, arcs, and curves. The path syntax is not really built to be written by hand, and all of our examples using paths will be created in a vector graphics application such as Inkscape and then imported to Raphaël. Be that as it may, it's important to have an understanding of the identifiers. If you have played with Turtle Graphics for the Logo programming language or some of the graphics packages for BASIC, you will feel right at home.

moveto and lineto

Unlike some of those early graphics libraries for BASIC and Logo, there isn't an explicit `penup` or `pendown` instruction. Moving the cursor in SVG parlance is the same as picking up the pen, moving it to another position, and putting the pen back down on the paper.

That position can be absolute or relative based on the current position of the "pen." It bears noting that almost all of our path instructions have absolute and relative versions. A `moveto` instruction is denoted by a lowercase *m* or an uppercase *M* and a Cartesian coordinate pair, indicating a relative or absolute instruction, respectively.

There are three variants of instructions for drawing lines: `lineto`, `horizontal lineto`, and `vertical lineto`. `lineto` is denoted by an uppercase *L* for absolute coordinates and a lowercase *l* for relative coordinates. You can specify a single point or a set of points. `horizontal lineto`, denoted by *H* or *h*, takes one or more x values. `vertical lineto`, indicated by *V* or *v*, performs the same action as `horizontal lineto` but on the y axis. Last but not least, we need a way to take our vertical, horizontal, and general polylines and make shapes out of them. The `closepath` instruction, marked by a *Z* or *z*, does just that in drawing a straight line from the current position to the start of the current subpath. *Z* and *z* do exactly the same thing but are including for symmetry with the other commands.

I promise you that you only have to endure a little bit of pain constructing these paths by hand for this section. No sane developer ever does this by hand. Just think of it like learning to calculate derivatives in Calculus class; once you fully understood the easy way, you never had to contend with the hard way anymore. Listing 6-8 moves the cursor to 100,100 and draws a rectangle with sides 40 units long, closes the path, and assigns a white fill color to it using horizontal and vertical lines. Afterward, relative coordinates are used to draw a rectangle with a black fill.

Listing 6-8   **Rectangular Paths**

```
var rect = paper.path("M100 100 h40 v40 h-40 v-40 z");
var rect2 = paper.path("M200,200 140,0 10,40 1-40,0 10,-40 z");
rect.attr({fill:"#FFF"})
rect2.attr({fill:"#000"})
```

curveto

Line segments can only take you so far. You can approximate a curve with `lineto` instructions, but scaling up the drawing will betray the method you used to draw them. And it wouldn't be that fun to have to construct all the segments to draw a curve anyway. Bézier curves can give us the precision we need while reducing the number of instructions required. Although he wasn't the creator of the curves named for him, Pierre Bézier, a French engineer for the Renault, created a computer-aided design system to use the curves to design automobile parts and bodies. Today, we use Bézier curves in the design of many consumer products and some font standards. It's fairly likely that the font used to print this text uses Bézier curves.

So now that you know how cool they are and where they are used in real life, what exactly are Bézier curves? They are defined by a starting point, an end point, and a set of control points. The curve doesn't pass through these control points, but they affect the path of the curve, pushing and pulling it like the poles of a magnet.

Bézier curves in SVG come in two varieties: cubic and quadratic. The difference between the two is that quadratic curves have one control point and cubic curves have two. SVG has several identifiers for each, with *C/c* and *S/s* denoting cubic Bézier curves and *Q/q* and *T/t* representing quadratic Bézier curves. *C/c* and *Q/q* take the absolute or relative coordinates for the control points followed by the endpoint. *S/s* and *T/t* are the shorthand versions of the aforementioned curves. They take the last control point in the previous curve and take the reflection of it to use as a control point. For quadratic curves, you only have to specify the new endpoint, but cubic curves require that you specify a second control point as well.

Exporting Paths from an SVG File

Now that you have slogged through learning how to draw lines and curves and all, let's discuss the easy way. Open up your favorite vector graphics editor, such as Inscape or Adobe Illustrator, use the Pencil/Pen tool to draw to your heart's content, and save the file as SVG. Then, look for a `path` tag and copy the contents of the "d" or data property. SVG-edit, pictured in Figure 6-7, allows you skip one of those steps by giving you an option to view the raw SVG from inside the web page.

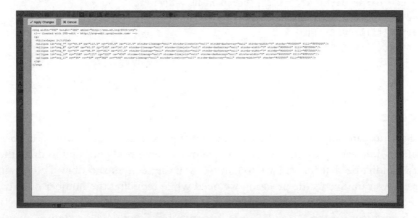

Figure 6-7   SVG-edit showing raw SVG code

Animating Along Paths

Raphaël comes with two functions to animate objects along paths: `animateAlong` and `animateAlongBack`. These functions animate an object starting at the beginning and end of a path, respectively. These functions take a path object or path string, the number of milliseconds the animation will span, an optional Boolean value for whether to rotate the object while animating it, and an optional callback function. Given a circle that we have already defined, we can animate it along one of our rectangle paths by executing the following line of code:

```
circle.animateAlong(rect, 2000, false);
```

One thing to note about `animateAlong` and `animateAlongBack` is that unless the shape's resting position is the same as the path it is moving along, it will move relative to its own space. For the preceding snippet, from its starting position, the circle will move 40 units to the right, 40 units down, 40 units left, and 40 units up, no matter where the rectangular path is drawn. Our ending screen uses a figure-8 path to animate the message "You win!"

Extending Raphaël with Plugins

Raphaël can be extended with plugins. Reasons for this could be the desire for deeper integration of third-party libraries as well as exposing as-yet-unimplemented features in the SVG specification. Raphaël is a compromise between the feature set in SVG, for non–Internet Explorer browsers, and VML, an Internet Explorer standard for drawing vector graphics. If a feature was not present in both standards, it was left out. Plugins can allow the developer to add back some of that missing functionality, albeit in a non-cross-platform way.

Adding Functions

Raphaël allows you to add functions to the paper or to elements as well as attributes. The key difference between functions added to the paper and those added to elements is that paper objects must be created before a paper is instantiated. Functions can be added to elements at any time and modified.

The ability to add functions to the paper is exposed by the `Raphael.fn` object. You are even able to use namespaces to modularize your code. The gRaphael charting library does just that. Element functions are exposed by the `Raphael.el` object. Adding a function to that object adds it to all Raphaël objects.

SVG Filters

SVG filters comprise sone area that benefits from plug-ins. Filters in SVG are not that unlike the filters present in many graphics manipulation applications such as GIMP and Adobe Photoshop. They allow you to alter the way a given object or set of objects is displayed. Because they aren't in core Raphaël, we'll discuss their capabilities but leave it as an exercise for the reader to integrate them. Table 6-9 shows an abbreviated list of available filters and their descriptions. Developer community members have created plugins supporting some filters, but as of the time of this writing, all filters have not been implemented. A good resource for what has been implemented is the Raphaël Google group. In the context of filters, "image" can refer to an actual raster image, such as a JPEG or PNG, a matte fill color, or a gradient color.

Table 6-9 **Abbreviated List of SVG Filters**

Filter Name	Description
feBlend	Combines the data of two components using one of the predefined blending algorithms
feDiffuseLighting	Defines a light that provides ambient lighting for the scene
feGaussianBlur	Blurs an image by applying a Gaussian function
feImage	Renders an image to a raster canvas
feOffset	Offsets an image by a given vector
fePointLight	Defines a light set at a specific point emitting in all directions
feSpotLight	Defines a light set at a specific point in space that is focused at a point with a bounding cone of influence
feTile	Fills a target object with a tiled repeated pattern
feTurbulence	Adds noise to an image

Speed Considerations

Compared to the much-newer technology HTML5 Canvas, which operates essentially as a bitmap buffer, SVG is a bit more heavyweight. The code for drawing 5,000 circles in a Canvas can be largely reused with translation instructions. An SVG drawing, on the other hand, has to create 5,000 discrete objects with full DOM representations for each. This is the price we have to pay for letting SVG handle most things for us. SVG is great for games with a low number of sprites on the screen, as in our examples, or games where the sprites will not change often. It would not be fruitful to use SVG for the whole of a first-person shooter game.

Summary

In this chapter, we dove deep into the internals of SVG with RaphaëlJS. You learned how to draw text, create objects, interact with them, and change them on the fly. You also learned how to bring color to objects in compelling ways, how to draw complex objects, and how to extend Raphaël. Lastly, we covered the conditions that would benefit from a game coded using SVG and those that would not. Knowing the innate capabilities of the tools and libraries you intend to use helps you down the line in assuring yourself you made the right decision and aren't trying to build a house with a screwdriver, so to speak.

Exercises

1. We briefly discussed the Cufón library, which can be used to convert fonts for use with RaphaëlJS. Use one of the open-source fonts found in the Google Font Directory (http://code.google.com/webfonts), convert it for use with Raphaël, and create a scene with any text string using that custom font.

2. Modify the card match game code to use a custom background for the cards.

3. Modify the card match game code to optionally include Jokers in the deck.

4. Draw a hexagon and pentagon using paths.

5. We used animation to flip playing cards. Make an animation that transitions between a triangle, a square, and a circle.

You can download chapter code and answers to the chapter exercises at www.informit.com/title/9780321767363.

7

Creating Games with WebGL and Three.js

In previous chapters, we took great pains to learn the hard way first before diving into libraries and frameworks that make our coding life simpler. WebGL is a beast. Based on OpenGL ES 2.0, which itself is a simplification of the much older Open GL API, it's still rather large. Although it stands to reason that one might use Canvas 2D or SVG without the benefit of a framework, the same is not the case with WebGL. There are many concerns to be taken into account, including lighting, texturing, depth of field, particle systems, and collision detection and response, that make operating without a framework much like walking a tight rope without a net. The framework we will be using extensively in this chapter is Three.js. Three.js is a 3D graphics library for modern browsers that, as mentioned before, can render to Canvas, WebGL, and SVG. It supports all that is possible in WebGL while allowing you to use the same code for all renderers, with some exceptions. The compatibility layer won't excuse you from doing extensive testing, but at the very least it gives you a possible fallback option if the client's computer isn't exactly the latest and greatest. Three.js abstracts many of the pointy edges away—for example, in dealing with materials and shaders. It has built-in helpers for some of the more common 3D geographic shapes such as spheres, cubes, and cylinders, and a full-featured particle system, texture mapping, and basic collision detection. In this chapter, we will endeavor to stay at a high, general level in some cases but dive into the low-level details in others—whatever seems appropriate for the task at hand. Let's begin the chapter by discussing OpenGL ES, the technology behind WebGL.

OpenGL ES, or OpenGL for Embedded Systems, is a specification for 3D graphics APIs running on devices such as mobile phones, tablets, and video game consoles. Most mobile device platforms (Android, iOS, Blackberry/QNX, WebOS) support some form of the spec. Video game implementers include Nintendo (Nintendo 3DS), Sony (PlayStation 3), and OpenPandora (Pandora). Although the names are similar and versions of OpenGL ES track to OpenGL, OpenGL ES is not OpenGL. OpenGL ES is a subset of OpenGL. Some key differences are the removal of `glBegin`/`glEnd` and `glVertex*` for drawing primitives. The use of display lists was deprecated in favor of vertex buffers. We won't be using them directly because Three.js abstracts them all away, but it is important to be aware of the differences.

Moving to Three Dimensions

When we were drawing on the 2D Canvas context, we didn't have to worry about an object's depth or its position, either near or far from us. We just had a rectangular viewport representing the things we could see. For WebGL, we do have to consider the depth, and this unsurprisingly makes our transformation calculations a more complicated. Don't worry—I'm not going into matrix math again. At least not yet. If you're a bit hazy on all this, take a moment and turn back to Chapter 5, "Creating Games with the Canvas Tag." We can control depth with the z-axis, as shown in Figure 7-1.

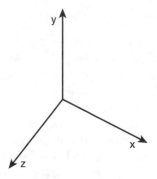

Figure 7-1   XYZ-axes

The addition of the third axis gives us a new construct for representing a point in space: the vertex. The following snippet shows the code needed to create a vertex in Three.js:

```
new THREE.Vertex(new Vector3(0, 0, 0));
```

Draw two vertices and you have a line. Draw three vertices and you can have a triangle. The options are limitless. Right now we can draw a bunch of vertices on the screen, but we won't be able to see them. That's because they don't have any relationship between them; at this point, they are just a bunch of random points in space. A **mesh** is a collection of vertices that describe an object. These vertices are arranged into faces that are composed of three or more vertices. To create a triangle, we need to perform the following tasks:

- Create a `Geometry` object to store the vertices.
- Add faces to tell the vertices how to arrange themselves.
- Create a mesh with the `Geometry` object and a material.

Don't worry about how to define the material just yet. We'll be covering materials a bit later in the chapter. We can see sample output in Figure 7-2 and the corresponding code to produce the mesh in Listing 7-1.

Figure 7-2   Triangle mesh

Listing 7-1   **Creating a Triangle**

```
geometry = new THREE.Geometry();
geometry.vertices.push(new THREE.Vertex(new THREE.Vector3(0, 10, 0)));
geometry.vertices.push(new THREE.Vertex(new THREE.Vector3(-10, -10, 0)));
geometry.vertices.push(new THREE.Vertex(new THREE.Vector3(10, -10, 0)));
geometry.faces.push(new THREE.Face3(0,1,2));
var triangle = new THREE.Mesh(geometry, geoMaterial);
```

Giving Your Objects Some Swagger with Materials and Lighting

We now have a context of how the different vertices relate to each other, but we still won't be able to see them. Why? We haven't told the world what they should look like. We do that with materials and lighting.

Understanding Lighting

Besides keeping humanity from freezing to death, lighting in Three.js isn't that dissimilar to what happens in the real world via the Sun. It has three types of lighting objects:

- **AmbientLight**—Ambient lighting is the average of all the light generated from all light sources in an area. Objects rendered with only ambient lighting will appear two-dimensional. That's because all vertices receive the same amount of light. One way to look at it is to consider ambient lighting to be like the thermostat on your air conditioner/furnace. Turning it on, in general, doesn't make individual rooms cooler or warmer, it brings them all approximately to the same temperature.

- **PointLight**—Point lighting is attenuated light coming from a specific location in world space. Light is emitted in all directions from the point and does make objects look more 3D. As an object moves further from the light source, the amount of light that can affect objects is less and less (attenuation, or colloquially "dropoff"). Point lights can also cause or contribute to specular reflections.

- **DirectionalLight**—Directional lighting can be viewed as similar to shining a bunch of lamps on a subject from the same direction. Whereas point lights will attenuate over distance, directional lights deliver the same intensity as they stretch toward infinity or the specified maximum distance.

Listing 7-2 shows examples of the three light types, starting with `AmbientLight`, which has a sole parameter. `intensity` corresponds to how bright the light rays should be, and `distance` refers to the longest light ray before total falloff. `castShadow` is Boolean that determines whether or not the object illuminated by `DirectionalLight` with cast a shadow. Although not listed in the constructors, you can set the position on `PointLight` and `DirectionalLight`. Parameters listed in brackets are optional.

Listing 7-2 **Lighting Examples**

```
new THREE.AmbientLight(hexColor);
new THREE.PointLight(hexColor, [intensity], [distance]);
new THREE.DirectionalLight(hexColor, [intensity], [distance], [castShadow]);
```

Using Materials and Shaders

Materials make our objects less ordinary by giving them colors and textures. We are covering materials after going over lighting because the lighting of a scene greatly affects how a material appears to the user. Many atmospheric components go into determining the final color of a vertex or face including, but not limited to, the following:

- Lighting (ambient, point, and directional)
- Shadows
- Shaders

- The blend mode
- Occlusion

We've already covered lighting, and shadows don't need much description, so let's press on with shaders. A shader uses software instructions to calculate rendering effects generally on the Graphics Processor Unit (GPU) but can be done in software as well. There are generally three types of shaders:

- **Vertex shaders**—Vertex shaders are run for each vertex in a mesh. They can alter properties such as the position, color, normals, lighting, and texture coordinates.

- **Pixel or fragment shaders**—Fragment shaders calculate the color and other properties for each pixel in a mesh when rendered onscreen.

- **Geometry shaders**—Geometry shaders are used to add or remove vertices on a mesh. One use is to add LOD (level of detail) effects to a scene—that is, to increase or decrease the number of vertices in a mesh as a object gets closer or further, respectively, from the screen.

WebGL and Three.js focus programmatically on the vertex and fragment shaders. The LOD aspect of geometry shaders is handled in Three.js, but a discrete object won't be covered in any detail in this chapter. Before we get to talking about shaders and materials, there's one important concept you need to learn about: the normal. It's a vector that is perpendicular to a surface or vertex. It is often used in lighting calculations, which also affects how materials appear and can be used to create greater detail in models without increasing the polygon count. Several shading algorithms are either supported natively in Three.js or easily implementable. Let's look at them briefly, from easy to difficult.

Flat Shading

Flat shading shades an object based on each polygon normal in a mesh. For very regular shapes such as rectangles, the calculations won't be that different from some of the most advanced algorithms we'll discuss. The problem with flat shading is that any model with a reasonable amount of polygons will look blocky, and users will be able to easily see where one polygon ends and another begins.

Lambertian Shading

Lambertian shading, put simply, reflects light equally in all directions. This causes models to look the same irrespective of the viewer's point of view. Unfinished wood, concrete, and other matte surfaces have this characteristic. Because of the lack of dynamism, Lambertian shading, like flat shading, is very easy on the GPU.

Gouraud Shading

Gouraud shading, at every vertex, applies a normal that is the average of all the surface normals for the polygons that the vertex touches. This gives us smoother illumination than flat shading but at a low cost to the CPU/GPU. Because it is an average of several vertices, some amount of error will be involved as the applied normal is an estimate and will be plus or minus what the actual normal value was. This can be especially evident in anything that causes specular highlights (bright spots on reflective objects). Figure 7-3 shows an infographic of how a plane normal is calculated.

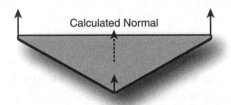

Figure 7-3   Gouraud shading normal calculation

Phong Shading

Phong shading is the most costly of the four. Also called per-pixel shading, it takes the vertex normals and calculates the intermediate normal values for each pixel. This produces a lighting model that improves greatly on the results from Gouraud shading but is costly to the processor.

Somewhat related but technical not a shading model per se is Phong reflection. Phong reflection considers how that very few objects are perfectly shiny or rough. As such, the surfaces on an object are a combination of the two properties (specular and diffuse reflection, respectively). The components for Phong reflection are as follows:

- An ambient color for the amount of light evenly distributed through the object
- A diffuse color that scatters light in all directions
- A specular color for the highlights, presumably caused by the light source

You might also specify a shininess or opacity. All of these work in tandem to produce the final material. For example, a totally unshiny material isn't going to consider the specular values.

Creating Your First Three.js Scene

One of the first things I learned to draw in OpenGL was a snowman scene from some random online tutorial. Snowmen are great because no one hates them but the sun, and it is easy to draw something that looks reasonably close to the subject. It also gives us a chance to discuss some of the built-in 3D shapes.

Setting Up the View

Before we get started, we need to do a little housekeeping to set up our environment to draw the snowman. In our truncated `init` function, we instantiate a renderer and scene. As mentioned before, Three.js can render to several different environments. Changing the renderer to `CanvasRenderer` or `SVGRenderer` is how you would do that. We also need to set the dimensions of the renderer. Three.js makes a best-effort attempt to render the scene with the given renderer. Although many effects and materials can be rendered with all the renderers, some are specific to WebGL. Below the `init` function, we have a pair of functions that handle our animation and rendering. `requestAnimationFrame` attempts to refresh the drawing as close to the monitor's refresh rate as possible while short-circuiting drawing if the window is not visible. You can see this code in Listing 7–3.

Listing 7-3   **Setting Up the Environment**

```
function init() {
        // ...
        // create a renderer and scene
        renderer = new THREE.WebGLRenderer();
        renderer.setSize (WIDTH, HEIGHT);
        // some code
        }
function animate() {
        requestAnimationFrame (animate);
        render();
}


function render() {
        renderer.render(scene, camera);
}
```

In this chapter, you might notice the use of both "scene" and "scene graph." The scene describes all the objects in the environment. The scene graph describes how the objects are arranged in relationship to each other. A scene graph is a collection of nodes arranged in a graph or tree structure. Each node may have child nodes. The essential point you need to know is that because Three.js is a scene graph, we only have to keep track of the objects we want to change. Otherwise, we add the node to the scene graph, call the render, and don't worry about it.

On the off-chance that a few of you have never seen a snowman or even snow, a snowman is shown in Figure 7-4. We can see that his body is more bulbous than humanoid and that he has sticks for arms and a carrot nose.

Looks pretty daunting, huh? That complete scene can be drawn with only three shapes: spheres, cylinders, and planes. We use those shapes in different sizes and with different transformations to create the snowman. A sphere, shown in Figure 7-5, is a perfectly round shape that is the result of taking a circle and spinning it around its center point. Basketballs, baseballs, and the Earth are all spherical shapes.

Figure 7-4   Snowman

Figure 7-5   Sphere

Listing 7-4 shows the code needed to draw the snow parts of the snowman's body. We start by instantiating a white material. Next, we draw three spheres, each successive one smaller than the one that preceded it. The first parameter in the Sphere constructor is the radius, followed by the number of steps to draw for the width and height. More steps give you a more round sphere but also add a lot more vertices to draw. Fewer steps yield an object that is quicker to draw but the lighting will not look as good. Lastly, we use the transformation functions on THREE.Mesh to move the spheres into place and then finish by adding them to the scene graph.

Listing 7-4   **Drawing the Snowman's Body**

```
var topSegment, middleSegment, bottomSegment;
var whiteMaterial;

whiteMaterial = new THREE.MeshLambertMaterial({
        color:0xFFFFFF
})
bottomSegment = new THREE.Mesh(
        new THREE.Sphere(8, 16, 16), whiteMaterial
);
middleSegment = new THREE.Mesh(
        new THREE.Sphere(6, 16, 16), whiteMaterial
);
middleSegment.translateY(10);
topSegment = new THREE.Mesh(
        new THREE.Sphere(5, 16, 16), whiteMaterial
);
topSegment.translateY(19);

scene.addChild(topSegment);
scene.addChild(middleSegment);
scene.addChild(bottomSegment);
```

The second shape we will use in the scene is a cylinder, as shown in Figure 7-6. A cylinder is formed by taking a circle and extruding it along a straight line. "Extruding" is just a fancy way of saying "duplicate the object, move it a little bit, and then rinse and repeat." Soup cans and some cups are cylindrical.

Figure 7-6   Cylinder

Listing 7-5 shows the code to draw the stick–like arms of the snowman. We start by declaring a brownish material. Next, we create the arms. The parameter list starts with how many steps to use, followed by the starting and ending radii, and the length of the cylinder. We have to do a bit more work this time to move them into place.

Listing 7-5 **Adding Arms**

```
var arm, arm2, armMaterial;

armMaterial = new THREE.MeshLambertMaterial({
        color: 0x8B5A00
});

arm = new THREE.Mesh(
        new THREE.Cylinder(20, 0.3, 0.3, 10),
        armMaterial
);
arm2 = new THREE.Mesh(
        new THREE.Cylinder(20, 0.3, 0.3, 10),
        armMaterial
);

arm.rotation.x = 30;
arm.rotation.y = 10;
arm.translateX(8);
arm.translateZ(1);
arm.translateY(15);

arm2.rotation.x = -30;
arm2.rotation.y = 10;
arm2.translateX(-7);
arm2.translateZ(1);
arm2.translateY(15);

scene.addChild(arm);
scene.addChild(arm2);
```

A plane, shown in Figure 7-7, gives our scene a little bit of depth. Think of it as a giant sheet of paper or, better yet, as a big rug.

Figure 7-7 Plane

Like the sphere and cylinder before it, the plane allows you to control how detailed the mesh is. After declaring the width and the height, you can set the respective step values. The code to draw a plane is shown in Listing 7-6.

Listing 7-6   **Drawing a Plane**

```
plane = new THREE.Mesh(
      new THREE.Plane(500,500, 20, 20),
      planeMaterial
);
```

Although we have three main types of shapes in the drawing, the snowman's nose can be thought of as both a cylinder and a new shape type: a cone, as shown in Figure 7-8. Some graphics libraries will differentiate between the two, but the relation is similar to that of rectangles and squares: All cones are cylinders but not all cylinders are cones. The extrusion is the same, but the radius of each subsequent circle gets smaller and smaller until it reaches zero.

Figure 7-8   Cone

You can see in Listing 7-7 that the only point of distinction between a cone and a cylinder is that one of the radii is close to zero.

Listing 7-7   **Drawing a Nose**

```
nose = new THREE.Mesh(
      new THREE.Cylinder(20, 0.8, 0.01, 3),
      noseMaterial
);
```

Viewing the World

If you tried to run the code we've written so far, you wouldn't see anything on the page and suspect that it is broken. The reason we can't see anything is because we haven't told Three.js where we will be located and what we will be looking at. Placing a `Camera` in the scene is how we can view it. Based somewhat on the human eye, cameras have attributes that determine what can or cannot be seen. The `Camera` object signature is shown here:

```
var cam = new THREE.Camera( fov, aspect, near, far, [target - optional])
```

The most important parameter and also the first is `fov`, or the field of view (FOV). The FOV determines the amount of the world that can be seen at one time. It is often talked about in degrees. We can calculate it by putting a camera (or eye if you want to make it gruesome) on a tripod and pointing it out in the distance toward some objects. Looking through the viewfinder and not moving the camera, you notice the rightmost object you can see and draw a line from your position to that point. You do the same for the leftmost object. Now draw a line between the two objects. We now have a triangle that we can use to find the FOV. An infograph of this is shown in Figure 7-9. Rest assured that you do not have to calculate this...ever. The computer does all the work for you.

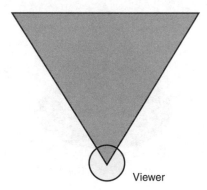

Figure 7-9   Calculating the field of view (FOV)

The next parameter is `aspect`, for the aspect ratio. You might recognize the term from the specs on your monitor or television. Aspect ratio is the ratio of the longer dimension of your viewport to the shorter. Most screens are somewhere in the area of 4:3 (standard definition) or 16:9 (widescreen). Aspect ratio works in collaboration with the FOV to determine how much of the world is cropped from view.

The next two parameters, `near` and `far`, represent the clipping planes for your world. In a scene with thousands of objects and textures being drawn at once, it would be taxing on the CPU and GPU to try and show everything. Even worse, it would be wasteful to draw the things you can't even see. The near clipping plane is usually relatively close to the user, whereas the far clipping plane is somewhere off in the distance. As objects cross the far plane, they spontaneously appear or disappear. Some games use fog to make the appearance and disappearance of objects more realistic. `target` is an optional parameter that allows you to designate an object to look at. Figure 7-10 shows how the first four parameters combined to make the viewing frustum.

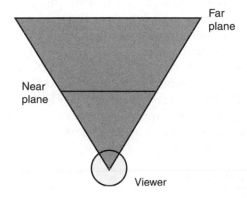

Figure 7-10   Viewing frustum

But, wait a minute, why didn't we have to deal with any of this when were drawing on the 2D Canvas? The short answer is that we were; Canvas was doing it for us behind the scenes. A frustum for a 2D scene can be created by making a camera with the `near` and `far` values being the same, which is also the z value for all drawn objects. In effect, that camera is constrained to seeing a specific slice of the world.

Loading 3D Models with Three.js

Having to create everything in code would get tedious very fast. You might be happy to know that Three.js supports loading 3D models in its own JSON format and has file exporter scripts for Autodesk 3ds Max and Blender.

Autodesk 3ds Max—or colloquially 3D Studio MAX or just MAX—is widely recognized as the industry standard for creating, animating, and rendering 3D models. It is widely used not only by artists for games but also in TV and film. Built in to the product is a scripting language called MAXScript, which can be used to build client-side plugins.

Blender (www.blender.org) is a cross-platform, free, and open-source advanced 3D modeling application. It can create complex effects supported in commercial 3D modeling software such as UV wrapping, texture, bones and rigging, and particle system effects. It also bundles a nonlinear editor and Python API for in-application scripting. Blender is managed by the non-profit Blender Foundation, chaired by Blender's creator Ton Roosendaal and developed by the Blender community (www.blenderartists.org/forum/). There is even a community magazine (http://blenderart.org/).

Part of the outreach the Blender Foundation conducts includes the Blender Conference (held annually in Amsterdam), the Suzanne Awards (which are competitively awarded to animators), and the production of several short films. Commercially, Blender has been used in television commercials, *History Channel* shows, and in the pre-production of *Spider-Man 2*.

The export scripts for both applications are located in the utils/exporters directory of Three.js. Check the appropriate vendor websites to find out how to install plugins, paying extra care to the version the plugin states it requires. Use a version newer than that required and it might not work correctly.

Listing 7-8 shows the code to asynchronously load a JSON model and add it to our scene graph. As you can see in Listing 7-9, the JSON model file can include materials that we can modify or use. The last line of `createScene1` may look a bit daunting at first, but let's break it down. Skipping the first two self-explanatory parameters, we have the global scale of the object, its x, y, and z positions, its rotation on the x, y, and z axes, followed by the material to use.

Listing 7-8 **Loading a Model File**

```
function drawCube() {
        var loader = new THREE.JSONLoader();
        loader.load( {model: "cube.js", callback: createScene1 });
}

function createScene1(geometry) {
        geometry.materials[0][0].shading = THREE.FlatShading;
        mesh = THREE.SceneUtils.addMesh( scene, geometry,
            250, 400, 0, 0, 0, 0, 0, geometry.materials[0] );
}
```

Truncated to the essence of what comprises the model file, Listing 7-9 gives you a gist of what is output from the Blender exporter. You can see the areas for the vertices, normals, materials, and faces. We'll hold off on explaining some of the other areas of the file until later in this chapter.

Listing 7-9 **Truncated Cube.js File**

```
var model = {

    "version" : 2,
    "scale" : 1.00,
    "materials": [        {
        "DbgColor" : 15658734,
        "DbgIndex" : 0,
        "DbgName" : "Material",
        "colorAmbient" : [0.0, 0.0, 0.0],
```

```
            "colorDiffuse" : [0.64, 0.64, 0.64],
            "colorSpecular" : [0.5, 0.5, 0.5],
            "shading" : "Lambert",
            "specularCoef" : 50,
            "transparency" : 1.0,
            "vertexColors" : false
            }],

        "vertices": [1.00...],
        "morphTargets": [],
        "normals": [0.577349,..],
        "colors": [],
        "uvs": [[]],
        "faces": [35,...],
        "edges" : []
};

postMessage( model );
close();
```

Programming Shaders and Textures

If you want to forgo using the built-in material features in Three.js and possibly create more advanced effects, you can dip into the WebGL features and create your own vertex and fragment shaders. In Three.js, you would create a material as demonstrated earlier in the chapter and attach your shaders. To write shader code, you need to learn a little bit about OpenGL Shader Language, or GLSL for short.

GLSL is a high-level language with a C-like syntax. Although structured like programs, and even called that in some cases (the combination of a vertex shader and fragment shader), the shaders are not compiled but passed around as strings. They can be created at runtime, as some are in Three.js, or read in from files or <div> tags on a web page. Some of the more dangerous operators such as pointers are not present in GLSL, but it closely matches the feature set of C, the operators of C and C++, and can do pretty much anything you'd want to do, including flow control and creating/calling functions. GLSL also has some bundled graphics-processing-specific convenience functions.

Listings 7-10 and 7-11 show the code for a GLSL program that colors all vertices with a white color. Listing 7-10 is where we assign the color using a vec4 to represent the desired red, green, blue, and alpha values.

Listing 7-10   **Sample Fragment Shader**

```
<script id="shader-fs" type="x-shader/x-fragment">
    #ifdef GL_ES
```

```
    precision highp float;
    #endif

    void main(void) {
        gl_FragColor = vec4(1.0, 1.0, 1.0, 1.0);
    }
</script>
```

Listing 7-11 shows the code for a vertex shader. When we view vertices, although drawn in 3D space, they are projected into 2D space when they are shown on the screen. gl_Position locates the final position of the vertex onscreen by multiplying the projection and model view matrices by the location of the vertex. Don't worry about the extra 1.0. That is present because in matrix multiplication, the dimensions have to match. projectionMatrix, modelViewMatrix, and position are all injected by Three.js for us. If you are adapting a GLSL program from another platform, you might see those programs explicitly declare these variables.

Listing 7-11   **Sample Vertex Shader**

```
<script id="shader-vs" type="x-shader/x-vertex">
    #ifdef GL_ES
    precision highp float;
    #endif


    void main(void) {
        gl_Position = projectionMatrix * modelViewMatrix * vec4(position, 1.0);
    }
</script>
```

To use the shaders in our application, we need to create a shader material for the objects that will use it. After this is instantiated, we can use it like any other material. Listing 7-12 shows the code to create a MeshShaderMaterial using the bare minimum properties. The code uses a JQuery-like library to get the contents of the script tags.

Listing 7-12   **Creating a MeshShaderMaterial**

```
var shaderMaterial = new THREE.MeshShaderMaterial({
                vertexShader: $('#vertexShader').get(0).innerHTML,
                fragmentShader: $('#fragmentShader').get(0).innerHTML
});
```

Often, shaders will need to do some advanced calculations, or you might want to pass data from your host application to your GLSL program. Shader variables let you do just that. There are three basis types:

- **Uniform**—The value stays the same during a render of a frame and is available to both shaders.
- **Attribute**—Read-only variables available to the vertex shader.
- **Varying**—Allows the vertex and fragment shaders to share data.

In Listing 7-11, `projectionMatrix` and `modelViewMatrix` are uniforms and `position` is an attribute. When creating our own variables, it is important to note that GLSL programs are not JavaScript and require explicit declaration of types. In addition to the primitive types available in C/C++, there are also some GLSL specific ones. Table 7-1 shows the possible vector types, whereas Tables 7-2 and 7-3 show the matrix and texture types, respectively.

Table 7-1   GLSL Vector Types

Type	Description
`vec2`, `vec3`, `vec4`	Floating-point vectors for 2D, 3D, and 4D
`ivec2`, `ivec3`, `ivec4`	Integer vectors for 2D, 3D, and 4D
`bvec2`, `bvec3`, `bvec4`	Boolean vectors for 2D, 3D, and 4D

Table 7-2   GLSL Matrix Types

Type	Description
`mat2`	2×2 matrix
`mat3`	3×3 matrix
`mat4`	4×4 matrix

Table 7-3   GLSL Texture Types

Type	Description
`sampler1D`, `sampler2D`, `sampler3D`	1D, 2D, and 3D textures
`samplerCube`	Texture for a cube map

Using Textures

Textures can range in shape and size, so we can't always map a 1:1 relationship between the size of a texture and the face it will be applied to. To compensate for this, instead of mapping with the actual pixel sizes, we map the relationship between the texture and the face it will cover with texels. A **texel**, also known as a texture coordinate or texture pixel, is a pair of two values that range from 0.0 to 1.0 for the x- and y-axes. We assign a texel for each vertex in the object we are texturing. You can see an example of this in Figure 7-11.

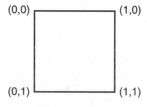

Figure 7-11   Texels

Instead of attempting to texture a complex object all at once like you would with a color, you can instead texture the individual faces of the object. This can optimize the texturing process and allow greater control over the look of the textured object. This process is called "UV mapping." You can see a simplified form of this in Figure 7-12 as a cube map. A cube map consists of six textures, one for the top, bottom, and four sides of the cube.

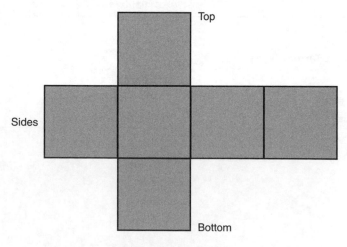

Figure 7-12   Cube map

If we supply one texture, it is repeated on all the sides of the cube. If a face in the object to be textured isn't present, the texture data for that face is discarded. Cube mapping allows us to use the same texture information for a cube, sphere, cylinder, or any other object.

With UV mapping, a template is created by unwrapping the triangles and laying them all flat. The artist could then paint on each individual face. Once textured, the object has the desired "skin." Take, for instance, the games of the *Dead Rising* franchise, which allow the protagonists to change their clothes at will. The game developer did this by layering multiple UV maps. There could be a map for the body and skin texture, then another for undergarments, and another for outer clothing.

Listing 7-13 demonstrates how to apply a texture to a sphere. To avoid needing extra lights to illuminate the model, we use a white ambient color on the material. Three.js will do a lot of the heavy lifting for us, leaving us mostly free to hand it a texture using the `map` property, and it then constructs the cube map for us. Figure 7-13 shows the model produced by the code in Listing 7-13.

Listing 7-13   **Texturing a Sphere**

```
function drawScene() {
        var texture   = THREE.ImageUtils.loadTexture(
            "200407-bluemarble.jpg" );
        var material = new THREE.MeshPhongMaterial( {
            color: 0xFFFFFF, ambient: 0xFFFFFF, map:texture
        } );

        sphere = new THREE.Mesh(new THREE.Sphere(32, 32, 32), material);
        scene.addObject(sphere);
}
```

In the case of Listing 7-13, which shows how to texture a sphere, the UV coordinates were created for us. The Three.js JSON format has support for UV coordinates, and all of the packaged exporter plugins can export them as well.

Figure 7-13   Textured sphere

Creating a Game with Three.js

Conway's *Game of Life* is a cellular automaton simulation where individual cells (or, in our version, spheres) abide by certain rules to determine their transition between different states. Conway's *Game of Life* is a great project because we don't have to worry so much about game play, but it requires us to manage many objects in the scene at the same time. Here are the general rules:

- A live cell with fewer than a certain number of live neighbors dies.
- A live cell with more than a certain number of live neighbors dies.
- A dead cell with a certain number of live neighbors comes alive.
- A live cell with a certain number of neighbors lives on.

Conway's is strictly 2D, and cells are born with three neighbors, die with more than three, and live on with two or three neighbors. Because we are using 3D and possibly different birth/death rules, we have to call the game "*Life*-like." Unlike the original, where the simulation has a reasonably large space to "roam," our simulation will be constrained to a customizable square grid with configurable birth/death rules. An added feature that is present in the Java3D application that inspired our app is different cell color based on the age of the cell. A screenshot of the running game is shown in Figure 7-14.

The code runs one cycle of 100 alive/dead transitions for each cell.

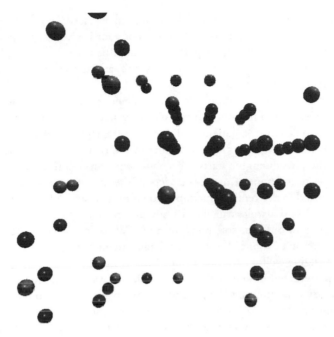

Figure 7-14   *Life* like game screenshot

Simulating the Real World with Game Physics

In Chapter 4, "How Games Work," we discussed some very basic ways to do collision detection and create particle systems. In that chapter, we used informal bounding boxes to determine whether a collision had occurred, which resulted in a very constrained response. We also dabbled a bit with particle systems. In this chapter, we apply physics properties to the particles in a more formal way.

When we think of what makes humanoid-based games look realistic, we are seeking physics engines at work—or more specifically, rigid body dynamics. One way to think of this is to consider rigid bodies to be like bones in the human body. The bones themselves don't bend but can be articulated at the joints and have a maximum of six degrees of freedom (translation and rotation in x, y, or z). We can also add constraints to restrict the motion so that our models aren't dislocating joints when they move. These constraints could be as simple as making the object immovable, like a wall or the ground, or by using joints. Joints allow us to connect and constrain rigid bodies. The two types of joints that most physics systems support are hinge and ball-and-socket. Hinge joints restrict motion to one axis. Examples in the human body are knees and fingers. Ball-and-socket joints, on the other hand, allow a freer range of motion on possibly all six degrees of freedom. Your shoulders and hip joints are good examples of ball-and-socket joints.

Rigid bodies also have physical properties such as mass, inertia, velocity, and so on. Whereas your bones only account for 30% to 40% of your body's mass, rigid bodies contain 100% of the simulated object's mass. Rigid bodies don't have to just be bone-like structures, they can be immovable objects such as walls and the ground or things encompassing one or many moving bodies.

Physics engines use a combination of primitive shapes to detect collisions, such as spheres, boxes, capsules, and free-form meshes. You are free to use as many as you want; for instance, you could detect a general collision with the right hand with one collision primitive and then drill down to the exact finger that was affected. After the primitives are all defined, the physics engine starts and slowly steps through time to check for collisions and changes to the transformation matrices of the objects and rigid bodies. These changes are reported to the render functions and combined with player input. There is another major type of dynamics called soft-body dynamics. Any type of cloth as well as fur, hair, and feathers would use soft-body dynamics. We won't be covering this in any detail as it is an advanced topic. However, it warrants mentioning.

The physics engine we'll be using for our demos is JigLibJS. It is a port of the Java variant of the popular JigLib library. JigLib is available at www.jiglibjs.org/. Although the original library is written in C++, in addition to JavaScript, JigLib has been ported to C# and Actionscript. Listing 7-14 shows the initial setup of our physics world. We begin by retrieving an instance of the `PhysicsSystem` and setting the gravity for the world and the type of solver to use. In this case, we used `FAST`, but the other options are `NORMAL` and `ACCUMULATED`. You give up a little accuracy for choosing `FAST`, over `NORMAL` and `ACCUMULATED`, but usually there isn't a noticeable difference.

Listing 7-14   **Setting Up JigLibJS**

```
function initJigLib() {
        system = jigLib.PhysicsSystem.getInstance();
        system.setSolverType("FAST");
        system.setGravity( jigLib.Vector3DUtil.create(0, -9.8, 0, 0) );
}
```

After we create the physics system, we need to create a mesh for the ground and a corresponding physics rigid body to represent the ground. The properties we need to set on the rigid body, for the most part, match what we set on the mesh, with the exception of the additional call `set_moveable(false)` to make the ground unaffected by external forces. This code is shown in Listing 7-15.

Listing 7-15   **Drawing the Ground**

```
// create the ground
var plane = new THREE.Mesh(
        new THREE.Plane(75,75,10,10),
        new THREE.MeshLambertMaterial({
            color:0x222222
```

```
        })
);
plane.translateY(-10);
plane.rotation.x = -70;
scene.addObject(plane);

var ground = new jigLib.JPlane();
ground.set_y(-10);
ground.set_rotationX(-70);
ground.set_movable(false);
system.addBody(ground);
plane.rigidBody = ground;
```

Next, we need to draw our sphere and assign a rigid body to it. The code to create a Three.js sphere is pretty straightforward, so I've excluded it in Listing 7-16. If you need a refresher, check out the sources. We begin with instantiating the JSphere, passing it a null for the skin and a value for the radius. After setting the mass on the object, we can orient it in 3D space using the moveTo function and the Vector3DUtil class. We could have set the point to move to using the individual set_x, set_y, and set_z functions, as we did with the ground or by just passing in an array of values as shown in the commented line. One reason why you might want to construct a Vector3D is if you plan to somehow transform it after you create it.

Listing 7-16   **Drawing a Sphere Rigid Body**

```
// create rigid body
var body = new jigLib.JSphere(null, 8);
body.set_mass(8);
body.moveTo(jigLib.Vector3DUtil.create(sphere.position.x,    sphere.position.y,
sphere.position.z, 0));
//body.moveTo([sphere.position.x, sphere.position.y, sphere.position.z, 0]);

system.addBody(body);
sphere.rigidBody = body;
```

Lastly, we need some code to update our objects. The updateDynamicsWorld function in Listing 7-17 begins with a calculation to find the elapsed time since the previous run. The system takes the elapsed time to figure out how to apply the forces to the system. We next iterate over all the objects, checking to see if they have rigid bodies attached. If so, we alter the transformations of the meshes to match. In Listing 7-17, we are dealing only with the translation and rotation, but the listed orientation variable is how we would access the full transformation matrix.

Frames per Second Versus Time-Based Animation

When games are created based solely on frames per second, they might be optimized for a particular class of system or processor and thus run differently on others. You might notice this if you dust off some of your old 3.50 or 5.250 floppies. If the game was developed for a 386 20MHz computer, it might be unplayable on a 3GHz machine. Also, frame-based animation inappropriately assumes that it won't have to share the processor with any other applications. CPUs, by design, rapidly switch between running processes. If a processor-hungry app is running in the background, such as a music player, you might see your frame rate rapidly decline.

Listing 7-17 **Updating the World**

```
function updateDynamicsWorld() {
        // find elapsed time from last update
        var t1 = new Date().getTime()
        var elapsedTime = t1 - t0;
        t0 = t1;

        system.integrate(elapsedTime/1000);
        for (var i = 0; i<scene.objects.length; i++) {
                var mesh = scene.objects[i];
                if (mesh.rigidBody) {
                    var state = mesh.rigidBody.get_currrentState();
                    var position = state.position;
                    var orientation = state.get_orientation().glmatrix;

                    mesh.position.x = position[0];
                    mesh.position.y = position[1];
                    mesh.position.z = position[2];

                    mesh.rotation.x = mesh.rigidBody.get_rotationX();
                    mesh.rotation.y = mesh.rigidBody.get_rotationY();
                    mesh.rotation.z = mesh.rigidBody.get_rotationZ();
                }
        }
}
```

Revisiting Particle Systems

Particle systems in Three.js solely deal with 2D objects. They use a concept called **billboarding**, wherein the textured face of the sprite is always facing the camera and/or user's viewport. Billboarding allows two-dimensional shapes to appear to have depth in a

3D world. Billboarding allows us to save polygons, where possible, and is not relegated to particle systems. Some LOD algorithms will transition between not drawing an object, drawing it with a billboard, drawing it with a low-poly model, and drawing it with the high-resolution model. To create a particle system in Three.js, we first need to create a `THREE.Geometry` object to hold the vertex locations of the objects to draw. We then pass it to a `ParticleSystem` object with the vertices and a `ParticleBasicMaterial` to use for the particles. In this case, we loaded a PNG image for the particles and set the size in the material to the dimensions of the image. In Listing 7-18, you can see that we don't ever instantiate the individual particles. After the geometry is assigned to the `ParticleSystem`, adding more particles has no effect even though it doesn't give an error when we try and it seems to work. Any transformations are applied to the particle system as a whole, and each particle system can only have a single texture for all the particles.

Listing 7-18   **Bubble Particle System**

```
// create texture
ballTexture = THREE.ImageUtils.loadTexture( "ball.png" );
var material = new THREE.ParticleBasicMaterial(
     { size:5?, depthFalse:false,
           transparent:true, map:ballTexture
});


// create vertices
geometry = new THREE.Geometry();
randX = Math.random()*100;
randY = Math.random()*100;
randZ = Math.random()*100;

for (var i = 0; i<numParticles; i++) {
      geometry.vertices.push(v(randX,randY,randZ));
}
particleSystem = new THREE.ParticleSystem(geometry, material)

scene.addObject(particleSystem);
```

Creating Scenes

Loading a single model is all fine and good, but what about loading a whole scene at once. Can we do that? We sure can. `SceneLoader` takes a JSON file and asynchronously loads the assets in it, freeing us to use ASCII and binary model files where appropriate.

Selecting Objects in a Scene

Figuring out which object on the screen is selected, also known as "picking," is a bit more difficult in 3D space that it is in 2D. In 2D, we could read the x and y mouse positions and be able to easily check them against our object constraints. In 3D space, the fact we're dealing with a 3D world projected onto 2D space creates a bit more work for us. One method is picking is to render the objects each in a unique color and then check the pixel color at the mouse's position. You could do this by using the scene graph to render an offscreen canvas exclusively for picking. Provided the polygon counts aren't that high or you are using a solely 2D canvas, color picking will perform very well. We could further increase speed by using lower detail models for our picking algorithms.

One of the drawbacks with color picking is that although it is great at locating the object that was picked, it is bad at telling us where the 3D projection of the selection point is located. To do this, we would have to give each face of each object a unique color. Doable, but not fun.

A more advanced method is to use **ray casting**, which is a means of testing for intersection by firing a beam toward a surface and reacting based on the first polygon encountered. A fork of Three.js (https://github.com/mindlapse/three.js/) contains code for picking using ray casting.

Animating Models

Making your models move like humans do is one way to make your games more realistic. A means of doing this is called "rigging," where, in addition to the mesh of vertices, we also give the object an armature of bones, each of which affects the vertices around it with a given weight. When you pick up a coffee cup, your brain has to make several calculations on how to move your shoulder, upper arm, forearm, and wrist to finally know how to move your hand to grab the cup. This is known as forward kinematics. Inverse kinematics uses the final position of the hand to backtrack and figure out where the rest of the joints will be. Instead of calculating the exact position for each frame of an animation, we calculate a couple of them, also known as keyframes, and interpolate the values between them. Keyframes help guide the animation in the right direction. Too few keyframes, especially if the start and end states are vastly different, can cause unhuman-like limb contortion. Although MAX and Blender both support inverse kinematics and forward kinematics, the export scripts do not. That gives us two choices: We can write an export script to get the rigging information, or we can pose our objects in the 3D modeling application, export the individual keyframes, and then stitch them together in the application. When they deal with a single object, keyframes can also be discussed with the more precise term, **morph target**. Whereas a keyframe can be a snapshot of an object's transformation or the individual locations of its object's vertices, a morph target only describes the latter. In order to produce smooth animations between two targets, morph target influencers are used. If one target represents 2 seconds into the animation and the next represents 4 seconds, and if the current time is 2.25 seconds, then the target at t = 2 will have a greater influence than t = 4. Morph targets are a new and lightly documented area of Three.js (as in about 3 days old at the time this chapter was being finished). Check the Three.js sources for examples and more details.

Sourcing 3D Models

Although it isn't hard to create inanimate objects such as trees, trunks, and basic furniture, creating photorealistic models and textures is outside the skillset of most people. If you know Photoshop or GIMP like the back of your hand and live and breathe Blender, Autodesk 3ds Max, or Maya, feel free to skip this section.

TurboSquid (www.turbosquid.com), formerly known as the Gamasutra Exchange, is an online marketplace for 2D/3D models, textures, materials, and application plugins. Over 200,000 models are available for download in a range of formats for open-source and commercial applications. The information page for each asset clearly lists the licensing terms.

If you use Google SketchUp (http://sketchup.google.com) to create models, you might be interested in the 3D Warehouse (http://sketchup.google.com/3dwarehouse). Even if you don't use SketchUp, you might be interested because the 3D Warehouse is a great source for models of historic and significant buildings as well as objects from the real world. For example, if you were doing a spy game based in London, the 3D Warehouse would be a great place to get models of Big Ben and Westminster Abbey. Limited exporter scripts are bundled with the free version of SketchUp. You can either pony up for the commercial version ($495) or try to find some community sources scripts on the Internet.

For the adventurous, there is MakeHuman (www.makehuman.org). It is an open-source project that started as a Blender plugin and allows you to create highly customized human models by specifying the ethnic features, gender, age, body tone, weight, and stature. These models are also fully rigged and textured, allowing you to quickly integrate them into your games. You can even edit facial expressions, and there is support for importing BVH (BioVision Hierarchy) files, one of the industry standards for providing motion-capture data that can be used with rigged models. Figure 7-15 shows the basic MakeHuman application.

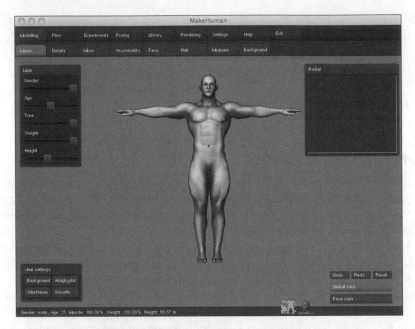

Figure 7-15   MakeHuman home screen

Benchmarking Your Games

Programming with WebGL takes an incredible amount of processing power and isn't always the most forgiving medium. One mistake that you might make early on is drawing too much. Whether you use raw WebGL or Three.js, drawing 100 spheres that are the same size doesn't mean you need to create a new set of vertices for each one. That is a sure way to use up more processing power than needed. An unoptimized version of the *Game of Life* demo did just that and used up 1.4GB of RAM before crashing the browser tab. WebGL will happily use a copy of vertices over and over again with different transformation matrices to produce objects. Let's discuss a couple of tools that will help you optimize and benchmark your applications.

Checking Frame Rate with Stats.js

Included in the sources for Three.js is a small utility library to measure the frame rate in WebGL scenes. Listing 7-19 shows the code to create a `stats` object with some optional CSS to position the element at the upper-left corner of the window. Call `stats.update()` somewhere in the `animate` function and you're all set.

Listing 7-19   **Creating a Stats Element**

```
stats = new Stats();
stats.domElement.style.position = 'absolute';
stats.domElement.style.top = '0px';
$("#container").appendChild(stats.domElement);
```

Using the WebGL Inspector

What Firebug and the Chrome/Safari Developer Tools are to HTML/CSS/JS, the WebGL Inspector (https://github.com/benvanik/WebGL-Inspector) aims to be for WebGL. The project, which is available as a Chrome extension, as a Firefox plugin, or can be bundled directly into an application, surfaces a panel to monitor what is going on in your WebGL application. You are able to see all the referenced textures and shader programs as well as capture individual frames. You can even walk though the calls that are being made on an individual frame, step by step. Figure 7-16 shows the WebGL Inspector running in a browser window.

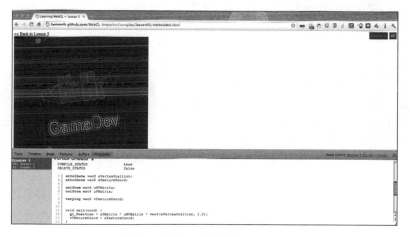

Figure 7-16   WebGL Inspector

Summary

It would be impossible to cover all there is to know about WebGL in one chapter. Instead we went with a more practical approach, discussing low-level details and concepts when needed while for the most part remaining high level, leveraging Three.js for the hard work. You can think of raw WebGL code as assembly code. Many learn it, but few have to use it from day to day. You learned how to leverage the low-level APIs for items such as shaders and how balance this with the abstractions for materials, texturing, and lighting that Three.js provides. You also learned how to integrate physics and 3D models into games. After we created a game with Three.js, you learned about some tools to help us optimize and benchmark our code.

Exercises

1. Load a model file and retrieve the material data from it.
2. Describe how to use texture coordinates to texture a triangle.
3. Write the code to texture a cylinder.

You can download chapter code and answers to the chapter exercises at www.informit.com/title/9780321767363.

8

Creating Games Without JavaScript

Html5 games without JavaScript, you say? Yes, I do. Well, sorta. JavaScript is considered by many as the lingua franca of the Internet. There isn't much you can do without it or by using some non-JavaScript plugin technology. So although the phrase "without JavaScript" could also mean using a plugin such as Flash or Silverlight, in this case, it doesn't. This chapter introduces several technologies that use an alternate language but output JavaScript code either at the compilation phase or at runtime. These technologies take advantage of the ubiquity of JavaScript to make it a sort of native code. It's similar to how a Java or C# compiler takes the code we write and makes something much less human readable but optimized for the machine running it.

Here are some reasons we might want to use an alternate language to build JavaScript applications:

- The existence of features not present in native JavaScript
- Possible speed increases in developing time
- A lack of knowledge or appreciation for native JavaScript

Whereas many developers don't dare venture to the bytecode/intermediary code level, we can enjoy the best of both worlds. You can wade through the compiled output or you can stay at the meta layer. So, presumably, a more descriptive title for this chapter might have been, "Creating Games with Alternate Technologies That Target JavaScript But Do Not Use It as a Primary Language." But that doesn't roll off the tongue.

Google Web Toolkit

Google Web Toolkit (http://code.google.com/webtoolkit/), also known as GWT, is a Java web application framework that allows developers to create AJAX applications using Java. The compiler converts Java code to JavaScript. Although a Java development environment is needed to develop applications, GWT places no such restriction on the server that runs the compiled code. Developers can use REST or their own method of communicating with a server in place of GWT's Remote Procedure Call mechanism. Several products within Google, such as Google Wave, AdWords, and Orkut were built using GWT.

GWT strives to reduce the pain usually experienced from browser-specific quirks by providing a set of standard widgets that operate similarly between browsers.

Understanding GWT Widgets and Layout

Instead of interacting directly with the Document Object Model as you would when creating a native JavaScript application, with GWT, you instead work with the Java widgets that are GWT representations of their HTML counterparts.

`RootPanel` is the widget that anchors the page to the HTML. It provides an interface between our Java code and the HTML page that hosts the application. We can use it to retrieve a specific element, like so:

```
RootPanel.get("buttonDiv")
```

Or we can use it o retrieve the page itself:

```
RootPanel.get()
```

Other than both variations of `get()`, the functions we will use the most are `add()` and `remove()`, which add and remove widgets from the page, respectively. Listing 8-1 shows the code to place a button on a web page. The button responds to button clicks with an alert message of "Hello, World!"

Listing 8-1   **GWT Hello World**

```
import com.google.gwt.core.client.EntryPoint;
import com.google.gwt.event.dom.client.ClickEvent;
import com.google.gwt.event.dom.client.ClickHandler;
import com.google.gwt.user.client.Window;
import com.google.gwt.user.client.ui.*;

public class MyFirstPage implements EntryPoint {

    public void onModuleLoad() {
        Button button = new Button("Click Me");

        button.addClickHandler(new ClickHandler() {
            public void onClick(ClickEvent event) {
                Window.alert("Hello, World!");
            }
        });

        RootPanel.get("buttonDiv").add(button);
    }
}
```

The call to addClickHandler in the listing is the equivalent of setting the onclick function. You can also see that there is a Window class to expose browser-level methods. The MyFirstPage class does nothing by itself. It needs an HTML page to host the JavaScript generated from our Java code and a specialized XML file whose filename ends with .gwt.xml and that tells the compiler which characteristics to include. Listing 8-2 shows the corresponding HTML page for Listing 8-1.

Listing 8-2   **Host Page for MyFirstPage Class**

```
<html>
    <head>
        <title>MyFirstPage Application</title>
        <link rel="stylesheet" href="MyFirstPage.css">
    </head>
    <body>
        <script type="text/javascript"
src="com.test.MyFirstPage.nocache.js"></script>

        <button id="buttonDiv"/>
    </body>
</html>
```

Listing 8-3 shows the module file for the MyFirstPage application.

Listing 8-3   **MyFirstPage Module File**

```
<module>
    <inherits name='com.google.gwt.user.User'/>
    <entry-point class='com.test.client.MyFirstPage'/>
</module>
```

The Java class and the .gwt.xml file define a module along side an HTML view. If we are packaging functionality for inclusion in other projects, creating an HTML page is purely optional. Inheriting from modules is how we can extend applications with new features. In Listing 8-3, the MyFirstPage module is inheriting the functionality from the User module. We'll visit a couple more examples later in this chapter.

Exposing JavaScript Libraries to GWT with JSNI

GWT would be somewhat useless if we didn't have a way to manipulate raw JavaScript. For those cases, we can extend GWT by using its JavaScript Native Interface (JSNI). JSNI uses a special format to signal to the compiler that the enclosed code calls from Java to JavaScript, or vice versa. Listing 8-4 shows a sample JSNI function to print out to the console log.

Listing 8-4   **A Simple JSNI Function**

```
public static native void log(String text) /*-{
   return console.log(text);
}-*/
```

JSNI also uses special identifiers $doc and $wnd to refer to the enclosing document and window, respectively. The RaphaëlGWT, Canvas2D (gwt-g2d), and WebGL (gwt-g3d) modules we will cover later in this chapter all use JSNI to expose their JavaScript code to Java.

RaphaëlGWT

In Chapter 6, "Creating Games with SVG and RaphaëlJS," we created a memory card game using RaphaëlJS. GWT has a complementary module exposing Raphaël function calls to GWT. When you create a circle or a path in GWT, thanks to JSNI, you are making the same function calls you would be making if you coded this by hand.

RaphaëlGWT functions in a different manner than its JavaScript counterpart. The library is structured so that you create a drawing by extending the Raphaël class and then add your objects to it. If you want to add a click listener or some other function to the object, you must create an inner class and implement the appropriate GWT handlers. Listing 8-5 shows an `Image` class that can accept click events.

Listing 8-5   **Raphaël `Image` Class**

```
public class RImage extends Image implements HasClickHandlers {
        public RImage(String src, double x, double y,
          double width, double height) {
           super(src, x, y, width, height);
        }

        public HandlerRegistration addClickHandler(ClickHandler handler) {
           return this.addDomHandler(handler, ClickEvent.getType());
        }
    }
```

This class would live in your extended Raphaël class due to scoping requirements. They can get very unwieldy quickly for all but the most simple games. For those brave souls out there, you could interact with the JSNI layer directly if you choose.

For a comparison with the JavaScript version, you can find a Java port in the source code for this chapter.

One area where RaphaëlGWT shines is creating paths. As you saw previously, path strings are long, unwieldy, and hard to read. `PathBuilder` creates paths by calling each instruction with its parameters, one at a time. Listing 8-6 shows a path created with `PathBuilder`.

Listing 8-6   **RaphaëlGWT `PathBuilder` Example**

```
PathBuilder pb = new PathBuilder();
pb.M(cx, cy)
   .m(-60, -20)
   .l(80, 0, 0, -40, 70, 60, -70, 60, 0, -40, -80, 0)
   .z();
```

Adding Sound with `gwt-html5-media`

`gwt-html5-media`, as its name suggests, is a module providing HTML5 audio and video functionality to GWT applications. You saw in Chapter 1, "Introducing HTML5," how we could create native audio elements using JavaScript. This library is a bit of scaffolding on top of that. Listing 8-7 shows how we can check for Ogg Vorbis support for audio files and default to MP3 if Ogg isn't available.

Listing 8-7   **Conditional Audio Loading**

```
void loadAudio() {
      if (!Audio.canPlayType("audio/ogg; codecs=vorbis")
        .trim().equals("")) {
           sndFlipCard = new Audio("/Game/sounds/flipcard.ogg");
           sndShuffle = new Audio("/Game/sounds/cardshuffle.ogg");
           sndWin = new Audio("/Game/sounds/fanfare.ogg");
      } else {
           sndFlipCard = new Audio("/Game/sounds/flipcard.mp3");
           sndShuffle = new Audio("/Game/sounds/cardshuffle.mp3");
           sndWin = new Audio("/Game/sounds/fanfare.mp3");
      }
   }.
```

Accessing the Drawing APIs with GWT

When it comes to the APIs for drawing, you aren't limited to just Raphaël. Many implementations of GWT libraries provide support for Canvas and WebGL. In this section, we cover gwt-g2d, which allows us to use Canvas from within GWT. gwt-g3d, which we won't cover in this chapter, provides similar support for WebGL.

The only dependency for gwt-g2d is the gwt-g2d.jar file (found at http://code. google.com/p/gwt-g2d/) or the gwt-g3d.jar file (found at http://code.google.com/p/ gwt-g3d/). gwt-g3d bundles the modules for gwt-g2d along side its own. We need to place gwt-g2d on the build path of own project and, as with all GWT libraries, we need to add a line to our .gwt.xml file and we are ready to go:

```
<inherits name='gwt.g2d.g2d'/>
```

The `gwt-g2d` analog to the Canvas context is the `Surface` class. It is our primary interface for drawing. `Surface` provides immediate noncached access to the Canvas. Listing 8-8 shows the initialization of a surface with a width of 640 pixels by 480 pixels. Next, a blue rectangle and some scaled black text are added to the surface. Lastly, our surface is added to the page.

Listing 8-8   **Basic Example Using Surface Class**

```
public class SurfaceExample implements EntryPoint {
    public void onModuleLoad() {
        Surface surface = new Surface(640, 480);
        surface.setFillStyle(KnownColor.BLUE)
            .fillRectangle(100, 175, 40, 40);
        surface.setFillStyle(KnownColor.BLACK)
            .scale(2).fillText("Hello from gwt-g2d", 100, 100);
        RootPanel.get().add(surface);
    }
}
```

There is also a higher-level API called ShapeBuilder that stores the commands internally until you batch them out to a shape. The shape can then be redrawn more easily. Listing 8-9 shows an example using ShapeBuilder. First, we describe a circle by drawing an arc of radius 25 with a center at 100, 100 from 0 radians to $2*\pi$ radians, which represents a full revolution around the center point. The shape is then drawn on the surface with a green fill color and with a yellow fill color and translated 75 pixels to the right.

Listing 8-9   **Example Using ShapeBuilder**

```
public class ShapeBuilderExample implements EntryPoint {
    public void onModuleLoad() {
        ShapeBuilder builder = new ShapeBuilder();
        builder.drawArc(new Arc(100,100,25, 0, Math.PI*2));
        Shape shape = builder.build();

        Surface surface = new Surface(640,480);
        surface.setFillStyle(KnownColor.GREEN).fillShape(shape);
        surface.setFillStyle(KnownColor.YELLOW).translate(75,0).fillShape(shape);
        RootPanel.get().add(surface);

    }
}
```

CoffeeScript

CoffeeScript is a Ruby- and Python-inspired language for JavaScript. It compiles to JavaScript and can use JavaScript libraries seamlessly. For those who have some experience with Groovy, a scripting language for Java, they will see some similarities as well. Ruby and Python have allowed developers to create web applications and iterate much quicker than with statically typed languages such as Java and C#. CoffeeScript can provide the same experience for JavaScript. CoffeeScript allows developers to code in a more object-oriented manner with a class and inheritance mechanism.

Ars Technica (the popular technology blog) and 37signals (the creators of Ruby on Rails) both have created iPhone applications using CoffeeScript. Anecdotal reporting has claimed that rewriting libraries in CoffeeScript has reduced the lines of code by as much as half.

Installing CoffeeScript

The CoffeeScript compiler is self-hosting and capable of compiling itself, and one of several implementations runs as a Node.js module. Node.js is an event-driven framework built on the V8 JavaScript engine that is commonly used for writing network applications. We will cover it and some other server-side JavaScript options in more detail in Chapter 9, "Building a Multiplayer Game Server," but for the moment, we'll just acknowledge its existence as something that can help us compile CoffeeScript. After cloning the Node.js and CoffeeScript repositories, you can install the compiler by running

```
sudo bin/cake install
```

in your CoffeeScript source directory. For instances where Node.js is not an option or difficult to install (for example, on Windows or Mac OS X, which requires XCode), these methods may alternatively be used:

- **Ruby**—`gem install coffee-script`.
- **Java**—JCoffeeScript is a library that uses the Rhino programming language to compile or to embed in a Java application.
- **Ubuntu/Cygwin**—Node can be installed on Windows using Cygwin (or if you have the space or know-how, you could install a Ubuntu virtual image and do your compilation inside of it). CoffeeScript is present in the Ubuntu repositories and can be installed with its dependencies by executing the following:

  ```
  sudo apt-get install coffee-script
  ```

For the purposes of this chapter, we will assume that you are using the Coffee executable provided by the Node.js installation method.

Compiling CoffeeScript Files

In most cases, we will invoke the CoffeeScript compiler by executing:

```
coffee *.coffee -c
```

This command creates a JavaScript version of every CoffeeScript file in the current directory. We could instead specify

```
coffee *.coffee -c -o [directory]
```

to create the JavaScript files in a different directory. Another useful switch is -P, which prints the output of the conversion to the console instead of a file. A full-fledged list of options can be found on the CoffeeScript website at http://jashkenas.github.com/coffee-script/#installation.

A Quick Guide to CoffeeScript

In this section, we'll dip into CoffeeScript. This isn't meant to be a canonical reference but rather a delta between traditional JavaScript and CoffeeScript.

Basics

One of the core differences with JavaScript is that most parentheses and semicolons are optional. When a set of parentheses can be implied, such as when there are multiple parameters, they can be omitted. Semicolons are only needed if we are putting more than one expression on one line. In CoffeeScript, whitespace is significant, a hallmark from Python. As you'll see later, this works hand in hand with the lack of curly braces. Listing 8-10 shows "Hello World" written in CoffeeScript. Notice that the first instance of `console.log` includes the parentheses to clarify the ambiguity that we want to refer to the function `console.log()` and not the property.

Listing 8-10   **Hello World in CoffeeScript**

```
console.log()
console.log "Hello World!"
```

The `var` keyword is also optional in CoffeeScript. Whereas in JavaScript, omitting `var` puts the variable into the global scope, CoffeeScript inserts the `var` for you and prevents you from overloading a variable in a function scope. Each script is also wrapped in an anonymous function to further make it hard to infect the global namespace.

Functions and Invocation

CoffeeScript functions follow a simplified form reminiscent of closures in Groovy. No function keyword is needed, only an optional parenthesized list of parameters, an arrow (`->`), and the function body. Listing 8-11 shows the CoffeeScript to calculate the circumference of a circle and its associated JavaScript.

Listing 8-11   Circumference of a Circle in CoffeeScript and JavaScript

```
#CoffeeScript
circum = (r) -> Math.PI * 2 * r
alert circum 10

// JavaScript
(function() {
    var circum;
    circum = function(r) {
        return Math.PI * 2 * r;
    };
    alert(circum(10));
})();
```

Another interesting addition is splats, or variable function arguments. Splats are indicated by three periods as the last parameter name in a function. Neither JavaScript nor CoffeeScript support function overloading, so we can use splats to indicate that the function can accept a variable number of parameters. Listing 8-12 shows a summation function using a splat. It also demonstrates the implied return value, which by default is the last expression in the function.

Listing 8-12   Summation in CoffeeScript and JavaScript

```
#CoffeeScript
sum = (x,y,z...) ->
    result = x + y
    for i in z
        result += I
    result
alert sum 1,2,3,4,5,6

// JavaScript
var sum;
var __slice = Array.prototype.slice;
sum = function(x, y) {
  var _i, _len, _ref, i, result, z;
  z = __slice.call(arguments, 2);
  result = x + y;
  _ref = z;
  for (_i = 0, _len = _ref.length; _i < _len; _i++) {
    i = _ref[_i];
    result += i;
  }
  return result;
};
alert(sum(1, 2, 3, 4, 5, 6));
```

To prevent the output from having a weird side effect such as "NaN" or "undefined," you have to supply the minimum number of parameters. Therefore, if a function calls for two normal parameters and one with a splat, you must supply at least two parameters to avoid any side effect.

Aliases, Conditionals, and Loops

Although you are free to use normal conditional statements and identifiers such as == and !=, CoffeeScript provides human text versions that can be more readable. Table 8-1 presents some of the common aliases and their equivalent values. The included parentheses are for clarity and aren't essential in real code.

Table 8-1   **CoffeeScript Aliases**

Expression	Alias
==	is
!=	isnt
!	not
if (exp != value)	unless (exp is value)
true	on, yes
false	off, no
this.property	@property
&&	and
||	or
while true	loop
while not (exp)	until exp

Conditional statements are able to be indicated before *or* after the expression to execute. The @property designation, lifted from Ruby, will help us later to differentiate local scope variables from class instance variables.

Enhanced `for` Loop and Maps

CoffeeScript introduces a new format of `for` loop to iterate over collections that is very similar to the notation in Python and Groovy. Instead of specifying initial, ending, and iteration conditions, you can use the more simpler syntax:

```
for item in collection
    doStuff(item)
```

Behind the scenes, this is iterating the loop, pushing the item referred to at index x into an object item that you are free to use within the function. If we needed for some reason to have access to the index, we could use the expanded form:

```
for item, index in collection
    doStuffWithIndex(index)
    doStuff(item)
```

We can iterate over maps using the same form with a slight difference, replacing in with the of keyword:

```
for key, value in map
    doStuff(key, value)
```

As you can imagine from seeing the code in Listing 8-12, the generated JavaScript code would be much longer.

Classes and Inheritance

One of the most exciting features of CoffeeScript is the ability to create classes in JavaScript. You could always create objects that act a bit like classes, but the delta between classes in a typical compiled language and JavaScript was a bit large.

CoffeeScript uses a new keyword (class), along with the significant whitespace, @property designation, and the new function format to create a reasonable facsimile of what we would consider a class. Listing 8-13 shows a simple Human class.

Listing 8-13   **A Human Class in CoffeeScript**

```
class Human
    constructor: (@name) ->
    setAge: (@age) ->
    getAge: -> @age
    setHeight: (@height) ->
    getHeight: ->
        @height
```

One change from traditional JavaScript that you can see here is the use of the constructor keyword en lieu of Human(parameters). The constructor doesn't require a body because the use of @name tells it to automatically save the value into an instance variable. For the same reason, our setters don't need a function body either. All @property variables are public, so given a Human object h, we could just get the height by calling

```
h.height
```

or

```
h.getHeight()
```

One way that we can guard against improper access is to change the signatures of the @property variables to be different from the general property names, whether by appending an underscore to the name or some other name mangling. Tactics like these will help us preserve state when it comes to inheritance.

Class inheritance is a computer science concept where receiving classes, or child classes, implicitly receive properties and method definitions from other classes, also known as parent classes. The implementer of the child class can choose to use the methods in the parent class unchanged or instead use their our logic. Listing 8-14 shows some of this in action.

Listing 8-14   **Extending the Human Class**

```
class Male extends Human
   constructor: (@name) ->
      super @name
      @gender = "male"
   getHeight: ->
      super() + 3
```

Every instance of our `Male` class is a `Human`. The `Male` class likes to fudge his height, so it retrieves the real height by calling `super()` and adds 3 units to it. `super` calls a function with the same name on the parent function with the given parameter list, if any. Another change we made is to declare the gender in the constructor function.

Alternate Technologies

Google Web Toolkit and CoffeeScript aren't our only non-JavaScript options. In this section, we briefly discuss a couple more options.

Cappuccino

280 North, which was acquired by Motorola in 2010, created the Cappuccino web framework, which uses the Objective-J programming language and ports of several GNUStep/Mac OS X Cocoa frameworks to create applications. The syntax of Objective-J is largely similar to that of Objective-C, but the former runs on top of JavaScript. In Objective-J, developers don't need to directly manipulate the DOM or create CSS; those capabilities are handled by the framework itself. Its relation to Objective-C might be helpful to current iOS developers in quickly porting applications.

Pyjamas

Pyjamas is a port of Google Web Toolkit using Python in the place of Java. Although it might tend to lag the features in GWT, it offers a more dynamic and possibly more rapid development environment than Java. Pyjamas supports HTML5 Canvas, but WebGL hasn't been implemented yet. Pyjamas does have a concept for interacting with JavaScript code similar to JSNI, so there is no barrier preventing a developer from porting WebGL to it. Pyjamas Desktop is a component of Pyjamas that allows applications to run unmodified on the desktop. Instead of compiling the code to HTML and JavaScript, the application runs the Python code, leveraging Python libraries for the Gecko, Webkit, and Trident browser engines, which power the Mozilla, Safari/Chrome, and Internet Explorer browsers, respectively.

Summary

In this chapter, we explored several technologies that allow us to use different languages to create games on the Web. We dove into the robust library support in the Google Web Toolkit and looked at the ways CoffeeScript can seamlessly integrate with JavaScript. In examining GWT, we took our memory card game from Chapter 6, created a GWT version, and added HTML5 audio. At the close of this chapter, we briefly discussed other options for making games where JavaScript isn't the primary language. Hopefully, this chapter showed you that a less-than-proficient knowledge of JavaScript is no longer a barrier to creating compelling HTML5 games.

Exercises

1. What are the alternate values for true in CoffeeScript?
2. What is the name of the protocol for calling JavaScript from GWT?
3. What is Pyjamas?

You can download chapter code and answers to the chapter exercises at www.informit.com/title/9780321767363.

9

Building a Multiplayer Game Server

In this chapter, we will build a game server to house the logic for our games and provide a communal experience for the players. Keeping in the spirit of the games we have been developing, we will be using the server-side JavaScript framework Node.js for our back-end work. This will allow us to deeply integrate between our game and server-side code. Assisting Node.js will be the socketing library Socket.IO.

Introduction to Node.js

Node.js is an asynchronous server-side JavaScript environment built on the Google V8 JavaScript engine. V8, which is written in C++, is the engine that runs JavaScript in the Google Chrome browser and is known for its speed. Node treats items such as sockets, HTTP, TCP/UDP, and file I/O as first-class citizens and provides little abstraction over them. Listing 9-1 shows the code for a simple Node.js application that responds to all requests with the text "Hello World." It begins with a require statement to retrieve the HTTP package for use in the applications. The `require` statements are similar to `require` and `import` statements from Ruby and Python, respectively, in that they make the contents of another file available for use by the currently running application.

Listing 9-1   **Simple Node.js Application**

```
http = require 'http'
http.createServer((req, res) ->
    res.writeHead 200, {'Content-Type': 'text/plain'}
    res.end 'Hello World\n'
).listen 8124, "127.0.0.1"
console.log 'Server running at http://127.0.0.1:8124/'
```

Using `require` statements is an easy way to modularize your code and make it more readable and maintainable.

It is important to realize that Node.js is a general-purpose event-driven framework and not the end-all and be-all for a web application. In most cases for any nontrivial example, you will want to use a Node.js web framework.

Node has been embraced by developers because it allows them to code from front to back in the same language. As a result, Node is being used for more than just web servers and is powering utility scripts, testing frameworks, and command-line applications. The official CoffeeScript compiler is implemented using Node. To further build on the work we did with CoffeeScript in Chapter 8, "Creating Games Without JavaScript," we will be using CoffeeScript for all the examples and demos in this chapter. If CoffeeScript isn't your favorite beverage-themed programming language, the CoffeeScript compiler produces reasonably readable JavaScript that you could use directly.

Extending Node with the Node Package Manager

By itself, Node is fairly lightweight. That's not to say you can't build fairly involved applications with just Node. Node can be extended using the Node Package Manager (or npm for short). npm functions like a software app store where the modules can be full applications in their own right or pieces that can be integrated into other applications. npm can be installed by executing the following command:

```
curl http://npmjs.org/install.sh | sh
```

If that fails, you can visit http://npmjs.org/ for further instructions. A list of available modules can be found at http://npm.mape.me/. Modules can be installed or uninstalled, respectively, by executing the following command:

```
npm install <name of module>
```

or

```
npm uninstall <name of module>
```

Managing Multiple Node Versions

Node is very much in its early days when it comes to stability. Some npm packages need to run against a specific version or have unpredictable behavior. As a result, you can save a bit of pain by installing Node using a version manager.

n (https://github.com/visionmedia/n) is a script file that allows you to manage your node versions. Not only can the versions exist along side each other, but you can specify a version of Node to be the default to route all commands through or you can selectively run commands through a certain version. You can install n by executing

```
npm install n
```

if you already have some version of Node installed, or by cloning the git repository and executing the following command:

```
make install
```

The command n `ls` lists the versions of Node available for installation, whereas the commands n `latest [or version]` and n `rm [version]` install/use the specified version and remove the specified version of Node, respectively.

Making Web Apps Simpler with ExpressJS

ExpressJS (http://expressjs.com/) is a rapid web application development framework for Node.js. Think of it as a focused web development layer over the more general-purpose Node. Express focuses on the following:

- URL routing DSL
- Middleware
- View templating and rendering
- Deep integration with Connect, a middleware layer for Node, to manage things such as cookies, sessions, and routing

Listing 9-2 shows a very basic ExpressJS application. After having installed Express with npm by executing npm `install express`, we need to tell Node to retrieve the Express library for us to use. We next create a server, a route (explained momentarily), and a port on which the server will listen. The `sys` package is imported to give us some status messages. `sys.puts` is equivalent to `console.log`.

Listing 9-2   **Example ExpressJS Application**

```
express = require 'express'
app = express.createServer()
sys = require 'sys'

app.get '/', (req, res) ->
    res.send('Hello World')
sys.puts "Server started on http://localhost:3000"
app.listen(3000);
```

Serving Requests with URL Routing

ExpressJS lets you define routes or URL endpoints to which your application can respond. Routes can respond to any of the verbs GET, PUT, POST, and DELETE. Listing 9-3 shows the definition of a route that responds to the base server URL and prints "Hello, World."

Listing 9-3   **Simple ExpressJS Route**

```
app.get "/", (req, res) ->
    res.send("Hello, World")
```

You can create separate blocks for each HTTP verb, or you could use `all`, which routes all verbs through the same block of code.

ExpressJS's routing API is fairly flexible, allowing you to route to a base URL, as shown in Listing 9-3, or to a static URL and formatted URLs, as shown in Listing 9-4. The use of a colon before a portion of the endpoint means that component will be exposed as a request parameter property. A question mark at the end of a fragment tells ExpressJS that portion of the endpoint is optional. We can separate the root and extended routes as we did with `/about` and `/about/:id` or combine them with conditional logic as we did with `/profile/:id?`. The final example, `/updateProfile`, uses a `POST`. It demonstrates how we can get access to the transmitted data by inspecting the `req.body` object.

Listing 9-4   **Advanced Routes**

```
express = require 'express'
app = express.createServer()
sys = require 'sys'
app.configure ->
    app.use express.logger()
    app.use express.cookieParser()
    app.use express.bodyParser()
    app.use express.static(__dirname + '/public')

app.get '/about', (req, res) ->
    res.send('About Page')

app.get '/about/:id', (req, res) ->
    id = req.params.id
    res.send('About Page for '+id)

app.get '/profile/:id?', (req, res) ->
    id = req.params.id
    if (id is undefined)
        res.send("Profile not found")
    else res.send(id+"'s Profile")

app.post '/updateProfile', (req, res) ->
    newData = req.body
    name = req.body.name
    doStuffWithData(data)
    res.send("Update successful.")

sys.puts "Server started on http://localhost:3000"
app.listen(3000);
```

ExpressJS has a middleware layer exposed to it by the bundled Connect (http://senchalabs.github.com/connect) library. Connect's middleware layer provides reusable functions for common things an application might need, including but not limited to authentication, logging, session management, cookies, and parsing request bodies. We've already written a few of the most basic middleware functions in our sample applications. Listing 9-4, which shows some advanced routes and uses the `bodyDecoder` middleware to enable seeing the `POST` request's body. It also specifies that there would be a static directory called public that serves up assets such as client-side JavaScript, images, CSS, and HTML.

Managing Sessions

In order to use sessions, we need to include a couple middleware components. You can see a sample route that uses sessions in Listing 9-5. `cookieDecoder` and `bodyDecoder` are required to be instantiated before `session`. The `secret` parameter of `session` helps the middleware to encode the GUIDs for the session IDs. The `session` object is created seamlessly for us behind the scenes, and we can attach [serializable] objects to it, as well as modify or remove them. If we don't specify a backing store, it defaults to in-memory. Although not bundled directly with either Connect or ExpressJS, backing stores are available for virtually every popular database.

Listing 9-5   **Logging Session Visit Count**

```
app.configure ->
  app.use(express.cookieParser())
  app.use(express.bodyParser())
  app.use(express.session({secret:'asdf'}))

app.get '/', (req, res) ->
    if req.session.visitCount == undefined
      req.session.visitCount = 1
    else
      req.session.visitCount = req.session.visitCount + 1;
      res.send "Session ID:"+req.session.id+"<br/>"+'You have visited this page '
+ req.session.visitCount + ' times';
```

Understanding the ExpressJS Application Structure

ExpressJS is pretty liberal when it comes to application structure, letting you set where to find the specific directories, as demonstrated in the following snippet:

```
# Set directory for views to render
app.set 'views', __dirname + '/views'
```

Be that as it may, all the applications in this chapter will follow the structure shown in Figure 9-1. It provides a clear separation of concerns and makes it easier to learn

ExpressJS. Views define how the information will be presented to the user. The public
directory holds static assets that the application will serve to users, such as CSS, images,
and JavaScript files. All applications should be tested in some shape or form, and the tests
directory will house those tests. Last but not least is the app.coffee (or alternatively app.js)
file. It initializes the server with our core logic for the application and sets up routes, logging, middleware, templating, and so on. It should be noted that executing the express
script in an empty directory will create a sample app.js file along with views, public, logs,
and tests directories.

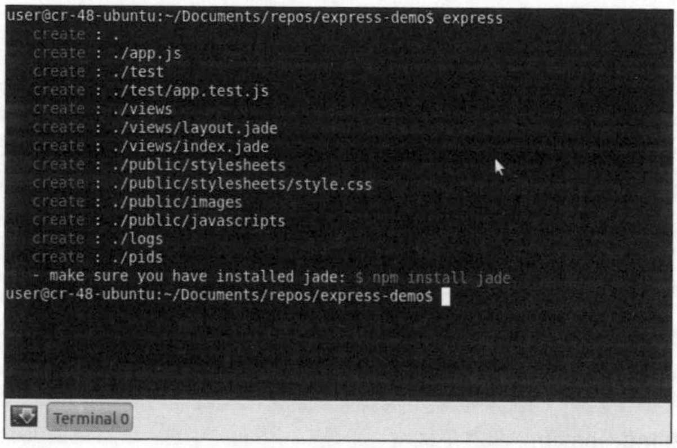

Figure 9-1   ExpressJS application structure

Templating HTML with CoffeeKup

CoffeeKup is a templatinge engine for HTML that allows you to create HTML entirely
by using CoffeeScript. Provided that Node.js is already installed, CoffeeKup can be
installed by executing

```
npm install coffeekup
```

on a command-line prompt. Frameworks that support CoffeeKup as a rendering engine
convert the CoffeeScript code at runtime into HTML and JavaScript. Listing 9-6 shows
the CoffeeKup code to create a simple HTML page and set the content of a `div` to
"Hello World!" Notice that we can assign and use variables inside the code.

Listing 9-6   **A Simple CoffeeKup Page**

```
@title = "Hello World"
doctype 5
html ->
    head ->
        title @title
    body ->
```

```
div id: 'content', ->

div id: 'fragment', ->
    @body

coffeescript ->
        document.getElementById('content').innerText = "Hello World!"
```

Listing 9-7 shows the HTML code that is generated when the preceding CoffeeKup file is served by ExpressJS.

Listing 9-7 **Generated HTML Code**

```
<!DOCTYPE html>
<html>
    <head>
        <title>Hello World</title>
    </head>
    <body>
        <div id="content"></div>
        <div id="fragment"></div>
<script>;(function () {
        return document.getElementById('content').innerText = "Hello World!";
        })();
        </script>
    </body>
</html>
```

So far, we have seen CoffeeKup generating full pages. Using it as a templating engine in ExpressJS means we can modularize our UI code and render fragments of pages on the fly using a set of common layouts. We can register CoffeeKup with ExpressJS by including the following snippet in our application file:

```
app.register '.coffee', require('coffeekup')
app.set 'view engine', 'coffee'
```

The code tells ExpressJS that, by default, we will be using views that are CoffeeScript files and that we can omit using the file extension when referring to them. Using the full filename allows us to mix layouts using the other libraries: Jade, Haml, JQuery Templates, and EJS. When a fragment file is referenced, the system looks for an associated layout file that describes the outer structure of the HTML to display. In the case of CoffeeKup, it searches for `layout.coffee` in the views directory, failing over to other directories if it is not found. Listing 9-6 is an example of what could be defined in a layout file. You might have noticed that there is a `@body` variable that hasn't been assigned a value and doesn't seem to appear in the generated HTML. When rendering a view, ExpressJS takes the content of the view we are rendering and puts it into the layout file as the value of the body variable. So given a view fragment named `index.coffee` that contains the code

```
div ->
    "The time is now #{new Date()}"
```

we could set up a route on `/getTime`, as shown in Listing 9-8, that, when visited, would return the composition of `index.coffee` and `layout.coffee`.

Listing 9-8 **Creating a Route for `/getTime`**

```
app.get "/getTime", (req, res) ->
    util.log "Client visited /getTime"
    res.render 'getTime'
```

View variables can also be passed at runtime. If we wanted to pass the time zone to the `getTime` page, we could modify the view as shown in Listing 9-9, passing the desired variables in a map property named `context`.

Listing 9-9 **Modified Route**

```
app.get "/getTime", (req, res) ->
    util.log "Client visited /getTime"
    res.render 'getTime', context:{timezone: 'America/Los Angeles'}
```

Persisting Data with Caching

In most applications, there will be a backing database of some sort to store data. Like a computer hard drive, reading the data is fairly quick—the time consuming part is finding the data. Caching allows us to have quicker access to data. Once data is accessed, it's fairly likely that it will be accessed in the future. Caching sets aside a bit of memory to store recently accessed objects. Caches don't have infinite storage; otherwise, they lose their advantage over databases. Caching strategies for choosing which objects to eject can vary greatly. Many of them center around some variant or combination of ejecting the Least Frequently Used (LFU), Least Recently Used (LRU), and Most Recently Used (MRU) objects. Alternatively, the cache can eject based on a period of inactivity, as is done with website sessions.

The node-cache project (https://github.com/ptarjan/node-cache) provides some basic functionality that we can further build upon. node-cache's API is pretty straightforward, providing the six functions listed in Table 9-1.

Table 9-1   **node-cache API**

Function	Description
`get(key)`	Retrieves the value for the given key; otherwise null.
`put(key,value,duration)`	Stores the given value with the specified key. If a time is specified, the key/value pair will be purged after the duration. Otherwise, it is stored until explicitly removed.
`del(key)`	Deletes the value held by the given key.
`size()`	Returns the number of non-null key/value pairs in the cache.
`memsize()`	Returns the number of key/value pairs in the cache.
`debug(bool)`	Turns debugging on or off.

Managing Client/Server Communication

In the early days of the Web, back when using the "World Wide" part of the name was still in vogue, interaction was pretty limited. You clicked a link, and it send you somewhere. You filled in a long form of data, clicked Send, and were routed to a new static page. Slowly but surely this static means of interaction became more dynamic as more websites began using AJAX to update their information without redirecting the user. The innovation didn't end there. Further advances brought server-side push, long polling, and has culminated in TCP sockets being supported natively in web browsers. Web Sockets in their current incarnation are new, but the concept itself is not. Early Java applets were able to open up a socket between the server and the client's browser.

Communicating with Socket.IO

Socket.IO is librarys for Node.js that seeks to provide a common interface that different transport mechanisms can use regardless of the destination or source of the message.

Socket.IO supports communicating using the following technologies:

- Native Web Sockets
- Adobe Flash sockets
- AJAX long polling
- AJAX multipart streaming
- Forever IFrames
- JSONP polling

This combination of transports allows Socket.IO to support almost all versions of every major desktop and mobile browser. In addition to the official Node.js implementation, there are unofficial server implementations for Java, Python, Google Go, and Rack (Ruby).

Setting Up a Simple Socket.IO Application with Express

Listings 9-10 and 9-11 show the server and client sides for a simple Socket.IO application that echoes back whatever the server or client send each other. The server has an event called `connection` that it listens for. When that even is fired, it prints to the console that a new client has connected and it registers a function to be executed whenever there is a message. It is empty in the code sample, but you can see that responding to the `disconnect` event is also possible.

Listing 9-10   **Server Code for Hello World**

```
# Setup socket.io
socket = io.listen app
socket.on 'connection', (client) ->
    sys.puts "new client connected."
    client.on 'message', (data) ->
        sys.puts data
        client.send data
    client.on 'disconnect', ->
```

Listing 9-11 shows the other side of the equation with the client's code. After including the requisite JavaScript file, we instantiate a new socket and register functions for the connection and message events like we did on the server.

Listing 9-11   **CoffeeKup Template for Hello World**

```
doctype 5
html ->
    head ->
        title "#{@title}"
        script src: '/js/socket.js'

    body ->
        coffeescript ->
            socket = new io.Socket 'localhost'
            socket.connect()
            socket.on 'connection', ->
                    console.log 'Connected.'
            socket.on 'message', (data)->
                console.log data
                socket.send "Hello World"
```

Making Web Sockets Simpler with NowJS

Socket.IO is great for simple communication, but complex conversations over sockets would require you to do something such as formatting messages as JSON, sending them over the socket, and decoding/encoding them on each side. As the number of conditions we have to handle grows, making our mini-language for all the features of our application becomes untenable. It would be so much easier for the server to be able to call the specific methods in the client's domain without complex message passing—and vice versa. With NowJS, we can do just that.

NowJS is a client- and server-side JavaScript library that enables clients and servers to make remote procedure calls over a Web Socket pipeline. NowJS uses Socket.IO for the communications bit by wrapping it with several important features. There are two shared namespaces, called `everyone.now` and `now`. The former is implemented on the server side, and the latter is the client's interface to NowJS. Any variables or object graphs set within the `everyone.now` namespace will be shared among *all* clients and the server. If the server calls a function in the `everyone.now` namespace and it exists on the client, it will attempt to execute the function of the same name in the client's now namespace. An example will help illustrate this better. One of the common tasks we will perform a lot on our game server is to retrieve player data. We are going to use NowJS to have the client request a list of the currently connected players. On the server we have a function in the `everyone.now` namespace called `getPlayerList`. It takes a callback to the client to return the code as its only parameter. Listing 9-12 shows only the code that would change from an initial application file.

Listing 9-12   **NowJS Demo Application File**

```
nowjs - require("now")

app = express.createServer()
everyone = nowjs.initialize(app)

everyone.now.getPlayerList = (callback) ->
    players = ['Jake','John','Cathy']
    callback(players)
```

Alternatively, we could have defined a function on the client to be called by the server. The server could have used this to communicate rather than a callback. Our client-side code, after the required now.js script file has been included, defines a function called `getPlayers` that calls the server's `getPlayerList` function and prints the results to the console. The last snippet of code is the call to `now.ready`. The `ready` function allows us to specify code to be executed when the connection has been successfully made to the server. This is shown in Listing 9-13.

Listing 9-13   **NowJS Client Code**

```
doctype 5
html ->
    head ->
        title "#{@title || 'NowJS Demo'}"
        script src: '/nowjs/now.js'

    body ->
    coffeescript ->
        window.getPlayers = ->
            now.getPlayerList (data) ->
                console.log(data)

        now.ready ->
            console.log('ready')
    div ->
        input type:'button', value:'Get Players', onclick:'getPlayers();'
```

Debugging Node Applications

With all those asynchronous callbacks firing, being able to effectively debug our applications becomes extra important. If we need to find the value of a single object for a short time, then console debugging (where we print out data to the console) might work. The sys object has a function called inspect that will convert all the details of an object to a String. We can use that with sys.put to output to the command line, as in the following snippet:

```
sys.put(sys.inspect(obj))
```

Great in a pinch, console debugging becomes untenable when you are trying to check flow control or when an error is several levels down. For those more advanced cases, a full-fledged debugger is more helpful, giving more control over the running application. The node-inspector project (https://github.com/dannycoates/node-inspector) provides this functionality for Node applications. You install node-inspector by executing the following command:

```
npm install node-inspector
```

You can then start the debugger with the following command:

```
node-inspector &
```

Now node-inspector is ready to start monitoring your applications. The last steps are to start Node in debug mode by executing either

```
node —debug <app file>
```

or

```
coffee —nodejs <app file>
```

and navigating to the address provided by node-inspector (generally
http://0.0.0.0:8080/debug?port=5858) in a WebKit-based browser. There, you'll see the
Developer Console repurposed to show details about the application. Turn back to
Chapter 1, "Introducing HTML5," if needed, for a refresher. One really cool feature of
node-inspector is that the Scripts tab shows you CoffeeScript files as the compiled
JavaScript that will actually run on the server side.

Creating a Game Server

A typical multiplayer game server includes several areas for users to interact, at minimum,
a game lobby, specific game rooms or areas, and a means for users to chat with one
another. In the coming sections, we will tackle each of these areas.

Making the Game Lobby

The game lobby is first part of our application that the users see. From the lobby, the
users can see games in progress that they can join, chat with other users, and create their
own game rooms.

Listing 9-14 shows the CoffeeKup code needed to implement the application's landing
page. On the left, we have a large container that will hold our Canvas. On the right is a
chat window for our players to communicate with others.

Listing 9-14   **Application Landing Page Code**

```
@title = 'Game Lobby'
div style:'float:left;height:600px;width:800px', ->
div style:'float:right;',->
    textarea id:'chat', rows:'10', columns:'50', style:'width:200px;height:550px'
    br ->
    input type:'text', columns:'40', id:'message'
    input type:'button', value:'Send',
        onclick:"distributeMessage($('#message').get(0).value)"
```

When the user clicks the Send button, it passes the content of the message text area to
our `distributeMessage` function, which in turn calls the function of the same name on
the server. `receiveMessage` is invoked by the server on all the clients when a client sends
out a `distributeMessage` call. We can see the client code in Listing 9-15.

Listing 9-15   **Client-Side Code to Send and Receive Chat Messages**

```
window.now.receiveMessage = (name, message) ->
    val = $('#chat').get(0).value
    val += name + ':' + message + '\n'
    $('#chat').get(0).value = val
    console.log('Received message: ' + message + ' from: '+name)

window.distributeMessage = (message) ->
    if now.name is 'Unknown'
now.name = prompt("What is your name?")
    now.distributeMessage(message)
```

Notice in Listing 9-16 that the server only has to implement the function where it is doing work. It calls `receiveMessage` with the blind faith that it will exist on the clients.

Listing 9-16   **Server-Side Code to Send and Receive Chat Messages**

```
everyone.now.distributeMessage = (message) ->
    console.log("Received message:"+ message + " from: "+this.now.name)
    everyone.now.receiveMessage(this.now.name, message)
```

Creating Game Rooms with NowJS Groups

From the lobby, players can select an existing game room they would like to enter or create one of their own. Each game room has properties with a preset range, such as the game in play for that room, the maximum set of players, and the game logic for the game. Shortly after all participants leave a game room, the server removes it from view.

NowJS allows you to segregate users by using groups. Groups have their own set of now objects that the clients share with the server. Groups make it so that the people not in our game room don't get bombarded with messages and notifications. `getGroup` retrieves an existing group with the name of the passed parameter or creates one. Listing 9-17 shows this in action in the bit of code we use to create our game rooms. After the game room is created, player entrances and exits are announced to the people in the room thanks to the on `'connect'` and on `'disconnect'` events.

Listing 9-17   **Creating a Game Room**

```
everyone.now.createRoom = (roomName, callback) ->
console.log("Created room: "+roomName)
    group = nowjs.getGroup(roomName)
    group.on 'connect', (clientId) ->
        group.now.receiveMessage(this.user.clientId +" joined the game room.")
    group.on 'disconnect', (clientId) ->
```

```
        group.now.receiveMessage(this.user.clientId + " left the game room.")
    gameRooms.push(group)
    callback(group)
```

Managing Game Participants and Moving Between Game Rooms

Now that we have our game rooms, we need people to put into them. That is where our game participants come into play. We can have two types of game participants: players and watchers. Players engage in the game and are affected by the game logic, whereas watchers can merely watch the play as the game unfolds. Either type of participant is able to broadcast messages to others in the game room. Listing 9-18 shows how the code we have wrapped around the NowJS objects to add or remove a user from a game room.

Listing 9-18   **Moving Between Game Rooms**

```
everyone.now.joinRoom = (roomName) ->
    group = nowjs.getGroup(roomName)
    group.addUser(this.user.clientId)

everyone.now.leaveRoom = (roomName) ->
    group = nowjs.getGroup(roomName)
    group.removeUser(this.user.clientId)
```

Managing Game Play

In this section, we get to the nitty-gritty of our game server. We will code the game logic for the Tic-Tac-Toe game we coded in Chapter 5, "Creating Games with the Canvas Tag."

Moving a game from running locally to running on a server is much like the transition in moving a web application from a traditional web framework to a purely event-driven model. Whereas you could just busy-wait for a single application running locally, on something like Node, you instead have to keep track of the dozens or hundreds of games at once. We will use the database and caching to allow us to manage many games at a time and to scale.

Back in Chapter 5, we used the Canvas to code some of the basics of tic-tac-toe, and in Chapter 4, "How Games Work," we coded the artificial intelligence powering it. We can use our game server to finish that effort and put the two pieces together.

After a room is created, users can create a new game. The now object for that game room stores the current state of the game board, which player is X and which is O, and whose turn it is. When a player takes his or her turn, the move is sent over the wire to the server's now object to validate and apply it if valid. Another change from the previous version is the use of the cache to store the current game state. Although groups have a now object, they cannot have arbitrary objects attached to it like the `everyone.now` object can. The cache also solves the problem of everything in the `now` object being shared between all clients. If we were to, for instance, store all the cards for a game in the `now` object, nothing would keep a less-than-honest player from easily peeking or changing the cards in his or her hand. You can see this code in Listing 9-19.

Listing 9-19   **Validating and Applying Player Moves**

```
everyone.now.completeTicTacToeMove = (room, x, y, player) ->
    rooms = cache.get("rooms")
    room = rooms[roomName]
    group = nowjs.getGroup(room)
    roomState = cache.get(room)
    board = roomState.board

    otherPlayer = if player is 'X' then 'O' else 'X'
    if board[x][y] is '-'
        board[x][y] = player
        # check for win

        cache.put(this.now.room, roomState)
    else
        roomState.message = 'Player #{player}, Please try again.'
        cache.put(room, roomState)
        group.now.receiveGameState(roomState)
```

We could just as easily wire in a computer player by having it calculate its moves and adjusting the game board on the server's `now` object. The `receiveGameState` function operates in a similar way to the `receiveMessage` function does with chat. The state on the server is treated as the source of truth. After each action, the game state is pushed to all the clients and they redraw their screens. The solution we used for tic-tac-toe works well for games that can be represented concisely, but fails as the scale of players goes up.

One way to handle scale, especially for free-roaming games such as arena-style first-person shooters, is to move most of the interaction to the server. Whereas in the tic-tac-toe game server example, the user could run specific functions on the server, albeit with some basic verification, other games might need more safeguards against cheating. One way to do that is to run most of the logic on the server and push updates to the client. On the client side, the client no longer can run functions—it can only send updates of what input keys were pressed. It is the server's job to make sense of what a button being pressed means. `RealtimeMultiplayerNodeJS` (https://github.com/onedayitwillmake/RealtimeMultiplayerNodeJs) exposes many of these features. Although it is outside the scope of this book to cover in any depth, it bears mentioning for the benefit of those who have their hearts set on massive multiplayer *Scrabble* or similar technology.

Summary

This chapter provided a crash course in the server-side JavaScript web framework and the surrounding ecosystems. You learned how to use ExpressJS to create routes for web pages and also how to template HTML to be served when the specific route is visited. You also learned how to use Web Sockets with the NowJS and Socket.IO projects for real-time communication between the server and clients. Next, we dove into data persistence using a simple cache. We finished this chapter with a tech demo around creating a game server.

Exercises

1. Write code that creates a NowJS group and prints "Welcome" to the console when someone joins the group.

2. What is the n command to install Node.js version 0.4.8?

3. Create a route that responds to the "location" and takes a parameter called `city`.

You can download chapter code and answers to the chapter exercises at www.informit.com/title/9780321767363.

10

Developing Mobile Games

It could easily be argued that the 2007 release of the iPhone was the genesis of mobile gaming and the "app-itization" of web content. Sales of content for mobile devices, including phones, tablets, and televisions has numbered in the billions. Although mobile games existed before, the appearance of smartphones was one of the first times that mobile devices could use the Web—the *real* Web—and not some watered-down version for consuming and producing content. In this chapter, we will discuss in part the dominant mobile phone operating systems, what is involved in developing for them, and some of the frameworks that work with them. Before we go into the how and why, let's briefly discuss the platforms themselves.

Choosing a Mobile Platform

In this section, we briefly cover the capabilities and peculiarities of the dominant mobile device operating systems.

iOS

Formerly known as the iPhone OS, iOS powers most of Apple's mobile and entertainment devices, including the iPhone, iPod Touch, iPad, and Apple TV. Considering only mobile devices, iOS has garnered approximately 16.8% of market share, at the time of this writing. iOS is a variant of the BSD-based Mac OS X optimized for touch interaction. iOS is restricted to Apple-branded devices. iOS applications that are not served by the browser are generally coded in the Objective-C programming language. The iPhone, iPod Touch, and iPad can connect to other devices using Wi-Fi and sometimes Bluetooth and CDMA/GSM cellular service. Webkit, a fork of the open-source KHTML layout engine, powers the browser experience for these devices. HTML5 is extra important to Apple because it forbids plugin technology such as Flash in its iOS devices. In addition to the iOS devices, on the desktop, Webkit is at the core of Google Chrome and Apple Safari, the third and fourth most popular desktop browsers. When it comes to implementing HTML5 standards, browsers that use Webkit have been at the forefront of the charge.

Android

Android is an operating system created by Google to run on mobile devices. Android has captured 36% of the market thanks to a multitude of carriers and device options. The first Android device launched approximately a year after the initial iPhone. One of the key differentiators between devices running Android and those running iOS is that, except in rare cases, Google doesn't assert control over the devices and or their specifications. Native Android applications can be written in a Java syntax that can be compiled for the Dalvik virtual machine. Communications options vary by device but are equivalent to those of the iOS devices. Android and iOS devices may also contain gyroscopes for directional positioning and accelerators to infer motion in space. Thanks to Android's open-source license, cellular carriers are free to install Android on any device or modify parts of the operating system without getting Google's permission. This has contributed to Android's gains in market share. A plethora of phones and tablets have emerged in the past three years spread across about five different versions of the operating system. Although this may cause some fragmentation in the capabilities of the core OS, it has less-tangible ramifications for HTML5 games. Android uses a variant of the Google Chrome web browser, which itself is derived in part from Webkit. Although some devices are still being released with the relatively ancient Cupcake and Donut versions (1.5 and 1.6, respectively), most new devices run Eclair (Android 2.0/2.1), Froyo (Android 2.2), or higher—which boast improved HTML5 support and faster JavaScript engines. Recent Android devices can also run Flash content, unlike their iOS counterparts. Because the operating system is open source, there tends to be a plethora of devices running different versions of Android. Although much hay has been made about fragmentation, at any given time, the number of versions run by a plurality of devices is generally only one or two.

WebOS

WebOS is a operating system creating by Palm, later acquired by HP, to run on mobile devices. The first devices launched in June 2009. Under Palm's tenure, only two devices were released: the Palm Pre and the Palm Pixi/Pixi Plus. WebOS, although using Linux for its core functionality, makes use of JavaScript, HTML, and AJAX for most user-facing applications. Since the acquisition, an updated Palm Pre 2 has launched and HP has announced its intention to use WebOS for mobile phones, tablets, and printers. WebOS only accounts for a scant sliver of the market. In mid to late August 2011, HP decided to exit the hardware business and discontinued production of the Palm Pre 2 and its tablet form factor device, the Touchpad. Existing devices have been marked down to fire sale prices with many consumers seeking devices in hopes that Android will be ported to it. HP says that their exit from hardware doesn't mean the end of WebOS. That remains to be seen.

Windows Phone 7

Last is the most recent entrant into the market, Windows Phone 7, created by Microsoft. The market share for Windows Phone 7 is somewhere below 3.3%. That figure includes Windows Mobile devices as well. The first Windows Phone 7 devices launched in late

2010. Windows Phone 7 is a break in compatibility to its predecessor Windows Mobile 6.5. Applications can be written in C# using either Microsoft's Internet application framework Silverlight, or the more gaming focused XNA project. For our needs, Windows Phone 7 at present is a nonstarter. The included browser is a blend of features from Internet Explorer 7 and 8, which support no HTML5 elements. Bear in mind that Internet Explorer 9 beta has a more complete implementation of HTML5 features.

In mid-2011, Microsoft and Nokia brokered a deal making Windows Phone 7 the standard OS for new Nokia devices. As these devices begin to roll out, Windows Phone 7 will begin to consume the 27.4% market share held by devices running Nokia's Symbian operating system. During that same time, Microsoft announced the "Mango" update to Windows Phone 7, which includes a mobile version of Internet Explorer 9 with HTML5 support. The update is due sometime in Fall 2011.

Flick, Tap, and Swipe: A Quick Guide to Mobile Gestures

If I take away your mouse and keyboard and give you a touch screen, you'll need a way to communicate with the system, and mobile gestures are just how you would do that. Gestures allow you to replace the mouse with your finger. Capacitive screens (or in laymen's terms, multitouch screens) allow you to interact with the screen using multiple fingers at one time. Multitouch screens allow you to do things that aren't usually possible with mice, such as making a pinching motion to zoom a map or drawing a letter to go to entries that start with that letter in an address book. The gestures that are usually present are tap and double-tap (cousins to the mouse click and double-click), possibly a long press, and some sort of swipe or flicking motion. Some of the mobile operating systems contain more or offer the ability to create new ones.

Deciding Between an Application and a Website

Launching your game as a website offers the following advantages over launching it as an application:

- Speed in development
- Portability
- Ease in deployment

A game that launches as a website has one hub of activity. Although some developers might test the game play on multiple devices, the website itself is treated as the main client for development and testing. Testing primarily in one place will greatly streamline development cycles to push new features or bug fixes. Having the game live on a website also simplifies the deployment strategy. There is one and only one place to push changes and fixes and to monitor for bugs. If you stay within the lowest common denominator of features between HTML5-compliant browsers, possibly with the help of a mobile framework, you could get a product that works reasonably well without the need for much testing.

Although all three major mobile platforms use some form or another of Webkit, they each have their own little quirks. These little nits might cause some unexpected behavior on these browsers. For example, Android devices running 2.2 or higher and newer WebOS phones could use Flash for audio, but Flash is stricken from iOS devices. In this case, using Flash audio on the website would break the experience on some devices.

To counteract these issues, we could deploy our games as applications for each individual platform. Deploying as individual products gives us the opportunity to do the following:

- Tailor the experience to each platform
- Market the applications better

Inversely, deploying for each platform individually increases the development costs both in maintenance of multiple apps and in finding developers who are mobile platform generalists. Later in this chapter, we will discuss in more detail some specific libraries that can help in packaging applications, but first let's talk generally about what is going on behind the scenes. Whether your game is launched as a website or a mobile application, the one point of commonality is your game assets: the HTML, JS, CSS, and whatever other assets you have created. The difference is in how they will be run. In a mobile application, the files are bundled and run locally. The application is, in its most basic implementation, just a widget of some sort to show HTML content with a little Java, Objective-C, or other native code to bind it all together. Frameworks that might interpret gestures sit at the outermost layer closest to the user. Figure 10-1 shows the breakdown of the individual layers in an Android application.

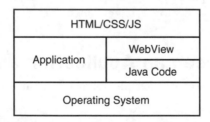

Figure 10-1   Android application layers

Native code is where we could define new gestures that only a specific operating system might support. In addition to OS-specific gestures, we might expose other features that are accessible only from native code, such as camera or accelerometer support. The biggest advantage to releasing your games as applications is better marketing opportunities. Most mobile platforms have app stores that feature apps that can run on their devices. Some, such as the iPhone App Store and the upcoming Amazon Android App Store, are curated environments, where each app is vetted to make sure it runs properly and as expected. Other stores, such as Android Market, allow the developer to deploy an app and have it almost instantly be available for download or purchase. If your game isn't packaged as an app, there is no way it can be a featured download in any of the stores. It can also be more difficult to get potential users to buy your game. If you use a website, you would have to set up payment systems as well as handle refunds and download errors. Releasing the app through a store moves that heavy lifting to someone else.

Making your game an application doesn't come without risks. Apps are vulnerable. They can be copied, cracked, and decompiled. If you make a good game, it may very well get pirated. All that being said, the opportunity for greater exposure, in my humble opinion, far outweighs the risks.

Storing Data on Mobile Devices

Most nontrivial applications have a need to store structured data. The general consensus for mobile devices has been to employ SQLite. In Chapter 1, "Introducing HTML5," we briefly discussed WebSQL, which is closely linked to SQLite. Note that mobile applications, for the most part, use the SQLite support built into the operating system rather than that of the browser. WebSQL (SQL in the browser) has been deprecated in favor of the NoSQL-like IndexedDB standard.

The application frameworks we will discuss later in this chapter—Appcelerator Titanium and PhoneGap—both allow you to make native OS database calls from your HTML5 applications. If you make extensive use of the database, it won't be optimal to use one method for the browser and another for mobile applications. Generally, the less code that has to change, the better. Enter Lawnchair.

Relaxing in Your Lawnchair: An Easier Way to Store Data

Lawnchair is a storage API created by some of the same folks behind PhoneGap. It allows us to use a single API to persist data in many backing data stores. We could use Lawnchair for something as simple as save states or as complex as game maps. It gives us a way to future-proof our code. Lawnchair supports the following backends:

- DOMStorage (localStorage)
- WebSQL (both Webkit and Gears)
- Window-Name
- BlackBerry
- IE User data
- IndexedDB

If you are familiar with NoSQL key/value stores such as MongoDB and CouchDB, you will feel right at home with Lawnchair. (Key/value store databases store their data in collections of objects that are maps of properties, generally as a JSON object.) You can create a database and just start populating things in it. You don't have to declare in advance what properties your objects will have. They can evolve naturally over time. As a result, all objects of the same "type" might not have the same set of properties. The install instructions can be found at http://westcoastlogic.com/lawnchair/. We need to include the Lawnchair.js file and one of the included adaptors.

Getting Started with Lawnchair

The first thing we need to do is create a Lawnchair store. You can think of it as a bag of objects that are generally alike. You can have as many stores as you want, up to the non-administrator limits of your browser (generally about 5MB, before the user is prompted for permission). Listing 10-1 shows the code to create a classes store and populate it with a couple objects using the `save` function. Alternatively, we could supply a function to be executed when the save operation is completed.

Listing 10-1   **Creating a Lawnchair Store**

```
var classes = new Lawnchair({name:'classes'}, function() {
    this.save({name:'Calculus 101', professor:'Jenkins'});
    this.save({name:'Physics 220', maxClassSize:30});
    this.save({name:'Advanced Physics', prerequisite:'Physics 220'});
});
```

Lawnchair supplies several functions to retrieve records: `each`, `get`, and `all`. Like its name implies, `each` iterates over each record in the store and runs a supplied function on the results. Listing 10-2 shows the code to print out all the names of our classes.

Listing 10-2   **Lawnchair each Example**

```
classes.each(function(record) {
    console.log(record.name);
});
```

`get` allows us to retrieve a record for a given key and, if found, run a function on the results. Until now, we haven't talked much about keys. If we don't specify one when we create our records, Lawnchair generates a GUID string to use as the key for us. Listing 10-3 shows the code to save some records with a custom key and a `get` function to find them.

Listing 10-3   **Lawnchair save and get Examples**

```
classes.save({key:"CISC650", name:"Intro to Computer Science"});
classes.save({key:"CISC615", name:"Analysis of Algorithms"});
classes.get("CISC615",
    function(r){console.log(r);}
);
```

Up until now, we haven't talked about removing records. r Lawnchair lets us remove a single record with `remove` or blow away the whole store with nuke. Listing `remove`, like `get`, takes the key of the object to remove. `nuke`, by default, doesn't take any parameters, but you can optionally include a callback function to be executed when the `nuke` is complete. Listing 10-4 shows both methods in action.

Listing 10-4   **Lawnchair `remove` and `nuke` Examples**

```
classes.remove("CISC615",
    function(r) {console.log("remove completed)}
);
classes.nuke();
```

Client-Side Scripting Simplified with JQuery and Zepto

Browser-based applications more and more are moving away from a list of static pages and toward one-page applications where interactivity is improved and portions are loaded dynamically. Although many options are available, we will be focusing on JQuery variants and Zepto. These were chosen based on the ubiquity of JQuery as a client-side scripting standard. On the lighter side, Zepto provides some touch screen gestures on top of a JQuery-like interface. JQueryMobile and JQTouch provide more of a framework for HTML5 applications. Their default themes look like native iOS apps, whereas you would have to define your own style sheets when using Zepto.

Using JQuery Variants

JQuery is a library for JavaScript that simplifies traversal of HTML documents, selectors, event handling, and AJAX animations. Polls and analysis vary greatly but the consensus is that for sites where the JavaScript library can be detected, between 50% and 78% use JQuery. JQuery's functionality can be expanded via user-developed plugins. JQuery is often recognized by its use of the $ and $. functions, the latter of which allows a single discrete function to be called, whereas functions of the former type can be chained together. The two generally used JQuery frameworks/plugins for optimizing a web application are JQueryMobile and JQTouch.

JQueryMobile (http://jquerymobile.com/) is a framework that focuses on providing a high-grade experience on today's mobile browsers. It is hosted on the JQuery website, and in theory, the advances made in JQuery will flow into JQueryMobile very quickly. The project attempts to gracefully degrade when displayed in a browser that doesn't provide full HTML5-compliant capabilities.

JQueryMobile supports many of the gestures that are supported in native mobile applications. In addition to sensing when you change the direction you are holding the device via the `orientationchange` event, JQueryMobile supports the following touch events:

- `tap`
- `taphold`
- `swipe`
- `swipeLeft`
- `swipeRight`

Earlier in this chapter, we discussed `tap`. A `swipe` event is fired when there is contact with the screen and movement of 30 pixels or more up or down (for a general `swipe` event) or left or right for `swipeLeft` or `swipeRight`, respectively.

JQueryMobile includes several CSS transitions for moving between pages. The following transitions are supported:

- `slide`
- `slideup`
- `slidedown`
- `pop`
- `fade`
- `flip`

We could a `pop` transition to an anchor tag by including the following code:

```
<a href="index.html" data-transition="pop">I'll pop</a>
```

Inversely, including `data-back="true"` will reverse the transition when the Back button is hit.

In addition to the smooth CSS transitions, JQueryMobile's components can be themed. It has a built-in theme that closely mimics the user interface of iOS applications. At present, there isn't a theme to make apps look more "Android like" (or for any other non-iOS platform). You could probably attribute this to the evolution of native apps on both platforms. Native applications from outside developers on iOS didn't arrive for nearly a year from the device launch. The advice from Apple at the time was to make web apps. Android, on the other hand, supported a software development toolkit from day one.

JQTouch (http://jqtouch.com/) shares a lot of ground with JQueryMobile. JQTouch focuses on smaller device screens, whereas JQueryMobile attempts to be device independent. Like JQueryMobile, JQTouch built-in themes support iOS devices and not much else. The number of built-in touch events is somewhat limited compared to JQueryMobile. Only `tap` and `swipe` are predefined. You can, however, build more gestures into your application by interpreting the return values from `touchmove`.

Using Zepto.js

Last but not least is Zepto.js (http://zeptojs.com/). It is not officially a JQuery variant but it does have a JQuery-compatible chaining syntax. It is also incredibly small. The library is under 5KB after being minified and gzipped. This comes at the expense of not including styling for components as JQTouch and JQueryMobile do. In addition to JQuery selectors and chaining, Zepto supports JQuery-style HTTP `GET`, `POST`, and AJAX calls and can sense the mobile operating system on which it is running. Touch event support is fairly robust with listeners for `tap`, `doubleTap`, `swipe`, `swipeLeft`, and `swipeRight`.

Architecting Your Applications with JoApp

Jo (http://joapp.com/) is a cross-platform JavaScript framework for HTML5 apps. The same code can be used to deploy an application in Safari, Chrome, Firefox, iOS, Android, and WebOS. Jo uses CSS3 as much as possible to handle presentation and animation. Jo also provides encapsulation for persistent storage and is able to unobtrusively work with other JavaScript libraries. Jo concerns itself with the visual elements of an application, leaving the device-specific minutiae to the enclosing framework—for example, Phone-Gap and Titanium, which we will discuss later in this chapter. Like the aforementioned JQTouch and JqueryMobile, Jo provides a fairly attractive iOS theme. Listing 10-5 shows the HTML for a basic Jo application. No other content is needed if the application creates all user interfaces in code.

Listing 10-5   **Basic Jo Application**

```
<html>
<head>
   <link rel="stylesheet" type="text/css" href="css/aluminum.css">
   <link rel="stylesheet" type="text/css" href="css/webkit.css">
   <!-- <link rel="stylesheet" type="text/css" href="css/webos.css"> -->
   <!-- <link rel="stylesheet" type="text/css" href="css/chrome.css"> -->
</head>
<body>

<!-- any static page content goes here -->

<!-- load jo library -->
<script src="jo_min.js"></script>
```

```
<!-- any application JavaScript files go here -->
<script src="hello.js"></script>

</body>
</html>
```

Jo includes a set of skinned components and controls to create user interfaces. These can be created using JavaScript or by using HTML. By default, HTML will ignore tags it doesn't recognize, so Jo can coexist with regular HTML code. Listing 10-6 shows the code to create a screen and embed a Canvas inside it.

Listing 10-6   **Displaying a Canvas in Jo**

```
//initialize jo
jo.load();

//define a wrapper for document.body
var scn = new joScreen();

var canvas = new joHTML("<canvas height="200" width="200"></canvas>");
scn.push(canvas);
```

Jo provides an easy means to meld together game content and the application using containers. Jo's interfaces use a stack architecture that's not unlike a deck of cards, allowing you to discretely separate screens.

Choosing an Application Framework

We have many options for creating applications using HTML and deploying them to mobile devices. The two frameworks we will discuss in this section—PhoneGap and Appcelerator Titanium—expose native mobile device functionality to JavaScript. Later in this section, we will package the same application with both of them targeting Android. The application we'll be developing uses Zepto.js to capture touch gestures and for determining the operating system. The app draws an HTML file that displays the OS and viewable window dimensions and also has a Canvas that responds to touch events.

PhoneGap

PhoneGap (http://phonegap.com) is a mobile application development framework created by Nitobi Software. The framework allows access to native components of mobile devices such as the accelerometer, camera, contacts, and the file system via a JavaScript interface. All application code is written using JavaScript and HTML and is bound at compile time to the corresponding Java or iOS APIs. Experienced developers could additionally expose other native APIs to the JavaScript interface. Currently, the framework supports developing applications using the following operating systems with varying levels of support for HTML5:

- iOS
- Android
- WebOS
- Blackberry
- Windows Mobile
- Symbian

Diving into the PhoneGap APIs

PhoneGap contains about a dozen APIs, listed next, for making applications. Virtually anything that can be done in a native app has a PhoneGap API:

- Accelerometer
- Camera
- Capture
- Compass
- Connection
- Contacts
- Device
- Events
- File
- Geolocation
- Media
- Network
- Notification
- Storage

Of the aforementioned APIs, the most important is the Events API. When an application loads, by virtue of the way HTML and JavaScript work, it is possible to call functions on objects before they are fully initialized. The Events API exposes an event called `deviceready` that fires when phonegap.js is ready to start receiving commands. Every PhoneGap application should subscribe to `deviceready`. Listing 10-7 shows a simple example of the code we would need to listen for the event.

Listing 10-7   **Listening for the `deviceready` Event**

```
document.addEventListener("deviceready", doStuff, false);

function doStuff() {
   // Now safe to use the PhoneGap API
}
```

In traditional browsers, JavaScript has no access to the local file system, thus handing that heavy lifting to code executing on the server side. This is a pretty hefty restriction for an application that doesn't have a server. Luckily for us, PhoneGap does give us a way to read, write, and upload files from JavaScript code. The `FileReader` object permits us to read files from the file system. The object only has three functions: `readAsText` takes a filename as a parameter and stores that text content of the file in the `result` property on the `FileReader` object. `readAsDataURL` returns the specified file as a base64-encoded URI string. For a refresher on how data URI strings operate, look at the section on images in Chapter 5, "Creating Games with the Canvas Tag." The `abort` function quits reading the file. In addition to the `result` property, there is also an `error` property to store any errors, a `readyState` property to initiate the status of the load in progress, as well as events that can be subscribed to for updates on progress and status.

The `FileWriter` object, like `FileReader`, contains properties for the `readyState` and errors. In addition to the expected `write` and `abort` functions, you can also seek to a position in a file and truncate it to the length of a specified number of bytes. Listing 10-8 shows the code to write a string to a file (test.txt) and truncate it to a length of 10 bytes.

Listing 10-8   **PhoneGap FileWriter Example**

```
var paths = navigator.fileMgr.getRootPaths();
var writer = new FileWriter(paths[0] + "test.txt");
writer.write("writing some text");
writer.truncate(10);
```

Lastly, the `FileUpload` object gives us a way to upload files to a server using HTTP POST. It has a sole-function upload that takes as parameters the file to upload, the URL to POST to, callbacks for success and failure, and an `options` object to pass additional information with the request.

The `isReachable` function on the `Network` object allows us to check for connectivity given a URL to connect to and a callback to execute when connectivity is determined. We can use the results to determine whether we are offline, connected to the carrier's network, or connected to Wi-Fi.

PhoneGap is capable of getting the user's attention with several different audio, visual, and sensory notifications. In addition to a stylized alert message that we would see in any browser, we can vibrate the phone for a number of milliseconds, make a beep sound a number of times, or show a confirmation dialog.

For further documentation, you can visit http://docs.phonegap.com.

Appcelerator Titanium

Appcelerator Titanium (www.appcelerator.com) is a software development toolkit that allows developers to create desktop and mobile application using web technologies such as HTML, JavaScript, and CSS. On the desktop, the experience is reminiscent of and is often compared to the Adobe AIR runtime.

For mobile devices, Titanium only supports Android and iOS. Although that is not technically cross-platform, iOS and Android account for most of the smart phones being sold. The reduced focus to cutting-edge mobile operating systems allows the creators to really refine the experience on iOS and Android.

Diving into the Appcelerator Titanium APIs

Whereas PhoneGap expects you to use HTML and CSS or another library altogether for laying out user interfaces, Appcelerator Titanium has its own set of JavaScript APIs to create UI elements. These elements produce native components during compilation and keep the secret that your app was built with Titanium. You are also free to develop your application using just HTML, JS, and CSS.

`Titanium.Filesystem`, and the object `File` it exposes, allows you to interact with the file system. Any operation that you would expect from a traditional compiled language—such as creating and reading files and directories, creating temporary files, and setting flags on them—is supported in this module. This is the only area where Titanium differs from PhoneGap. Having to only deal with Android and iOS, which are fairly feature rich, makes it easier to enable this functionality.

Titanium's Network module is equally robust. Like the PhoneGap counterpart, it can detect network connectivity and determine whether the host is connected via Wi-Fi or cellular service. The module can create and receive HTTP and TCP requests and search for connected Bonjour/Zeroconf services. Bonjour is the name of Apple's implementation of Zeroconf, which allows computers, servers, and peripherals such as printers and scanners to connect with little configuration from the user.

Packaging Android Applications with Titanium and PhoneGap

Now that we have talked about Titanium and PhoneGap, let's dig into them a little bit more by packaging an application with them. The application is fairly basic in nature, displaying some information about the mobile browser and responding to some events. To assist us with mobile gestures, we will be using Zepto.js. The core HTML file we will be using is shown in Listing 10-9. It uses `window.innerHeight`/`innerWidth` to retrieve the height and width of the browser window and properties on the `$.os` object to show the operation system and version

Listing 10-9   **HTML File for Mobile App**

```
<!DOCTYPE HTML>
<html>
        <head>
                <script src="zepto.min.js"></script>
                <title>Test Application</title>
        </head>
        <body>
    <div id="t"></div>
                <canvas id="canvas" height="200" width="200"
        tabindex="1">
                </canvas>
                <div id="os"></div>
                <div id="browserWidth"></div>
                <div id="browserHeight"></div>


        <script>
            function determineOS() {
                if ($.os.ios == true || $.os.iphone == true || $.os.ipad == true ) {
                return "iOS/iPhone/iPad " + $.os.version;
                } else if ($.os.android == true) {
                return "Android "+ $.os.version
                } else {
                return navigator.userAgent;
                }
            }

            $("#os").text("Operating System:"+ determineOS());
            $("#browserHeight").text("Height: "+window.innerHeight + "px" + "\n");
            $("#browserWidth").text("Width: "+window.innerWidth);

            $('#canvas').bind('click', function(event){ $("#t").text('tapped at
➥'+new Date()) });
                        $("#canvas").bind('tap', function(evt) {
            $("#t").text('tapped at '+new Date());
                        });
                </script>
        </body>
</html>
```

Sound on Android Devices

Although there is far better support than usual for the audio element, some Webkit
browsers, such as the one in Android 2.2, don't natively support it. A workaround for this
lack of support is to use a video element with the audio file as the source and then call
`play()`. If you're using a framework such as PhoneGap or Titanium, this won't be a problem, but it is something to be aware of if you are rolling your own solution.

Packaging an Application with Titanium

Creating a project with Titanium is simple, requiring only a few filled-in text boxes and a few button clicks. Figure 10-2 shows the New Project screen for a sample Titanium application.

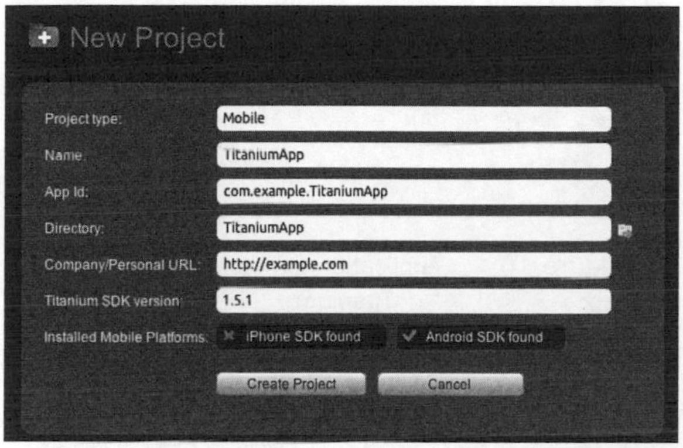

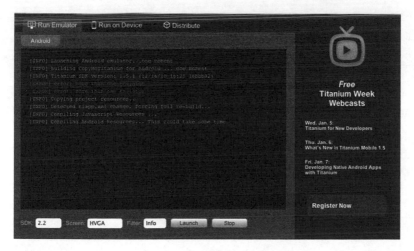

Figure 10-2   Creating a new project in Titanium

From the Titanium application, we can run our apps in the Android or iOS emulator, on physical devices, or deploy them to their respective app stores, as shown in Figure 10-3.

Figure 10-3   Running an emulator in Titanium

Figure 10-4 shows a list of the files for our application. Of particular note to us is the Resources directory (which houses all our application code) and tiapp.xml (which describes how our app will behave on iOS and Android).

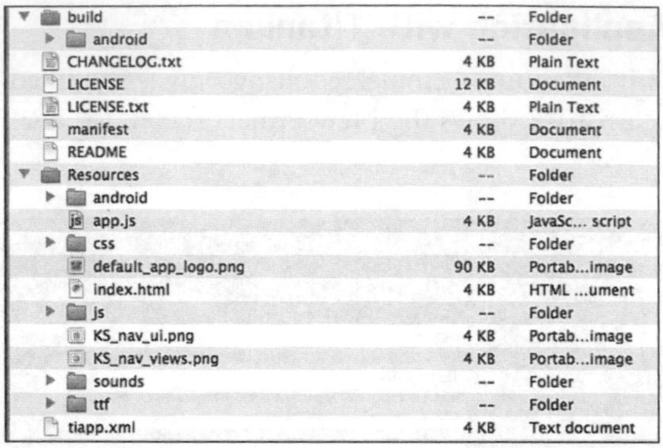

▼ 📁 build		--	Folder
▶ 📁 android		--	Folder
📄 CHANGELOG.txt		4 KB	Plain Text
📄 LICENSE		12 KB	Document
📄 LICENSE.txt		4 KB	Plain Text
📄 manifest		4 KB	Document
📄 README		4 KB	Document
▼ 📁 Resources		--	Folder
▶ 📁 android		--	Folder
📄 app.js		4 KB	JavaSc... script
▶ 📁 css		--	Folder
🖼 default_app_logo.png		90 KB	Portab...image
📄 index.html		4 KB	HTML ...ument
▶ 📁 js		--	Folder
🖼 KS_nav_ui.png		4 KB	Portab...image
🖼 KS_nav_views.png		4 KB	Portab...image
▶ 📁 sounds		--	Folder
▶ 📁 ttf		--	Folder
📄 tiapp.xml		4 KB	Text document

Figure 10-4   Application directory structure in
Titanium

Titanium maintains its own Android images just for Titanium. Any modifications won't be persisted, as Titanium regenerates them from time to time. Behind the scenes, when you deploy to the emulator, Titanium launches the selected image and compiles and deploys the application.

Titanium uses a file named app.js to describe the user interface and logic of your application. Listing 10–10 shows the code to use Titanium's JavaScript API to create a window, populate it with a `WebView`, and show it to the user.

Listing 10-10   **Sample Application app.js File**

```
// this sets the background color of the master UIView
//(when there are no windows/tab groups on it)
Titanium.UI.setBackgroundColor('#000');

//
// create root window
//
var win1 = Titanium.UI.createWindow({
    title:'App',
    backgroundColor:'#fff'
});

var webview = Titanium.UI.createWebView({
    url:'index.html'
});

win1.add(webview);

// open window
win1.open();
```

After we place our index.html and zepto.min.js files in the same directory as app.js, we are ready to run our application.

Packaging an Application with PhoneGap

Instead of using a customized emulator launcher like Titanium does, PhoneGap relies strongly on the existing Android tool chain. This means that you can use the Android plugin with the Eclipse IDE like a native application would. Components of the AndroidManifest.xml configuration file that are automagically created for you in Titanium have to be coded by hand with PhoneGap. For the purposes of this example, we assume you have the Android plugin installed in your IDE of choice.

Creating a project is pretty straightforward and bears no hallmarks that are different from creating a native application. Figures 10-5 and 10-6 show the creation screens for our project. In Figure 10-6, we left the option "Create 'Hello World!' project" selected because that reduces the amount of Java code we will have to write.

PhoneGap exposes Java functionality to HTML applications using two files: a Java library named phonegap.jar and its JavaScript counterpart, phonegap.js. phonegap.jar needs to be placed somewhere on the application path. We will leave phonegap.js for a bit later.

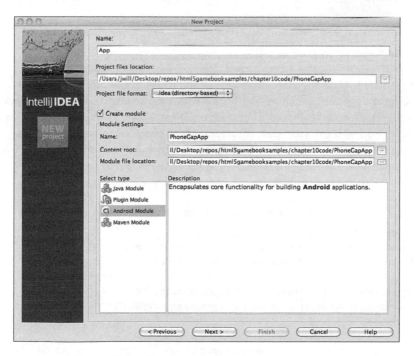

Figure 10-5   Creating an application using PhoneGap

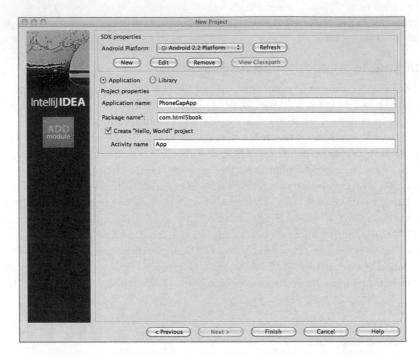

Figure 10-6   Creating an application using PhoneGap (continued)

Listing 10-11 shows the additions we must add to AndroidManifest.xml to allow
PhoneGap to do its work. The snippet begins with a tag telling Android what types of
screens this application is allowed to operate on. Next is a series of enabled permissions
for components of the device, such as camera access, contacts, audio, and GPS. In
Android, every application must explicitly declare which permissions it will use. For our
sample application, the sole permission we use is `android.permission.INTERNET`, but
Listing 10-11 shows the required permissions to enable all features of PhoneGap.

Listing 10-11   Additions to AndroidManifest.xml

```
<supports-screens android:largeScreens="true"
android:normalScreens="true" android:smallScreens="true"
android:resizeable="true" android:anyDensity="true"
/>
<uses-permission android:name="android.permission.CAMERA" />
<uses-permission android:name="android.permission.VIBRATE" />
<uses-permission
android:name="android.permission.ACCESS_COARSE_LOCATION" />
<uses-permission android:name="android.permission.ACCESS_FINE_LOCATION" />
<uses-permission
android:name="android.permission.ACCESS_LOCATION_EXTRA_COMMANDS" />
<uses-permission android:name="android.permission.READ_PHONE_STATE" />
```

```
<uses-permission android:name="android.permission.INTERNET" />
<uses-permission android:name="android.permission.RECEIVE_SMS" />
<uses-permission android:name="android.permission.RECORD_AUDIO" />
<uses-permission
android:name="android.permission.MODIFY AUDIO_SETTINGS" />
<uses-permission android:name="android.permission.READ_CONTACTS" />
<uses-permission android:name="android.permission.WRITE_CONTACTS" />
<uses-permission
android:name="android.permission.WRITE_EXTERNAL_STORAGE" />
<uses-permission android:name="android.permission.ACCESS_NETWORK_STATE" />
```

To the application tag in the AndroidManifest.xml file, we also need to add the following:

```
android:configChanges="orientation|keyboardHidden"
```

This tells Android that when the specified changes happen (in this case, the user rotating the device and sliding in/out the keyboard), this application will handle it and not to execute the default behavior and relaunch the application.

Next, we need to make some changes to the sample Activity file Android has created for us. Activities represent a single screen display. Unless you have a really good reason to or would like to tweak Java code, you can get along with solely the changes shown in Listing 10-12.

Listing 10-12   **Sample Application Activity File**

```
package com.html5book;

import android.app.Activity;
import android.os.Bundle;
import com.phonegap.*;

public class App extends DroidGap {
        @Override
        public void onCreate(Bundle savedInstanceState) {
                super.onCreate(savedInstanceState);
                super.loadUrl("file:///android_asset/www/index.html");
        }
}
```

Just as we only had to concern ourselves with the Resources directory in Titanium, after initial setup, there is just one primary directory in which we will be working on PhoneGap. We even saw a hint of this when modifying the Java file. We need to create a directory and subdirectory on our path named assets and assets/www, respectively. This is where all our HTML-related application files will live. android_asset is a link to assets. To expose our Java functionality to the application, we just need to copy the phonegap.js file to assets/www. Figure 10-7 shows the application directory layout for our application.

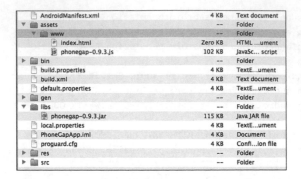

Figure 10-7   Application directory structure in
PhoneGap

As opposed to needing a special application to build, launch, or install our application, we can use our favorite IDE or work directly from the command line using the build.xml file.

Summary

In this chapter, we discussed various libraries and frameworks to create HTML5 applications on mobile devices. We focused on libraries that expose touch events and storage options. We looked in detail at two frameworks to package applications: PhoneGap and Appcelerator Titanium. Finally, we used those frameworks to package some applications.

Exercises

1. What is a workaround for playing audio using HTML5 in Android 2.2 browsers?

2. What are the pros and cons of using Appcelerator Titanium versus PhoneGap?

3. What is an advantage of using Lawnchair or any other NoSQL-inspired storage solution over a SQLite database?

4. Which operating system is currently a no-go if you want to create HTML5 applications?

You can download chapter code and answers to the chapter exercises at www.informit.com/title/9780321767363.

11

Publishing Your Games

The first ten chapters of this book dealt primarily with learning about HTML5 and associated technologies and developing games. In this chapter, we shift our focus and cover how to deploy your games with a good measure of optimization thrown in. Applications on the Web live and die based on their speed. Optimization and effective use of offline cache are important pieces of the puzzle when pushing out your work to the masses.

Optimizing Your Game's Assets

We are making games, so lots of our payload will be in the games' logic. In an attempt to write code that you will understand in six months' or a year's time, you may have painstakingly commented and formatted your code. Or not. The problem with all those comments is that they take up space in your files and your users don't care that you've explained how something works, just that it does. The smaller your files are, the faster they will download. **Minification** is the process of making code smaller. Often, this will include removing white space and comments as well as renaming functions and variables.

Minification with Google Closure Compiler

Google Closure Compiler is a code analyzer, optimizer, and minimizer, all rolled into one package. Most minimizers will do the standard function and variable renaming, comment removal, and then call it a day. Closure Compiler goes one step further and walks the abstract syntax tree for your code and notes which code can be removed because it is unreachable or can be simplified by inlining, which is replacing a function call with code from that function. It can also identify mistakes in your code. We won't be using the advanced features in this chapter, but you are encouraged to research this more if you are so interested. Closure Compiler does require Java to be installed to run the application, so go ahead and take a moment to grab it if you don't already have Java installed on your machine.

Download and extract compiler.jar from the zip file located at http://closure-compiler.googlecode.com/files/compiler-latest.zip. The compiler doesn't have any external Java dependencies. We can optimize a file by executing

```
java -jar compiler.jar
```

at the command line, followed by the options and values we desire. The useful flags for our needs are `--js`, `--compilation_level`, and `--js_output_file`.

You can see the available command-line options, including the ones we won't be covering at all, by executing the following:

```
java -jar compiler.jar --help
```

`--js` specifies files to be minified. We can include as many as we want, as long as each file has its own `--js` flag. We have three choices for the `--compilation_level`:

- `WHITESPACE_ONLY`
- `SIMPLE_OPTIMIZATIONS`
- `ADVANCED_OPTIMIZATIONS`

As mentioned before, we will leave `ADVANCED_OPTIMIZATIONS` for another place and time. The `WHITESPACE_ONLY` identifier only removes white space and comments. `SIMPLE_OPTIMIZATIONS` executes the `WHITESPACE_ONLY` optimizations and additionally mangles top-level variable and parameter names. `--js_output_file`, as its name hints, allows us to specify an output file to hold the optimized JavaScript. If we passed multiple files via `--js`, they will be concatenated into a single file. You can see an example of how a call to optimize several files with simple optimization would look here:

```
java -jar compiler.jar --js Game.js —js zepto.min.js
--js_output_file outfile.js --compilation_level SIMPLE_OPTIMIZATIONS
```

The amount of white space and comments will determine how small the minified version is. On some of the project files from other chapters, I noticed an average 40% reduction in size after minification. Think about that for a moment: that's 40% less data to download and in most cases a reduction in files to download (because they are concatenated together). It's a clear win. If you are running your own server, you should know that most web servers allow you to go a step further in gzipping your assets. You might have to install an additional module or plug-in, but it is something to consider because minifying then gzipping can yield a reduction in file size in the high double digits. When a client requests a file from the server, the server will respond to the request with a gzipped version that the client then extracts. The web page that requested the asset has no idea that it was served a gzipped resource.

CSS can also be minified and gzipped. Closure Compiler doesn't do CSS minification. Most of your games will probably be light on CSS and heavy on JavaScript, so CSS minification is not likely to make a significant difference.

Images can likewise be optimized. Every image included in a document is a separate HTTP request. Combining them into a sprite sheet allows us to save precious time by providing them all in one go.

Running Applications Offline with Application Cache

One of the trends that has been ushered in with HTML5 is a desire to blur the lines between online and offline access. In Chapter 1, "Introducing HTML5," we talked briefly about how the now-defunct Google Gears allowed you to store data for offline access; that concept has been carried forward with HTML5 Application Cache. It takes away the binary decision users had to previously face: whether to be online and able to access the app, or not. A properly structured app could retain some subset of functionality while offline. Although you won't be able to hit an external server (for instance, to post leader board scores), other tools, such as localStorage, can cache data locally and re-transmit it to the server when connectivity is re-established.

Listing 11-1 shows a basic Application Cache manifest file. All manifests must begin with the line CACHE MANIFEST. The manifest listed is using the default behavior to cache all indicated files if there are no section headers.

Listing 11-1   **Basic Application Cache Manifest**

```
CACHE MANIFEST
/game.css
/game.js
```

The sections we can specify in a cache manifest are as follows:

- CACHE
- NETWORK
- FALLBACK

These indicate to always cache, to never cache, and how to handle a request for an uncached file, respectively. CACHE is the default. Listing 11-1 is equivalent to the code shown in Listing 11-2.

Listing 11-2   **Basic Application Cache Manifest**

```
CACHE MANIFEST

CACHE:
/game.css
/game.js
```

The NETWORK section can be specified in one of two ways. We can either specify explicitly which assets can only be accessed online, as we did for cached assets in Listings 11-1 and 11-2, or we can specify wildcard (*) values. Listing 11-3 shows a manifest were we exclude all Ruby files from caching. If we had omitted the .rb extension, the manifest would require network access for everything we didn't explicitly list in the CACHE section. Any line whose first non-white-space character is a # is treated as a comment. Unlike comments in programming languages, these must be on their own lines. The reason for this is that the # is also used in URLs as a fragment indicator. A comment on the same line as a URL would be ambiguous to the browser.

Listing 11-3   Application Cache Manifest with Network Section

```
CACHE MANIFEST
# Manifest with CACHE and NETWORK sections
CACHE :
/game.css
/Game.js


NETWORK:
*.rb
```

The last and arguably the most important part of the manifest file is the FALLBACK section. The pairs in the FALLBACK section help your user cope with offline access. The first value in the pair is the URL pattern to match. It is followed by the asset to serve in its place. We might show a generic avatar for some users if they are viewing the leader board offline. We could also route them to a page stating that they are offline and certain features will be unavailable until they reconnect. The goal again is to give them as much functionality of the app as possible. Listing 11-4 shows a manifest file that serves generic_avatar.png for all requests made to the /images/avatars/ directory and shows offline.html for all uncached HTML files.

Listing 11-4   Application Cache Manifest with All Sections

```
CACHE MANIFEST
#Manifest with all sections
CACHE:
/game.css
/Game.js

NETWORK:
*.rb

FALLBACK:
/images/avatars/ /generic_avatar.png
/ /offline.html
```

Now that we have a manifest with all sections defined, we need to tell our application to serve it to users. You might have noticed that we never specified any HTML files to be cached. We both indicate the HTML to be cached and serve the manifest to users by adding a property value to our code, as shown in Listing 11-5.

Listing 11-5   **HTML File with `manifest` Property**

```
<!DOCTYPE html>
<html lang="en" manifest="/offline.manifest">
      // Stuff goes here
</html>
```

The filename can be anything, but it must end in .manifest. It should also be served with the MIME type `text/cache-manifest`. That's of less concern than the filename. Most web servers will properly guess the MIME type of files based on their extension and contents. If we have a single-file app, after adding the code from Listing 11-5, we're done. For a multipage app, we need to include the `manifest` property in each page that should be cached. Although you can list the HTML files in the manifest itself, it is less messy to have the property be a part of your templates and omit it, as necessary to prevent caching rather than trying to maintain a massive list of HTML files in the manifest.

A common misconception is that changing files on the server without changing the manifest will somehow automagically retrieve the changed files and leave the unchanged files alone. That simply is not the case. Changing the manifest file is how the browser is notified of changes to the files. One quick-and-easy way to change the manifest is to add a comment line with a version number or identifier and to increment the number when you change assets referenced in the file. When you visit the site, it looks at the manifest file and checks whether it has viewed the file before, firing a `checking` event along the way. The manifest is checked against the local version if one exists; if they match, the browser fires a `noupdate` event and the function ends. If the local version doesn't exist or the browser notices a change, a `downloading` event is fired and *all* assets are downloaded again. Periodically during the download process, `progress` events will be fired to give updates on the download status. When complete, either a `cached` or `updateready` event will be fired for the site without or with a previous manifest, respectively. Although caching occurs, unless you force an refresh on receipt of the `updateready` event, the user's session will not be swapped to use the cached assets. The cached assets will be used on the next refresh after caching occurs.

Hosting Your Own Server

When it comes to running your own server, you can choose to physically run the equipment at your home or place of work or you can use a hosting service. Some services give you a curated experience, where you just log in to an online dashboard to upload files; others give you a clean instance of a server to install the software you need to run on it.

If you are anything like me, even if you have been diligent about gifting your slow machines to non-gamers, you still probably have one or two usable machines around the house. One of my castoffs was a laptop whose screen went bad but has a decent processor and 2GB RAM in it. With an external monitor to do the initial setup, that is the perfect machine to run a site.

The Domain Name System (DNS) translates human-friendly domain names to their IP addresses. When you have an instance at Rackspace or Amazon, the IP address is not going to change for the lifetime of that instance. Residential Internet providers, on the other hand, routinely invalidate and reassign the IP address assigned to your cable modem. This presents a problem for your users if the IP address for your site changes often. It's the equivalent of someone changing their e-mail address every month. At first, you would try to keep up and actively seek them out, but eventually you would get lost and lose interest. Dynamic DNS services solve this problem by running software that reports the IP address back to the host at short intervals so that it catches changes quickly. Many modern wireless routers have this functionality built in. DynDNS and No-IP.com are two of the better-known and trusted dynamic DNS services. In addition to handling the routing of your domain name, they offer a number of free branded domain names you can use to get started.

When a user types in the domain for your website, several operations take place. First, the root servers, which contain the canonical information for the top-level domains (TLD; that is, .com, .uk, .fr, .me, and so on) are contacted to find the address of the TLD your site uses. The TLD is then queried to find the name server for your domain. Those servers are queried to get the IP address of your site. The last hop before returning the IP address is where dynamic DNS would fit in. Dynamic DNS doesn't work for all situations, especially those that need 100 percent uptime. However, it is a great way to test ideas before growing to a hosted server.

Deploying Applications on Hosted Node.js Services

At the time of this writing, only a few companies specifically target deploying Node.js applications. This situation is expected to improve as Node.js becomes more of a mainstay. The advantage of using such a service is that you don't have to worry about the minutiae of maintaining a hosted server, such as opening and routing to ports, enforcing separation between apps sharing the box on different domains, and operating system updates. A disadvantage of using such a service is lack of control. You don't have a say in what equipment your site will run on and can't do much if intermittent connectivity issues arise. Due to their elastic replication nature, you won't be able to save new files into the application instance while it is running. This is an issue easily handled with online storage services such as Amazon and Rackspace, but it is certainly something to think about. In this section, we will focus on the services offered by Nodester.

Nodester (www.nodester.com) is a open-source hosting platform for Node.js applications. Nodester uses Git to track changes as well as to start and stop your applications. Provided you have Node.js and NPM installed, you can get started by installing the nodester module with the following command:

```
npm install nodester-cli -g
```

Next, you need to request a registration token:

```
nodester coupon <email address>
```

Within a couple hours or so, you should have a welcome e-mail with your registration code and some basic "Getting Started" instructions. The e-mail takes you through the steps to create a new user, generate an SSH key, and provide a password. We will conveniently skip those steps here and instead focus on what makes Nodester cool: its API.

Nodester's command-line interface is a bridge over common tasks from Node, NPM, and Git. When you create a Nodester application with the command

```
nodester app create <app_name>
```

you are actually creating a remote Github repository for the application. You can manage NPM modules by just running the following command:

```
nodester npm <install|uninstall> <modules>
```

You can start, stop, or restart an app at any time by running this command:

```
nodester app <start|stop|restart> <app_name>
```

These commands only affect the code that is on the remote server. Any local changes need to be committed and pushed to the remote server before they will show up.

Having an application run from appname.nodester.com is fine for proof-of-concept apps, but real apps will need their own domain. Nodester can accept redirects from your own domain. You can manage aliases from your app name to your domain by executing the following command:

```
nodester appdomain <add|delete> <app-name> <domain-name>
```

You also need to add an A record to your DNS host pointing from your domain to Nodester's IP address, currently 50.16.203.53. You can discover the other available commands by running `nodester` on the command-line with no parameters.

Nodester puts forth a novel solution to the hosting problem by providing hosting and version control deeply integrated into the same package. One area where it falls short is in persistence. Nodester doesn't offer a built-in database for you to use—and probably with good reason. It would be hard to build a solution that solves the needs of most developers and keeps data properly segregated. Fortunately, the cloud database-hosting industry is fairly strong with offerings from MongoHQ (MongoDB), Cloudant (CouchDB), and Amazon (SimpleDB/SQL).

Publishing Applications on the Chrome Web Store

The Chrome Web Store is a place where you can purchase apps, themes, and extensions for the Chrome web browser. Estimates place the number of Chrome users at somewhere around 120 million worldwide. The Chrome Web Store is also the primary means for

Chromebooks (Netbooks running Chrome OS) to install applications. Computers running Chrome OS have a Linux core, but the sole interface with which users will interact is the Chrome browser. The Chrome browser updates itself mostly silently in the background, so you don't have the concerns that you have with other major browsers in supporting legacy versions. Applications distributed through the Chrome Web Store also have the ability to have updates pushed to users with little effort. With the Chrome Web Store, you can lean forward and code to the cutting-edge capabilities of the browser. That's not to say you won't have to do a little sniffing to determine capabilities of something such as WebGL or hardware acceleration, but targeting a single browser reduces the pain. We've talked a lot throughout the book about what apps are, but we haven't really discussed themes and extensions. A **theme** modifies the look and feel of your Chrome application window with custom images and fonts. **Extensions** are mini-applications often have only a single purpose. An example of an extension would be a tool that "linkifies" text that appears to be a Twitter handle. In this section, we focus on packaging applications. When it comes to apps, the Chrome Web Store gives you two options for delivery to your users. You can deploy an app hosted on your servers or a packaged app that the user downloads.

Describing Your Application's Metadata

Every installable app—be it a hosted or packaged app—needs some metadata about it to be described in a file called manifest.json. In the manifest file, we describe essentials, such as the name, description, and version of the application, icons, URLs (either external or bundled), and what permissions the application will use. Listing 11-6 shows a sample manifest.json file for a packaged app.

Listing 11-6   **Sample manifest.json File**

```
{
    "name":"Copy Me Game",
    "version":"0.0.1",

    "description":"A Simon-like 'repeat the pattern' game",
    "app" : {
        "launch": {
            "local_path": "index.html",
            "container":"tab"
        }
    },
    "icons": {
        "16": "icons/icon_16.png",
        "128": "icons/icon_128.png"
    }
}
```

Deploying a Hosted Application

Hosted apps are not just glorified bookmarks. The manifest file allows you to request additional permissions at installation. Listing 11-7 shows a typical manifest file for a hosted app. One notable change from the previous example is the web_url key/value pair. It indicates the website that will be launched when the app is started. The site will also be approved for the requested permissions.

Listing 11-7   **Sample Hosted App manifest.json File**

```
{
    "name":"Copy Me Game",
    "version":"0.0.1",

    "description":"A Simon-like 'repeat the pattern' game",
    "app" : {
        "launch": {
            "web_url": "http://copyme.example.com/index.html",
        }
    },
    "icons": {
        "16": "icon_16.png",
        "128": "icon_128.png"
},
"permissions": [
        "unlimitedStorage",
        "notifications"
]
}
```

In the case of Listing 11-7, users will be presented with a single pop-up listing all the requested permissions, as opposed to multiple requests in succession. Here's a list of the permissions we can request for an app:

- background
- geolocation
- notifications
- unlimitedStorage

In Chapter 1, we discussed using geolocation and notifications, so turn back to that chapter for a refresher. unlimitedStorage removes the 5MB restrictions on localStorage and database storage. Without the permission, users would be shown a pop-up when they have reached the threshold. If they decline, it might negatively affect your application. Therefore, if you are going to be saving any sort of substantial data, it's better to request it than not.

The background permission allows an app to load as soon as Chrome is started and run even if the user isn't actively interacting with the app or Chrome. It runs a background HTML page that it can use to run miscellaneous tasks. The Twitter client, Tweet-Deck, uses background pages to check for new tweets and sends browser notifications when a user is mentioned or direct-messaged. In the context of a game, this might be where you would send and receive the game state, messages, and moves. In order to use the background permission, you also have to add a `background_page` key/value pair to the manifest.

Deploying a Packaged Application

Packages applications are great for offline access and, like hosted applications, use a zipped file that contains a manifest.json file. In addition, all of the app code is included. Packaged applications can also leverage the Licensing API, but that functionality does come with a couple words of caution. Because the whole application is downloaded to the user's machine, a motivated user can alter files to circumvent your security. If your application is free, this won't be a concern at all. For an application that is free but uses in-app payments for content, perhaps, it likewise might not be that much of an issue.

Testing Your Applications Locally

Chrome gives you the ability to rapidly test your applications locally without having to redeploy to the web store. The Extension Options pane, which can be accessed from Tools | Extensions or by typing chrome://extensions in the omnibar, allows you to install a working copy of your application as well as configure, uninstall, or disable other themes, extensions, and applications. Figure 11-1 shows the Extensions pane with the Developer Mode collapsible pane expanded. You would click the Load Unpacked Extension button and navigate to the root directory of your application.

Figure 11-1   Chrome Extensions pane

Uploading Your Application to the Chrome Web Store

When you have tested locally to your heart's content, it's time to take it to the next level with either beta testing or full deployment to the world. If you go to the Chrome Web Store from a new tab, near the bottom will be a Developer Dashboard link. From this dashboard, you can manage updates or add new themes, extensions, and apps for the Chrome Web Store. If you weren't grandfathered in during the beta period, you will have to pay a $5 fee to distribute applications through the Chrome Web Store. Like the

Android developer fee, that is not an annual recurring fee—it's a one-time fee. After you sort out the registered developer situation, you can navigate to the dashboard. Figure 11-2 shows a dashboard with a couple of apps that are in beta test.

Figure 11-2   Chrome Web Store Developer Dashboard

In beta test mode, these applications show up in the Chrome Web Store, but only for the creator and any testers the creator has white-listed. Below the listed apps is a "so big you can't miss it" button permitting you to add a new item. When you click the button, you are greeted with a simple web form asking you to upload an archive file, as shown in Figure 11-3.

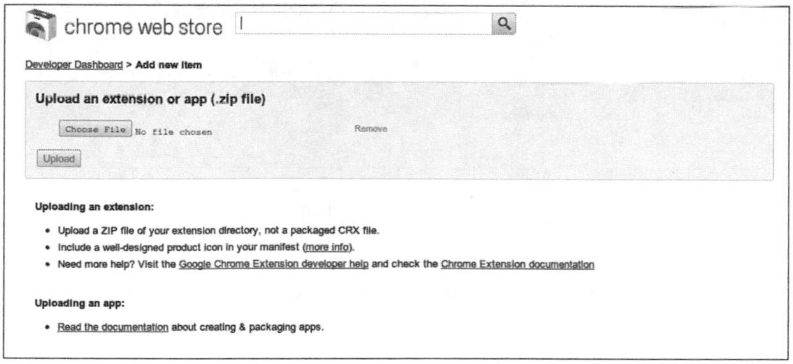

Figure 11-3   The Add New Item screen

When you attempt to submit the file, the server parses it to make sure that it has, at the very least, a manifest.json file, a small icon (16×16 pixels) for the browser tab, and a large icon (128×128 pixels) for the New Tab app dashboard of all installed apps. Forget to include any of these items, and the server will refuse to upload the file.

To the far right of the applications in Figure 11-2 are two links: one to toggle whether the application is published or unpublished, and link to edit an item. The latter link allows us to configure the app with more granularity than the manifest file allows.

Configuring Your Application

Figure 11-4 shows the first portion of a large form for configuring app attributes. You can see that it populates some basic information from the manifest file, including the app name, version, and description. You can also select which countries' users will be able to see the app in the Chrome Web Store. From this form, we can also load an icon and add screenshots, a link to a YouTube video, or a link to Google Docs presentation.

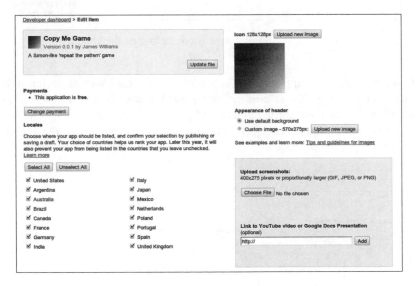

Figure 11-4   The Edit Item screen

The second portion, shown in Figure 11-5, gives you a chance to select preset categories for the app or to add your own. There is also the area for providing a detailed description as well as upload buttons for promotional banners in the event your app gets featured. Lastly, there is a default language designation. Chrome provides built-in localization for themes, extensions, and apps so you can include all messages in deployment instead of deploying several versions of the app.

The third and final portion, shown in Figure 11-6, allows you to associate the item with a verified website you own, mark the content as "Mature," attach links, and designate the use of OpenID authentication. It is important to note that if you are using Chrome Web Store Payments, you must use OpenID authentication so that the purchase can be verified and attached to the user's Google account. All the documentation on the matter suggests using OpenID because it purportedly makes the path to transitioning from a free to a paid app easier and improves the user experience.

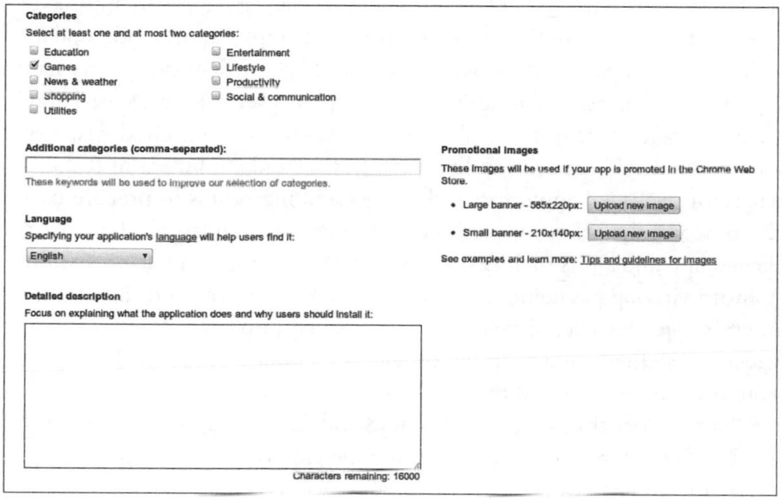

Figure 11-5   The Edit Item screen, continued

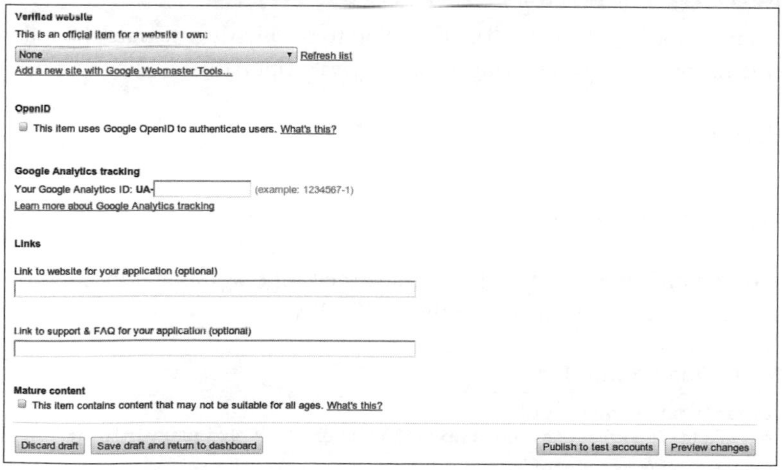

Figure 11-6   The final portion of the Edit Item screen

Deciding Between Packaged and Hosted Chrome Apps

The decision on whether to make your application a hosted or packaged app depends on many factors. Free apps can use either model with ease, whereas paid apps have to take extra pains for verification if deployed as packaged apps. Although the app updates can be made available to users with a simple button click, updating packaged apps takes more steps for the user. Although both hosted and packaged apps require code updates and loading to your or Google's servers, users of a hosted app will automatically have the updated application whereas there might be a delay for users of a packaged app.

Google encourages developers to allow their users to have a limited free trial of their applications. Hosted applications can handle both trial and paid users in the same code-base, whereas for packaged applications, the suggested method is to prepare two packages: one for the trial and the other for paid access. Size is also a concern. The maximum size for a packaged app and all its included assets is 10MB. Though in beta at the time of this writing, Chrome in-app payments will provide a way to convert a trial version to a paid version of your app. However, developers aren't locked into using Chrome Payments; they can also elect to use their own payment providers—either directly in the application or by requiring users to register and provide credentials on their website. The video-streaming service Netflix does this with its native iOS and Android apps. Users have to register and pay for Netflix before they can use the mobile application. The mobile app simply asks for username and password.

Publishing Applications with TapJS

TapJS is a game-hosting platform that allows you to seamlessly integrate the following social elements into your games using a concise JavaScript API:

- Achievements
- Leader boards
- Player accounts

Integrating with TapJS is simple: Just include the script tags shown in Listing 11-8 in your `head` tag and you are ready to use the TapJS APIs.

Listing 11-8 **TapJS Script Tags**

```
<script type="text/javascript"
src="https://ajax.googleapis.com/ajax/libs/jquery/1.4.4/jquery.min.js"></script>
<script type="text/javascript"
src="http://YOUR-GAME-URL.tapjs.com/api/js"></script>
```

Creating a TapJS Application

It's also simple to create a TapJS game: Simply fill in a title and click Continue, as shown in Figure 11-7, and you are brought to a long form shown in sections in Figures 11-8 through 11-12. Figure 11-8 shows the areas where you can describe your app in more detail, and Figure 11-9 shows the limited set of themes and layout options as well as achievements.

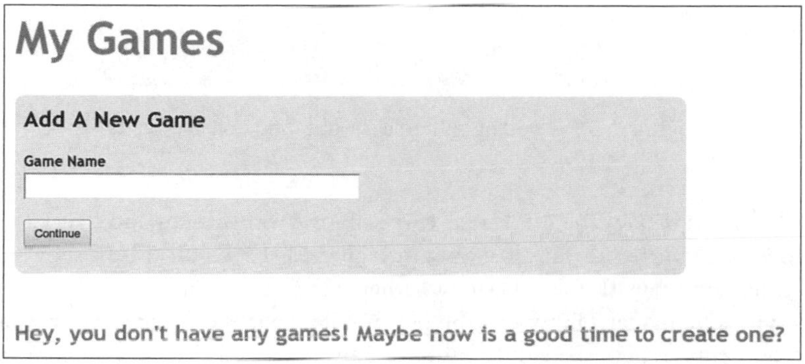

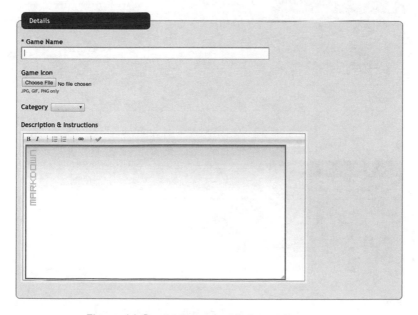

Figure 11-7   The Add a New Game screen

Figure 11-8   Adding a description and category

Page Style And Layout

Layout Theme Dark ▾

* iFrame Height (px)

400

Typically it is a good idea to set this to 20-50px larger then the height of your game board.

Display Highscores Yes ▾
Select "Yes" if you want to display high scores on your game page.

Display Badges Yes ▾
Select "Yes" if your game uses Badges.

Display Comments Yes ▾
Select "Yes" if you want to display comments on your game page.

Display "AddThis" bar Yes ▾
AddThis is the bar that allows people to easily share your game via Facebook, Twitter and a long list of other services.

Figure 11-9   Adding a theme, layout, and achievements

The subdomain defines the URL that you will give your friends and that Facebook will use to access your game. This is shown in Figure 11-10. Figure 11-11 shows the permissions your game can ask for—that is, whether Internet Explorer 7 and 8 users will be told to download a modern browser, whether mobile devices can access your game, and whether your game is published and playable. Lastly, Figure 11-12 shows where you would enter the Facebook-specific details.

Domain

* Subdomain

.tapjs.com

The value will show up as subdomain.tapjs.com

Or, Us A Custom Full Domain Name

If you wish to use your own domain name, enter it here and point the A record to 173.255.231.213
Note A subdomain value is still required.

Figure 11-10   Adding a subdomain

Permissions

Allow IE 7 & 8 No ▾
If you do not allow IE 7 & 8, players using Internet Explorer 7 or 8 will be shown an error message and links to download either IE9, Google Chrome or Firefox.

Allow on mobile devices No ▾
If you do not allow your game on mobile devices, players using mobile devices will be shown a message that this game is not available on mobile devices

Status De-activate ▾
Only games with a status of ACTIVE will be displayed and playable.

Private No ▾
If you DO NOT want your game promoted on other TapJS game pages, set it as private. You may also want to keep it private while testing.

Figure 11-11   Adding permissions

Figure 11-12   Adding Facebook integration

Packaging an Application for TapJS

Packaging an app for TapJS is as easy as creating a zip (archive) file and you're all set. You can include any of the following file types in the zip file:

- .html
- .css
- .ttf
- .js
- .swf
- .jpg, .png, .gif
- .mp3 and .ogg

You are free to use any folder structure you prefer. The only requirement is to include the aforementioned script tags somewhere in your application and an index.html file.

Publishing a TapJS Application to Facebook

TapJS can also deploy applications to be used on Facebook. This choice does come with compromises in regard to what functions you can call. You will first need to create a Facebook application. We covered this briefly in Chapter 9, "Building a Multiplayer Game Server," but let's revisit it with the changes needed for a TapJS application. Figure 11-13 shows the Web Site tab of the Facebook Developer Application console. You needed to set the Site URL to the URL you picked when you created the game on TapJS (generally http://YOURGAME.tapjs.com).

On the Facebook Integration tab, the Canvas URL and Tab URL fields should be set to your TapJS URL. The IFrame Size option should be set to Auto-Resize. The Canvas Page and Tab Name fields should be set as well. Figure 11-14 shows a screenshot of this part of the developer console.

Figure 11-13   Facebook Application Web Site tab

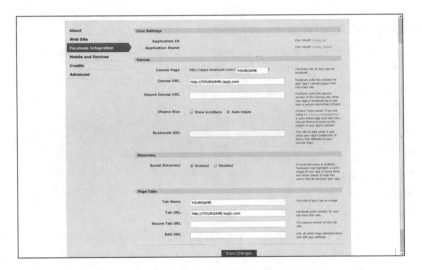

Figure 11-14   Facebook Application Facebook Integration tab

TapJS's Facebook API is rather concise. There are three functions on the `tapjsSocial` object. Their signatures are listed here:

- `tapjsSocial.fbCheck ([callbackFunction] )`
- `tapjsSocial.fbApp ([callbackFunction] )`
- `tapjsSocial.fbWallPost (message [,link] [,caption] [,description]`
  `[callbackFunction] )`

`fbCheck` determines whether the user is accessing the application from a Facebook Canvas. This can be called to give your applications hints on Facebook-specific features to turn on or off. One in particular is the Facebook ban on AdSense ads. `fbApp` retrieves information about your app, such as the app ID and Canvas page URL. `fbWallPost`, as its name implies, allows you to post to a user's Facebook wall. The TapJS API doesn't currently support in-app payments such as Facebook Credits and Google Payments, although in-app payments are listed on the roadmap. Using TapJS to deploy on Facebook is a good means for performing a smoke test rollback on Facebook before trying to do something more tailored to the platform.

Publishing Games with Kongregate

Kongregate is a online game-hosting platform that originally supported only Flash and Unity games but is now able to host HTML5 games. It is very mature and boasts a large number of users and developers. Konduit, its application platform, incorporates many of the same elements as TapJS, and more, including the following:

- Chat integration
- Micropayments
- Guest game players (not signed in to Kongregate)
- User profiles

One point of interest is that when you deploy to Kongregate, you are also deploying to Android. Kongregate publishes an Android app that grants access to all the games on its platform. Konduit is a bit large to discuss with any justice here, but interested readers are encouraged to read up on it at www.kongregate.com/developer_center/docs/konduit-platform.

Publishing HTML5 Applications to the Desktop

As mentioned before, Webkit, the browser engine that powers Google Chrome and Apple Safari, started its life as an open-source project called KHTML. Webkit's open-source roots means that it is addressable from many different programming languages that interface with C/C++. Developers can write their own bindings from their language of choice to Webkit or choose from ready-made solutions using the GTK (http://en.wikipedia.org/wiki/GTK) or wxWidgets (http://en.wikipedia.org/wiki/WxWidgets) widget libraries, each of which has bindings for many programming languages. These libraries are additionally cross-platform. These bindings allow you to make your application as rich or as basic as needed. You could just code a shell app that loads the application like any other browser (as if often the case with XULRunner apps), or you could allow your app to use gamepads or other peripherals that wouldn't be available in a regular browser.

XULRunner (http://en.wikipedia.org/wiki/XULRunner) is the runtime engine in Mozilla products that allows you to build applications. XULRunner lags in language support behind Webkit and isn't as open to being embedded as Webkit is. With a XULRunner solution, you aren't actually coding as much as you are composing an application. Your application runs in an XULRunner instance, and for the most part, besides some XUL layouts, you don't address the app internals.

HTML5 applications have even been published to the Mac App Store (www.apple.com/mac/app-store/) with no changes to game code and only a little code to wrap a WebView around the game. On Linux, the Ubuntu Software Center (http://developer.ubuntu.com/), which initially allowed you to install free apps and libraries, as of late 2010 has added a paid app area. At the time of this writing, it was only open to a few partners and eventually will be rolled out to the general public.

Summary

We covered a lot of ground in this chapter. We opened with some techniques to reduce file sizes and make your apps run faster. We had a crash course in DNS routing for those of you who might want to host your own site on commodity hardware lying around your house. We then transitioned to looking at dedicated cloud Node.js hosting. For those who don't want to manage your own server, we discussed the social options that TapJS provides—both as a standalone application on TapJS's servers and as an embedded Facebook application. We dove into the options provided by the Chrome Web Store and had a healthy discussion of the desktop options for deploying HTML5 applications, including the Mac App Store (not to be confused with the iOS App Store) and the Ubuntu Software Center. We also discussed the upcoming options (in beta at the time of this writing) for in-app payments in Chrome apps and paid apps on the Ubuntu Software Center.

Exercises

1. How would you force new assets to be cached using a manifest file?
2. Does localStorage have a limit when accessed from a website not packaged in the Chrome Web Store? If so, what is it?
3. What are the pros and cons of using TapJS to deploy applications to Facebook?

You can download chapter code and answers to the chapter exercises at www.informit.com/title/9780321767363.

Numerics

N

transitions

JQTouch, 187

JQueryMobile support, 186

Trident.js, 79

easing, 81–82

keyframes, 81

spritesheets, 83

timelines, reversing, 81

timelines, creating, 80

TurboSquid, 143

U

unsupported media elements in HTML5, handling

listing multiple sources, 14–15

with Modernizr, 15

updateDynamicsWorld function, 139

uploading applications to Chrome Web Store, 208-210

URL routing with ExpressJS, 163-165

user input, 53

UV mapping, 134

V

V8, 161

var keyword (CoffeeScript), 154

variables for shaders, 132

vectors, normal, 121

verifying Geolocation API support on browsers, 8

vertex, 118-119

vertex shaders, 121, 132-133

video tag (HTML5), 13-14

viewing snowman scene in Three.js, 128-129

W

web browsers

Geolocation API support, verifying, 8

Google Chrome V8, 161

Google Gears, 3

MIDI files, playing, 89

web notifications

creating, 11–12

interacting with, 12

permission to display, requesting, 11

web server tools, 23

Web Sockets

simplifying with NowJS, 171

Socket.IO, 169–170

Web Storage, 7-8

Web Workers, 4-5

WebGL, 16, 117

WebGL Inspector, 145

webhosting

hosted applications, deploying, 207–208

hosted Node.js services, Nodester, 204–205

hosting your own server, 203–204

packaged applications, deploying, 208

WebOS, 45, 180

websites

CSS, 315

launching games as, 181

Nodester, 204

PhoneGap, 190

WebSockets, 4

WebSQL API, 6-7

while loops (JavaScript), 36

widgets (GWT), RootPanel, 148-149

informIT.com

THE TRUSTED TECHNOLOGY LEARNING SOURCE

PEARSON

InformIT is a brand of Pearson and the online presence for the world's leading technology publishers. It's your source for reliable and qualified content and knowledge, providing access to the top brands, authors, and contributors from the tech community.

♦Addison-Wesley · Cisco Press · EXAM/CRAM · IBM Press. · QUE · PRENTICE HALL · SAMS · | Safari Books Online

LearnIT at InformIT

Looking for a book, eBook, or training video on a new technology? Seeking timely and relevant information and tutorials? Looking for expert opinions, advice, and tips? **InformIT has the solution.**

- Learn about new releases and special promotions by subscribing to a wide variety of newsletters.
  Visit **informit.com/newsletters**.

- Access FREE podcasts from experts at **informit.com/podcasts**.

- Read the latest author articles and sample chapters at **informit.com/articles**.

- Access thousands of books and videos in the Safari Books Online digital library at **safari.InformIt.com**.

- Get tips from expert blogs at **informit.com/blogs**.

Visit **informit.com/learn** to discover all the ways you can access the hottest technology content.

Are You Part of the **IT** Crowd?

Connect with Pearson authors and editors via RSS feeds, Facebook, Twitter, YouTube, and more! Visit **informit.com/socialconnect**.

FREE Online Edition

Your purchase of *Learning HTML5 Game Programming* includes access to a free online edition for 45 days through the Safari Books Online subscription service. Nearly every Addison-Wesley Professional book is available online through Safari Books Online, along with more than 5,000 other technical books and videos from publishers such as Cisco Press, Exam Cram, IBM Press, O'Reilly, Prentice Hall, Que, and Sams.

SAFARI BOOKS ONLINE allows you to search for a specific answer, cut and paste code, download chapters, and stay current with emerging technologies.

Activate your FREE Online Edition at www.informit.com/safarifree

> **STEP 1:** Enter the coupon code: MSGZKCB.

> **STEP 2:** New Safari users, complete the brief registration form.
> Safari subscribers, just log in.

If you have difficulty registering on Safari or accessing the online edition, please e-mail customer-service@safaribooksonline.com